T0323388

Collaborating for Our Future

Collaborating for Our Future

Multistakeholder Partnerships for Solving Complex Problems

Barbara Gray and Jill Purdy

OXFORD
UNIVERSITY PRESS

OXFORD

UNIVERSITY PRESS

Great Clarendon Street, Oxford, OX2 6DP,
United Kingdom

Oxford University Press is a department of the University of Oxford.
It furthers the University's objective of excellence in research, scholarship,
and education by publishing worldwide. Oxford is a registered trade mark of
Oxford University Press in the UK and in certain other countries

Published in the United States of America by Oxford University Press
198 Madison Avenue, New York, NY 10016, United States of America

British Library Cataloguing in Publication Data

Data available

Library of Congress Control Number: 2017947528

ISBN 978–0–19–878284–1

Printed and bound by
CPI Group (UK) Ltd, Croydon, CR0 4YY

Foreword

James L. Perry

I got my first exposure to collaboration in the early 1990s when US national service programs expanded and the Corporation for National and Community Service was created. The philosophy behind these programs, championed by both Presidents George H. W. Bush and Bill Clinton, was grounded in cross-sector collaborations and partnerships. One of the first pieces of scholarship to which I was exposed because of my interest in collaboration was Barbara Gray's *Collaborating: Finding Common Ground for Multiparty Problems*. After almost three decades, I am delighted that Barbara Gray and Jill Purdy are revisiting the subject for which Gray's 1989 book was so influential. I expect this new book, which synthesizes, interprets, and advances the scholarship and practice that has blossomed in the intervening period, will become a new standard to guide scholarship and practice for the next generation.

At this juncture, it would be hyperbole to place the late twentieth century ascendance of collaboration as an organizing form on the same plane as bureaucracy as a modern organizational form, but the hindsight of future developments may lead us to a different assessment. I cannot address now how history will assess the significance of multistakeholder partnerships, but can speak to present realities. We know that multistakeholder partnerships appeal to the *aspirations* of leaders, affected parties, and citizens who are searching for solutions to complex problems. The *reality* of today involves the problematics driving multistakeholder partnerships. The problems span political jurisdictions, exceed the capacities of any single sector to solve them, and have solutions that may please some stakeholders but not others, or are publicly contested in ways that might undermine their implementation.

To illuminate the problematics and build explanations and understanding to support action, Gray and Purdy have written a book whose breadth is impressive. In fact, the contents of the book are a model of the cross-boundary relationships that are at its substantive core. The case studies in Chapter 4, which the authors use in subsequent chapters to illustrate key ideas, are drawn from several complex policy arenas globally. The cases range from a private Dutch firm's (Rabobank) partnerships with NGOs to improve its carbon footprint worldwide, to the collaborative design of a relicensing process for hydroelectric plants regulated by the US Federal Energy Regulatory Commission (FERC), to the International Monetary Fund's efforts to address conflict over water contamination by a Peruvian gold mine. The book draws attention to these cases from around the globe, but the authors remind us that multistakeholder partnerships run the gamut from small local initiatives to multiparty global initiatives.

Gray and Purdy cross boundaries in other ways, too. Their attention to the multidisciplinary foundations of evidence for multistakeholder partnerships is particularly prominent. They weave together content from business, economics, management, public administration, political science, psychology, sociology, and other fields and disciplines. Given recent tendencies within disciplines and applied fields to hive off knowledge by creating silos bounded from other fields, the authors' openness to ideas across disciplines is both intellectually effective and refreshing and assures the book's comprehensiveness. Not only is there "something for everyone" studying multistakeholder partnerships, there is also sage advice to guide practitioners who are engaged in them.

The book reconnects readers with two traditions in the social sciences, institutions, and power that simultaneously situates the subject matter in familiar territory and provokes thoughtful reconsideration of assumptions and existing theory. Gray and Purdy add considerably to our conception of how multistakeholder partnerships influence institutional fields and the mechanisms by which partnerships, over time, may change institutional fields. Their attention to institutions elevates this book to a commentary about emergent structural consequences associated with growing involvements in partnerships.

The authors' story about institutions and institutional change is intertwined with the concept of power. For the most part, the attention to power is about the "realpolitik" of partnerships, about how some agents are able to dominate interactions that create, affirm, or enforce existing patterns of dependence, and others pursue strategies to alter patterns of domination. The attention to power realities is also inspiring because it takes us to a place where we ask fundamental questions, like "To what vision of the future do we want to commit?" which the authors pose in the concluding chapter.

The authors also keep us anchored in another reality—multistakeholder partnerships are not a panacea. The problems that coalesce stakeholders often involve conflicts and power struggles over values, ends, and means. This is a reality about which we are regularly reminded by both scholars and practitioners. Our understanding and mastery of multistakeholder partnerships is not a story for which the last chapter has been written, far from it. Thus, this book is a source for important questions about theory and the practice of collaborating.

This book is ultimately about solving problems, the type of problems so common today that are complex, not resolvable by any single organization, that spill across institutional boundaries. I applaud the authors for succeeding at offering readers a rare trifecta—a theoretically grounded book that is simultaneously readable and practical. This book is an ideal instrument for moving the conversation about multistakeholder partnerships forward.

James Perry is Distinguished Professor Emeritus, School of Public and Environmental Affairs, Indiana University, Bloomington. He was senior evaluator in the Corporation for National and Community Service in 1999–2000. He served on the Indiana Commission on Community Service and Volunteerism for six years, chairing it in 2004–05. He was Editor in Chief of *Public Administration Review* from 2012 to 2017. He is a fellow of the National Academy of Public Administration.

Preface

In 1989 when Barbara wrote *Collaborating: Finding Common Ground for Multiparty Problems*, she observed, "finding creative solutions in a world of growing interdependence requires envisioning problems from perspectives outside our own. We need to redesign our problem-solving processes to include the different parties that have a stake in the issue. Achieving creative and viable solutions to these problems requires new strategies for managing interdependence" (Gray, 1989: xviii). Since then, the number of multistakeholder partnerships created to tackle civic, environmental, social, and other kinds of problems has increased exponentially. Many of these partnerships were successful, bringing together strange bedfellows to knock heads together and bridge conflicts in order to tackle difficult issues. On the other hand, many also fell short of achieving the goals to which they aspired or met formidable obstacles, even though the partners agreed on steps to address them.

We set out to write this sequel to *Collaborating* to capture these new partnership developments. Toward that end, we document and analyze successful, unsuccessful, and difficult partnerships undertaken in the last several years. In many cases the practice of collaborating has grown more complex and difficult as the world has grown smaller and more interdependent through globalization and the help of the Internet. Nonetheless, serious problems persist and have proven unresponsive when solutions are proffered by single organizations or a subset of all those who are implicated in the problem. MSI Integrity and its partners recently documented forty-five complex, global standard-setting partnerships that have been convened to address human rights and environmental concerns alone (MSI Database, 2017). These partnerships link prominent companies, governments, civil society organizations, and community groups in voluntary collaborative forums. These data alone suggest there is an imperative to learn more effective processes for finding collaborative solutions to the world's problems. Of course, countless partnerships have also emerged at regional and local levels around the globe—to address sustainability, climate change, human trafficking, refugee issues, education, hunger, housing, and the list goes on.

Our theorizing has also progressed in the past twenty-nine years. When *Collaborating* was written much of the relevant theorization was practical in nature, cobbled together by academic/practitioners from fields such as law, public policy and negotiations and from their own fledgling experiences in the field. While we retain much of that practical focus in several chapters, this book draws heavily on an institutional theory lens as an overall framing to explain both the reasons for partnership formation and its broader consequences on institutional fields. Partnerships are envisioned both as a consequence of institutional interactions and as drivers of new field-level institutional configurations. Power dynamics also play a central role in our theorizing and, unfortunately, if not adequately addressed, can be a primary reason why partnerships fail.

Although we are certainly advocates for collaborative partnerships, we also insist on high standards for what constitutes an effective multistakeholder collaboration—not the least of which includes broad stakeholder representation, constructive conflict, creative problem solving, a level playing field among partners at the table, and skillful facilitative leadership. These are tall orders so it is no wonder that many partnerships fall short of the mark. We sincerely hope that this book will help many would-be partners to carefully calibrate their expectations and invest in cultivating the necessary wisdom, skills, and persistence to establish robust partnerships capable of effecting sorely-needed societal changes.

Our relationship as coauthors of this book also reflects a long-standing partnership. Our partnership began in the early 1990s in the Department of Management and Organization at Penn State University when Jill joined the Ph.D. program where Barbara was serving as a faculty member. While engaging in many joint projects and publications as well as separate and unique experiences as our careers unfolded, we decided it made sense to capitalize on our synergistic thinking and tap our divergent experiences to produce this book.

We have many people to thank for setting us on this course. Among them are Barbara's mentor at Case Western Reserve University, Dave Brown, who encouraged her initial efforts to write about collaborating and has taught many partners to collaborate, Eric Trist who inspired the 1989 book, early collaborators Joe McCann and John Selsky with whom fledgling ideas about collaborating were piloted at the Academy of Management in the mid-1980s and Chris Huxham from the University of Strathclyde, who took the first of many initiatives to create a network of researchers studying collaborative partnerships by inviting twelve of us to Ross Priory on the shores of beautiful Loch Lomond in the midsummer of 1993. That meeting generated fertile ground for what eventually became the MOPAN (Multi-Organizational Partnerships, Networks, and Alliances) Conference, which continued to promote research on collaborative partnerships for many years and created lasting relationships among many of us who regularly participated. More recently, the Conference on Cross-Sector Alliances and Partnerships (CSSP) has performed a similar role as did other conference and workshops where we could test out our ideas with like-minded scholars and practitioners.

Consequently, many scholars offered insights that were important to this volume. Among them were: Noelle Aarts, Charles Abdullah, Lisa Blomgren Amsler, Shaz Ansari, Chris Ansell, James Austin, Gail Bingham, Oana Branzei, John Bryson, Rene Bouwen, Chris Carlson, Amelia Clark, Andy Crane, Marc Craps, Barbara Crosby, Tina Dacin, Art Dewulf, Frank Dukes, Kirk Emerson, Archon Fung, Pieter Glasbergen, Cynthia Hardy, Maddy Jansens, Sanjiv Kharam, Tom Koontz, Tom Lawrence, Eliza Lee, Tina Nabatchi, Rosemary O'Leary, Jim Perry, Nelson Phillips, Sandra Schrujer, Mae Seitanidi, Eva Sorenson, Marietta van Huijstee, Rajesh Tanden, Katrien Termeer, Jacob Torfing, Lee Vancina, Siv Vangen, Steve Waddell, Sandra Waddock, Nancy Welsh, Frances Westley, Frank Wijn, Julia Wondolleck, Donna Wood, and countless others who have each in their own way helped to pioneer the theory of multistakeholder partnerships over the last forty years. Their insights have been inspirational for us and invaluable as we sought to bring coherence to our ideas.

We also appreciated the opportunity to learn from the many people and organizations that design, lead, and evaluate multistakeholder partnerships: Tima Bansal, Brandon Brockmyer, Gregg Carrington, Jane Covey, Peggy Dulaney, Ann Florini, Juan Pablo Guerrero, Theresa Haas, Michael Kern, Ernst Ligteringen, Peter Lund-Thomsen, Ken Obura, Bill Potapchuk, Rinalia Abdul Rahim, The Global Governance Group, The Institute for Development Research, MSI Integrity, Policy Consensus Initiative, RESOLVE, The William D. Ruckelshaus Center, Synergos Institute, and also the CSSI community of scholars.

We are also appreciative of funding that facilitated our collaboration in researching and writing this book that was provided by The Dispute Resolution Research Center at Kellogg Graduate School of Management led by Jeanne Brett. Funding from the Network for Business Sustainability at Ivey Business School, Western Ontario University, provided the grist for a larger project from which Chapter 8 was drawn. That project was conducted with Jenna Stites with oversight from Tima Bansal at Ivey.

We are also immensely indebted to our families for the patient, loving support they provided throughout the process of writing this book: To our spouses, Dom and Chris, as well as our children Sophia, Helen, and Lara, Dan, and Elizabeth, and their spouses, all of whose needs had to be put on hold on many occasions when we were closeted to solve some dilemma or meet a deadline to complete this project. We are so appreciative that we could count on your patience and support over the last several years. Thank you for believing in us and in this work. We hope we have made you proud.

And to the editorial staff at Oxford University Press, our editors, David Musson, who believed in our project from its inception, and Clare Kennedy, who gently nudged us along, Vasuki Ravichandran and Martin Noble for editing and technical support during the production process, Stephen York for proof reading, we are immensely grateful. We also want to thank Ginny Smith for her assistance in preparing the manuscript and Sheryl Rhinehart for turning our pictures into artwork. And we are especially grateful to Jim Perry, a dear friend and colleague, for graciously agreeing to write the Foreword for this volume.

We hope that the ideas we have expressed here can stimulate further investigation of the issues we have raised and improve the practice of partnering across the globe.

Barbara Gray and
Jill Purdy

August 2017

Contents

List of Figures   xv
List of Tables   xvii

1. The Rise of Partnerships: From Local to Global   1
2. Multistakeholder Partnerships in Context   14
3. An Institutional Lens on Multistakeholder Partnerships   36
4. Three Diverse Examples of Multistakeholder Partnerships   48
5. Designing Multistakeholder Partnerships   68
6. Conflict in Multistakeholder Partnerships   96
7. Power and Collaboration   117
8. Partnerships for Sustainability   131
9. Collaborative Governance   156
10. Cross-Level Dynamics   172
11. How Partnerships Can Transform Institutional Fields   184

References   201
Index   237

List of Figures

1.1	Types of multistakeholder partnerships	3
3.1	Frame amplification	43
4.1	Rabobank and NGOs partnership	51
4.2	Process for collaboration on hydroelectric licensing rules	53
5.1	Phases of partnership formation	71
6.1	Restoration of trust following a breach	99
8.1	Increase in articles about sustainability partnerships	132
8.2	The Natural Step's Sustainability Criteria	133
8.3	Types of business—NGO partnerships	135
8.4	CSR sustainability continuum	138
10.1	Partnerships as cross-level phenomena	181
11.1	Issue field configurations	190
11.2	Pathways of change in field configurations	193

List of Tables

2.1	Business motivations for partnering	29
2.2	NGO motivations for partnering	31
2.3	Purposes of partnerships	33
5.1	Driving and restraining forces for partnership formation	72
5.2	Interventions to enhance partnerships	74
6.1	Additional strategies for dealing with conflict	112
7.1	Actor capacities based on forms of power and power orientations	121
7.2	Orientation toward field creation or restructuring in collaboration	124
8.1	Positive and negative partnership outcomes by sector	146
11.1	How collaborative partnerships impact field structure	189

1

The Rise of Partnerships: From Local to Global

For the past several decades, organizations have been turning to partnerships to meet challenges, which as single organizations they cannot handle on their own. These partnerships often couple unlikely bedfellows to address problems such as healthcare delivery, poverty, human rights, watershed management, and education, and or to take advantage of opportunities in which partners' interests overlap such as sustainability, innovation, or economic development. Partnerships may involve as few as two or three partners (such as when one business and one NGO team up) or bring together fifty or even over one hundred stakeholder organizations in global initiatives such as the Global Reporting Initiative or the Voluntary Principles on Human Rights.

Whether they are large or small, multistakeholder partnerships (MSPs) attempt to join various stakeholders in a process of collaboration. Collaboration has been defined as a process that engages a group of autonomous stakeholders interested in a problem or issue in an interactive deliberation using shared rules, norms, and structures, to share information and/or take coordinated actions (Wood & Gray, 1991: 11). This process may simply involve stakeholders informing each other about the issue of interest, but more often it includes negotiating a common set of norms and routines that will govern their future interactions and remain open to revision as they renegotiate their relationships over time. We distinguish collaborative partnerships from purely contractual exchange relationships in which one party provides services for another. For example, a nonprofit agency may be retained by a city government to provide shelter, meals, and mental health services for the homeless, but this falls outside our definition of multistakeholder partnerships. However, an MSP would exist if nonprofit agencies and city leaders jointly developed and implemented a plan to alleviate the problem of homelessness. Among their many purposes, such partnerships may be formed to tackle knotty societal problems, to promote innovation, to provide public services, to expand governance capabilities, to set standards for a field, or to resolve conflicts that impede progress on critical issues. Multistakeholder partnerships may adopt many forms ranging from networks of small rural farmers working with micro-financiers in Africa, to government-led efforts to manage natural resources or design transportation infrastructure, to efforts to improve preschool education for low-income children, to industry-level certification bodies such as the Forest Stewardship Council or the Soya Roundtable, and even to efforts to fight human trafficking or regulate the future of the Internet.

Mapping Stakeholders and Types of Collaboration

Stakeholders refer to all individuals, groups, or organizations that can directly influence the focal problem or issue by their actions or are directly influenced by actions others take to address it. Our use of the term here is different from that used in the strategy literature where stakeholders are associated with a focal organization such as a corporation (Freeman, 1984). Instead, we follow Eric Trist's (1983) notion in which stakeholders are associated with a problem domain or, as we will say through this book, an issue field. Issue fields (such as homelessness or deforestation or healthcare) are comprised of actors who share an interest in that issue or problems associated with it. The objective of collaboration is to create a richer more comprehensive appreciation of the issue/problem than any of them could construct alone by viewing it from the perspectives of all the stakeholders. A kaleidoscope is a useful image to envision what joint appreciation of a problem is all about. As the kaleidoscope is rotated, different configurations of the same collection of colored shapes appear. Collaboration comprises building a common understanding of how these images appear from the respective points of view of all the stakeholders. This, in turn, forms the basis for choosing a collective course of action to address the problem or issue (Gray, 1989).

Figure 1.1 identifies four generic types of stakeholders that may participate in collaborative partnerships (businesses, governments, nongovernmental organizations (NGOs), and civic society) and diagrams the possible relationships among them. Six types of bilateral partnerships are possible. When business and government join forces, their venture is labeled a public–private partnership. When businesses and NGOs link up, these alliances are known as business–NGO partnerships. SLENs (Sustainable Local Enterprise Networks) are formed when NGOs team up with civic society members (Weber, 2009: 670). Businesses also engage directly with communities (as in stakeholder engagement forums), but because building these relationships is often difficult for businesses because they lack routine interactions with civic society

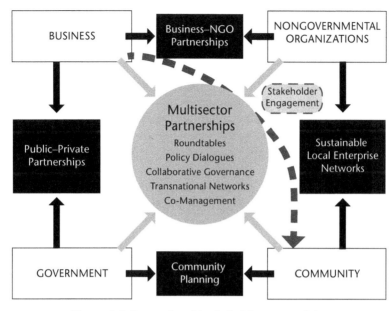

Figure 1.1 Types of multistakeholder partnerships

partners, NGOs often broker relationships between businesses and civic society (Wheeler et al., 2005).

When three of more types of stakeholders are engaged we refer to these partnerships as multistakeholder partnerships.[1] *Multistakeholder partnerships* "are generally defined as initiatives where public-interest entities, private sector companies, (NGOs) and/or civic society organizations enter into an alliance to achieve a common practical purpose, pool core competencies, and share risks, responsibilities, resources, costs and benefits" (Utting & Zammit, 2009: 40). As the circle in the center of Figure 1.1 shows, these partnerships can assume many different forms including policy dialogues, co-management of natural resources, and transnational networks among others. For example, when governments partner with civic society and NGOs, and even business on some occasions, these arrangements have been termed *collaborative governance*—which serve as a means for governments to augment their own governance efforts. We devote Chapter 9 to investigating this type of partnership, which has been growing in use in recent years (Amsler, 2016; Ansell & Torfing, 2014).

Why Partnerships and Why Now?

The frequency of multisector partnerships has increased dramatically over the last several decades, yielding many new examples of structures, processes, achievements, and challenges. The rise in such partnerships can be attributed to several factors. First, the world has been transformed by technology such that local issues may be broadly communicated and thus draw the interest of actors across a much wider swath of society than before. This allows opportunities for collaboration to be more easily recognized and acted upon. Similarly, technological and economic development has enabled people to more easily organize around shared interests and operate collectively (Held, 2007). As a growing share of the world's population has experienced increased income, mobility, and leisure time, their capacity to engage with issues, problems, and opportunities has also grown, resulting in an increasing number of local and transnational social movements (Khagram & Alvord, 2008). Much of this engagement occurs through the auspices of for-profit, not-for-profit, or governmental organizations. Yet another factor supporting the growth of multistakeholder partnerships is a rising awareness of the complex, systemic nature of both the problems and opportunities faced by societies. Few organizations contain sufficient knowledge and resources to fully analyze issues and take action on them unilaterally. Further, as actors attempt to solve problems and make new discoveries, they are also more likely to be scrutinized and held accountable for the environmental impact, social justice, unintended consequences, and long-term viability of their actions. Finally, significant changes in economic, political-legal, sociocultural institutions across the globe have raised questions about the domains in which issues should be raised, who has the legitimacy and authority to address them, and how the interests of various constituencies should be weighed. These factors have collided to propel the growth of partnerships locally and globally.

Despite this impetus to partner, stakeholders' motivations for participating in multistakeholder partnerships may vary considerably. For example, businesses may pursue partnerships for sustainability out of a desire to enhance their reputations for corporate social responsibility (CSR) (Austin & Seitanidi, 2012), to find leaner ways to produce (Hall & Vredenburg, 2003), or to reduce their environmental footprint (Dienhardt & Ludescher, 2010). For governments, partnerships are becoming the governance structure of the future (Ansell & Gash, 2008) that supports legitimacy and public engagement. For NGOs the challenge involves taking up the role that, in many cases, governments are no longer able to fulfill because of shrinking resources or weakened social mandates (Yaziji & Doh, 2009). For communities and civic society, the desire to escape poverty, eliminate human rights abuses, ensure sustained natural resources, and enhance their overall health and well-being are paramount (London & Rondinelli, 2003; Selsky & Parker, 2005; Wheeler et al., 2005). Partnerships tap different competencies of partners to tackle problems that individual organizations (or even whole sectors) cannot solve, or cannot solve as well, when working independently (Bryson et al., 2006; Gray, 1989; Gray & Stites, 2013; McGuire, 2006).

Collaborative relations between these four sectors of society are believed to increase our prospects for tackling the pressing social, economic, and environmental challenges and make important contributions to societal development as well as benefit the various partners in the collaboration (Brown & Ashman, 1999; Gray, 1989; Innes & Booher, 2010; Miller and Ahmad, 2000). For the public sector, partnerships with NGOs and the private sector may result in capacity building through which the design and implementation of policies can be improved and the legitimacy of the public sector enhanced (Miller and Ahmad, 2000). For NGOs, partnerships may involve organizational development, the provision of additional and much needed resources, and increased recognition and status whereby the organizations' political influence can be strengthened (Miller and Ahmad, 2000). For businesses, several benefits of multistakeholder partnerships are possible. Corporate community involvement may lead to business benefits like improved reputation and brand value, license to operate, innovation, development of local markets, improved risk management, and greater ability to attract, and retain their employees (Austin & Seitanidi, 2012; Emerson, 2003; Googins & Rochlin, 2000; Laasonen, Fougère & Kourula, 2012).

Examples of Multistakeholder Partnerships

The various partnership types depicted in Figure 1.1 may also include other partners such as arts, education, or religious organizations too. Typically, governments and civic society each have a stake in criminal justice issues so they may form a bilateral partnership or team up with educational or religious organizations. Similarly, governments, agricultural businesses, and environmental groups have shared concerns with farm run-off that creates agricultural pollution and may enter into a multistakeholder partnership to address this issue. Over the last thirty years, multistakeholder partnerships built around problem and issue fields have grown in use at all levels of society (Gray & Stites, 2013; Khagram, 2017). For example, creating eco-labels to certify the sustainable production of commodities such as fish, coffee, or concrete products is of interest to business, governments, and various environmental groups, and may also be of interest to governments seeking competitive advantage for their national industries. Similarly, partnerships that bring together healthcare professionals, public health officials, communities, and pharmaceutical manufacturers to eradicate malaria, AIDS, and other diseases are often organized on the global level (Ulbert, 2008). One example of this type of partnership is the GAVI Alliance (The Global Alliance for Vaccines and

Immunization), which seeks to eradicate basic childhood diseases among young children in developing countries around the world. The partnership, which began in 2000, includes: national governments; international organizations, such as the United Nations Children's Fund (UNICEF), the World Health Organization (WHO), and the World Bank; philanthropic institutions, such as the Bill and Melinda Gates Children's Vaccine Program and the Rockefeller Foundation; the private sector, represented by the International Federation of Pharmaceutical Manufacturers Associations (IFPMA); and research and public health institutions.

With nearly one in four children remaining without immunization for the basic vaccination package known as EPI (which covers measles, polio, pertussis, diphtheria, tetanus, and tuberculosis), the amount of resources and coordination needed to deliver these medications is phenomenal. At the country level, governments collaborate with the Alliance partners through a national Inter-agency Coordinating Committee (ICC), which explores ways of strengthening immunization services and the financing of those services through national, bilateral, and multinational resources (http://www.who.int/mediacentre/factsheets/fs169/en/). One measure of GAVI's success is reduction in child mortality rates. In countries where GAVI is operational, the average child mortality rate fell an average of 3.6 percent per year from 76 to a projected 63 deaths per 1,000 live births between 2010 and 2015. This is attributable to an acceleration in the introduction of new vaccines and increased coverage for existing vaccines (http://www.gavi.org/progress-report/#section2). Such improvements would be unheard of without the cooperation of many local, national, and global partners.

Another equally fascinating and successful partnership is Honey Care Kenya. This partnership began in 2001 as an alliance between an NGO and local farmers in Kenya whom it trained to become beekeepers. As Honey Care Kenya grew, the NGO sought the help of a business entrepreneur to underwrite the endeavor, which has now grown into a very profitable business that sells honey on the global market and is expanding its operations to several other African countries (Wheeler et al., 2005). Although this partnership began between two sectors, as it grew it branched out to include partners from the business sector as well as additional members from the community and NGO sectors. At this juncture, the partnership (now part of Honey Care Africa) operates in several African counties, and its Africa partners include ASHOKA, USAID, The William Davidson Institute at the University of Michigan, KIVA, the World Economic Forum, the World Bank, ROOT Capital (a nonprofit investment firm), Lundin Foundation, Grameen Foundation, and the Swiss impact investor AlphaMundi.

Multistakeholder partnerships can also involve designing and planning for the future as in the Planning for Livable Military Communities project. This project, funded by a US Department of Housing and Urban Development (HUD) Community Challenge Grant, is a partnership with the North Central Texas Council of Governments and seven cities (Benbrook, Fort Worth, Lake Worth, River Oaks, Sansom Park, Westworth Village, and White Settlement in conjunction with Tarrant County) surrounding the Naval Air Station Fort Worth, Joint Reserve Base (NAS Fort Worth, JRB). The focus of this planning grant is to evaluate transportation options; to support economic development initiatives; to evaluate housing and retail markets in the area; to complete local government comprehensive plan updates; and to encourage housing and transportation choices closer to the base (www.nctcog.org/trans/aviation/jlus/hud.asp).

One arena in which multistakeholder partnerships are burgeoning is sustainability, a topic we explore in depth in Chapter 8. Bilateral initiatives between business and NGOs are very common (Austin, 2000; Gray & Stites, 2013). Other partnerships in this issue field also involve governments and civic society. For example, on Brazil's northeastern Amazon frontier, deforestation was running rampant—the consequence of governmental decisions to relocate ranchers to this remote area of the country during the 1960s and 1970s and subsequent migrations in later years as soy farming replaced cattle ranching in other parts of Brazil. This resettlement was accompanied by substantial deforestation in the Amazon region. Facing global pressure to stop these practices, the Brazilian government gradually shifted its priorities away from resettlement and toward sustainability. It began to partner with the NGO, the Nature Conservancy, to develop a land registry and to encourage ranchers to sustainably manage their land. IBM also assisted to develop software for tracking deforestation. New forest legislation introduced in 2012 made the registration process mandatory. In addition to reducing deforestation, the partnership taught ranchers more efficient husbandry practices and to diversify their income by replanting native species such as cacao, banana, and hardwoods (Smith, 2016).

Partnerships across sectoral boundaries are also prevalent in the fields of healthcare (Milward et al., 2009; Ollenschläger et al., 2004; Ulbert, 2008), arts and culture (Gazley, 2008), education (Kagan, 1991; Selden, Sowa & Sandfort, 2006), public services (Bryson et al., 2006; Sullivan & Skelcher, 2002), and international development (Brown, 2008). In a recent review of the literature, Morris and Miller-Stevens (2016) note the remarkable array of settings in which collaborative partnerships have been studied. In fact, partnerships have been variously referred to as the "collaboration paradigm of the 21st century" (Austin, 2000: 44), and the "new organizational zeitgeist in dealing with societal issues" (Vurro, Dacin & Perrini, 2010: 40).

What Does It Mean to Collaborate?

Despite its now widespread use, the meaning of the term "collaboration" differs from setting to setting. Some definitions confound the terms *collaboration* and *partnership* by using them interchangeably. Although partnerships are often referred to as collaborations, we believe it is important to distinguish between these terms because not all partnerships satisfy the more rigorous definitions of what constitutes collaboration let alone achieve collaborative outcomes.

As a result, the term collaboration has become "hopelessly ambiguous" (Donahue, 2010: S151). Despite efforts to find consensus, partnerships can also be fraught with conflict that may not be resolved (Gray, 2004) or they may not realize the aspirations they set out to achieve and, instead, may even generate unintended or negative consequences. As we see it, the essential components of a rigorous definition of collaboration include:

- The actors are interdependent with respect to the problem or issue, and none of them can solve the problem on their own;
- It is an emergent process that uses shared rules, norms, and structures;
- It involves constructively wrestling with differences using formal and information negotiations and consensus-building to find trade-offs that create value for all;
- Partners bring different competencies and need to respect and learn from each other's expertise;
- Partners assume joint risks and responsibilities for the outcomes of their joint efforts.

The key is that collaboration can be viewed either a process or an outcome or both with specific process characteristics. Let's explore each of these features in more detail.

Interdependence

Collaboration establishes a give and take among the stakeholders that is designed to produce solutions that none of them working independently could achieve. Because each one's actions to address the problem have implications for the others, they need to understand how their interdependent relationships work in order to forge a collective solution (Gray, 1989; Trist, 1983). Initially, the interdependence may not be fully appreciated by all the parties. Therefore, the initial phase of a collaboration usually involves calling attention to the ways in which the stakeholders' concerns are intertwined and how each is implicated in solving the problem. Heightening stakeholders' awareness of their interdependence often kindles renewed willingness to search for trade-offs that could produce a mutually beneficial solution. In some cases, an unexpected external stimulus is needed to trigger actors' exploration of their interdependence.

Interactive Process Using Shared Rules, Norms, and Structures

A critical component of collaboration is management of the process by which partners interact (Wondolleck, 1985). Despite partners' best intentions, conflicts frequently arise during deliberations. Agreeing on expectations and ground rules for how these will be handled goes a long way to keeping the deliberations constructive and civil (Wood & Gray, 1991). From the outset agreements need to be reached about who has a legitimate right to participate in the partnership, what they can contribute to the deliberations, how the participants will be organized, for whom they can speak with authority and how each party will purport themselves during the deliberations (Thompson et al., 2008; Wood & Gray, 1991). For complex global multistakeholder partnerships, thinking through an effective structure for coordinating the participation of what may be hundreds of stakeholders is an important preliminary step. Often these global initiatives will appoint a steering committee to manage the sheer logistics of the interactions among stakeholders and may devolve other structural arrangements including topical subcommittees to enable multiple facets of the problem or issue to be explored simultaneously.

Constructively Dealing with Differences

Respect for differences is an easy virtue to champion verbally and a much more difficult one to put into practice in our day-to-day affairs. Yet differences are often the source of immense creative potential if they can be harnessed in constructive ways (Ansell & Gash, 2008; Fisher & Ury, 1981; Gray, 1989; Lax & Sebenius, 1986). This is a key benefit of collaborating.

Like the wise men in the parable about the blind men and the elephant, most of us routinely make a number of assumptions that limit our ability to recognize and capitalize on the creative potential of differences. One assumption that we frequently make is that our way of viewing a problem is the best. "Best" to us may mean the most rational, the fairest, the most intelligent, or even the only way. No matter what the basis, we arrive at the conclusion that our way is superior to any other. In doing so, we lose sight of the possibility that multiple approaches to the elephant yield multiple perceptions about what is possible and desirable.

Even if we grant that multiple perspectives are possible, we can easily fall prey to another common assumption; that is, we conclude that different interpretations are, by definition, opposing interpretations. But here we need to distinguish between interpretations that differ from each other and those that are truly opposed. As Fisher and Ury have aptly pointed out, "Agreement is possible precisely because interests differ" (1981: 44). Without differing interests, the range of possible exchanges between parties would be nonexistent. Because parties' interests do vary, as do the resources and skills they bring to bear on a problem, they may able to arrange trade-offs and to forge mutually beneficial alliances (Lax & Sebenius, 1986). It is also frequently the case that, as we strive to articulate our differences, we discover that our underlying concerns are closer to others' than we originally thought. These underlying shared concerns may have been masked by the different ways we described or framed the problem or may have obscured by strong emotions that deafened us to the message coming from others. Parties in conflict are known to engage in selective listening and to pay more attention to information that confirms their preconceived stereotypes of their opponents. Stereotypes cause us to discount the legitimacy of the other's point of view and cause both sides to ignore data that disconfirm their stereotypes (Sherif, 1958). Consequently, they may miss clues about shared or differing interests that may contain the seeds of an agreement. Collaboration operates on the premise that the assumptions that disputants have about the other side and about the nature of the issues in contention are worth testing. The premise is that testing these assumptions and allowing a constructive confrontation of differences may unlock heretofore disguised creative potential.

Respecting and Learning from Each Other's Expertise

As we have just noted, partners bring diverse knowledge and expertise to a partnership. Some of this knowledge is technical, such as the appropriate medical treatment for diseases or alternative farming practices while others offer more contextual expertise pertinent to the locales where the partnership's decisions will need to be implemented. Far too often, this latter expertise is misunderstood and/or underestimated (Dewulf & Bouwen, 2012; Simanis & Hart, 2008; Teegan et al., 2004) which can prevent effective implementation of plans where they are most needed. In North/South partnerships, for example, the potential for local partners to feel that their expertise is discounted in favor of the views of Northern donors is often a recurring theme (Jaumont, 2016). These partnerships highlight the delicate issues of establishing the legitimacy of all partners' views in collaborative decision making and the difficulty of doing so despite well-intended efforts of Northern partners (Jaumont, 2016; Maasen & Cloete, 2006; Whiteman, 2009). To successfully collaborate, "partners need to respect each other's expertise" and "explore how what they know can productively and usefully be juxta-posed with the expertise of others" (Michaels, 2009: 998).

Partners Assume Joint Ownership and Responsibility for Partnership Outcomes

Joint ownership means that partners in a collaborative venture are directly responsible for reaching an agreement on a solution (Gray, 1989). Unlike litigation or regulation, in which intermediaries (courts, regulatory agencies, legislatures) devise solutions that are imposed on the stakeholders, in collab-orative agreements the parties impose decisions on themselves. They set the agenda and the ground rules; they decide what issues will be addressed; they decide what the terms of the agreement will be and the enforcement criteria. Any agreements reached may be free-standing contracts, or they may serve as input to a legal or public policy process that ratifies, codifies, or in some other way incorporates the agreements. At the national level, collaborative agree-ments cannot serve as a substitute for constitutional decision-making proced-ures, but they can generate more legitimacy for formal decisions. At the transnational and global levels, decisions reached by multistakeholder part-nerships provide a form of soft power governance in the absence of an authorized governing authority although enforcement of such agreements is limited. The Paris Agreement on Climate Change is a good case in point as it requires ratification and implementation by many countries to have a meaningful effect.

Nonetheless, Partnerships Are Not Panaceas

Despite the unprecedented interest in partnerships locally and globally, partnerships are not panaceas. Simply teaming up with other stakeholders does not offer a magic bullet for tackling an issue or problem. For many reasons, on which we will elaborate in Chapters 5, 6, and 7, just agreeing to collaborate will not ensure success. The problems or issues that bring stake-holders together are often fraught with conflicts over values, desired out-comes, and methods for achieving these outcomes (Saz-Carranza & Ospina, 2011). Designing partnerships to capitalize on differences rather than being stymied by them requires skillful leadership (Bryson et al., 2006; Chrislip & Larson, 1994; Gray, 2008), including the ability to build a shared vision of a collectively desirable future. It also requires careful process design and facilita-tion and the ability to wrestle constructively with conflict. It also means getting the right stakeholders to come to the table in the first place and adapting to shifting conditions (such as cuts in resources or loss of key partners) as the project proceeds. When the scope and scale of partnerships are large and they cut across multiple levels of governments (e.g., are cross-level by nature), this adds considerable complexity to designing and managing the deliberations and to implementing joint solutions in vastly different contexts (e.g., nations with fragile governments, little infrastructure or few resources). As we will argue in Chapter 5, without careful attention to stakeholder inclusion and design of the process by which stakeholders will interact, well-intended collaborative partnerships can unravel. An example of a public–private partnership in Iceland serves as a useful example.

In 2003 an agreement was reached to build a new hydroelectric plant called Kárahnjúkar in eastern Iceland. The parties behind the proposal were Iceland's state-owned power company, which would build and operate the plant, and the American aluminum company Alcoa, which planned to buy nearly all of the plant's electricity for a new smelting operation. This public–private partnership boded well for Iceland economically. As a geographically remote country with abundant natural energy resources, the project sought to create jobs and revitalize the economic prospects of East Iceland by attracting energy-intensive industry while reducing the greenhouse gases caused by aluminum smelting. Little engagement with other organizations seemed necessary or desirable. However, a 1998 attempt to construct a hydroelectric dam in Iceland's northeast highlands had caused "the most bitter environmental debate Iceland has yet seen and literally divided the country into two opposing camps" (Thórhallsdóttir, 2002: 99). Despite this, the partners on the Kárahnjúkar project did not expand their collaboration to include other affected stakeholders, resulting in disruption and unrest within the country. When environmental activists outside of Iceland learned that the proposal would flood 57 square kilometers of pristine Arctic wilderness (Krater & Rose, 2009), they formed an international network called Saving Iceland. The plant's construction was condemned by World Wildlife Fund, Royal Society for the Protection of Birds, Birdlife International, and the International Rivers Network (Bosshard, 2003) for the environmental harm it would cause. Protestors occupied the construction site intermittently for five years as the project moved through legal challenges into construction. The disruption caused by a lack of wider collaboration extended beyond environmental issues to include community and diversity issues as well. With foreign workers comprising more than 70 percent of the construction workforce, local communities struggled to deal with social challenges as the non-Icelandic population swelled and job opportunities shifted away from the traditional fishing economy. In this case, the original partners' failure to involve other interested stakeholders resulted in unanticipated strife and negative consequences for the host region.

Intention of This Book

Our intention in this book is to conceptualize partnerships as forms of organizing that hold promise for transforming institutional fields. We will argue that actors in issue fields form partnerships to cope with changing or conflicting institutional demands. These demands may emanate from the partners' efforts to shape the field to their individual advantage or because of pressures in adjacent fields that have ripple effects for the partners in the focal field of interest. In forming a multistakeholder partnership, partners not only hope to gain shared control over these forces while at the same time gain advantages for themselves. Partnerships also can have reciprocal effects on fields (Vurro & Dacin, 2014). Bringing an institutional lens to bear on our analysis of partnerships enables us to highlight how meanings and power shift within the field as partners renegotiate the rules and norms that govern the field. We introduce this theoretical perspective in Chapter 3.

Overall, this book provides an understanding of partnerships rooted in organization theory, and in particular, from the lens of changing institutional fields. We hope that adopting this vantage point will provide new insight for both academics studying partnerships and practitioners who are in the trenches inventing and reinventing them every day.

Note

1. Interestingly, because partnerships are studied by a number of separate but sometimes intersecting literatures, many different terms have evolved that are roughly synonymous. These include multistakeholder partnerships (MSPs), multiparty collaborations, multistakeholder initiatives (MSIs), cross-sector social partnerships (CSSPs), and global action networks (GANS) (when the issues are global in nature). We will consistently refer to them as multistakeholder partnerships unless quoting from another source that uses other terminology.

2

Multistakeholder Partnerships in Context

Collaborating to Deal with Wicked Problems

In this chapter we ask and answer the questions: Why do partnerships form? What motivates potential partners to align themselves with others to pursue their organizational objectives? The recent literature offers a number of reasons why partners may want to team up. For example, pooling resources has become a necessity for addressing many social problems because problems no longer fit neatly into the domain of one kind of organization. To illustrate, successful primary and secondary education is no longer just the province of schools. Whether children, particularly those in disadvantaged communities, can function in school often depends on whether they have eaten, can secure appropriate medical care, and have safe places to go after school. Thus, successful education depends on adequate social services. Additionally, governments are finding that the problems they are charged with managing outstrip the resources they can muster to cope with them. As a result they seek partners who can help them provide the necessary public services they are charged with providing (Sandfort & Milward, 2008). Many nongovernmental organizations are resource poor which increases the appeal of partnering with corporations. Partnering also affords enhanced legitimacy for many businesses (Oliver, 1997; LaFrance & Lehman, 2005) enabling them to "do well by doing good" (attributed to Benjamin Franklin). Private sector firms may also seek partners to gain collaborative advantage within their industry or network, to improve sustainability (Gray & Stites, 2013) or to spur innovation—a motivation that applies also to governments (Ansell & Torfing, 2014; Torfing, 2016).

Because partnerships have cropped up in so many different kinds of societal fields, answering questions about "why partner?" requires a deeper level of analysis. It necessitates examining a variety of changes in the contexts in which organizations conduct their affairs. The breadth and variety of contextual changes contribute to the turbulent conditions faced by many organizations because actions taken by one organization negatively impact others, often in a different sector of society (Emery & Trist, 1965; Trist, 1977; Wildavsky, 1979). These "contextual factors" have spurred organizations to seek partners that differ from them and offer valuable, complementary resources. Instead of acting independently, organizations have become increasingly interdependent (Fiorino, 1999; Carlsson, 2006; Termeer et al., 2015; ECOSOC, 2016)—embedded in both formal and informal networks and subject to challenge from many different actors. Consequently, the freedom of organizations to pursue an independent course of action (Gray, 1989; Bryson et al., 2015) is rapidly disappearing.

As a result of this increasing interdependence, more and more societal problems have become "wicked problems" that involve many actors and defy resolution (Rittel & Webber, 1983; Roberts, 2000). Wicked problems are "ill-defined, ambiguous, and contested, and feature multilayered interdependencies and complex social dynamics" (Termeer et al., 2015: 680) and are mired in political intractability (Selsky et al., 2014). Because the actions of one party have implications for many others, individual efforts to solve wicked problems are precluded. Instead, wicked problems are plagued by complexity, conflicts, and entanglements that impede easy resolution (Gray & Purdy, 2014; Selsky et al., 2014). Further wicked problems have no "stopping rule" whereby "additional efforts might increase the chances of finding a better solution" (Rittel & Webber, 1983: 162). Therefore, any hope of unpacking solutions requires the attention and commitment of many interdependent players over considerable time.

> When the kinds of issues demanding policy and management attention cannot be neatly compartmentalized in one sector—one public organization—but instead span fields, sectors, specialties, and extant institutional arrangements, new and often collaborative cross-organizational forms may be the preferred structural choice (Hicklin et al., 2009: 97).

Even forming a partnership to address a wicked problem may be insufficient unless partners come to understand the complexities underlying the problem's persistence. Wicked problems test the process of collaboration, yet are the very reason that an alternative to traditional forms of top–down managerial or bureaucratic decision making by individual organizations and adversarial forms of debate are all inadequate to address them (Gray, 1989; Ansell & Gash, 2008; Roberts, 2000; Termeer et al., 2015).

In the next section we look at several wicked problems facing global society. Dealing with them is creating an impetus for collaboration on a grand scale across the globe.

Collaboration in the Context of Globalization

At this juncture, the conditions and contexts propelling the need for collaborative partnerships have only intensified in breadth and urgency. According to Rein and Stott (2013: 81), contextual factors promoting partnership formation:

> include a wide range of variables, such as: regional, national and local environments; economic, political, cultural and social conditions; linkage with international bodies and with networks promoting partnerships; the presence or absence of intermediary organisations and/or key individuals.

These factors are usually not independent of each other, but instead intersect in dynamic ways that influence how partnerships emerge and develop.

One key contextual factor propelling collaboration today is increasing globalization resulting from "the development of global markets in goods and services and the changing infrastructure of global communications linked to the IT revolution" (Held, 2007: 243). While this does not mean that the world is now homogenized and that national differences have disappeared, increasing globalization has contributed to a host of changes at the global level that make the need for partnerships all the more apparent. Additionally, at the same time there is a curious fusing of the local and the global referred to as "glocalization" that "interlaces worldwide similarity with cross-national variation" (Drori et al., 2013: 3). Glocalization acknowledges that a variety of global models for action have become widely diffused but are customized to local conditions. "The so-called global is a collage of local practices, behaviors, and tastes, while the so-called local is increasingly constructed within the scripts drafted by global forces" (Drori et al., 2013: 5). Our research suggests that partnerships often result when local instantiations of global issues arise and collaboration is required to respond. Similarly, over forty-five multistakeholder initiatives have been organized in recent years to address global issues (MSI Database, 2017) including the UN Global Compact, the Global Reporting Initiative, the Roundtable on Sustainable Palm Oil and ICANN, a consortium charged with developing regulations for the global internet.

For example, many partnerships have emerged to respond to compelling global problems such as those identified by the World Economic Forum in their annual Global Competitiveness Reports (Schwab, 2015; 2016). We synthesize these into the following list of glocal contextual factors that generate the need for collaboration:

- deepening income inequality;
- growing importance of health in the economy;
- environmental degradation including climate change, water crises, and the need for sustainability;

- large-scale involuntary migration;
- increases in extreme weather events;
- continued decline in the ability of governments to handle complex problems.

These contextual factors are not necessarily discreet or unrelated. Nonetheless, below we explore each of them individually and provide some detail on how they have spurred the growth of cross-sector partnerships locally and across the globe.

Deepening Income Inequality

Although the number of people in extreme poverty[1] worldwide has fallen faster than ever before in history over the last thirty years (Roser & Ortiz-Ospina, 2017), figures for income inequality tell a very different story. According to figures released by Oxfam in 2016, "the richest 1% now have more wealth than the rest of the world's population combined. Global inequality is worse than at any time since the 19th century" (BBC News, 2016). Anand & Segal (2015) report "that inequality has exploded over the past few decades" with the Gini coefficient rising from 0.57 in 1988 to 0.72 in 2005 (with 1 as the maximum and 0 as the minimum possible).[2]

While income inequality has persisted for centuries, many factors have fueled the recently widening rift between the rich and the poor. "Our economies may be growing but the number of available jobs is largely failing to keep pace" (Schwab, 2015:7). In addition, globalization has affected international labor markets which results in migration of unskilled labor from the Third World to the First. Recent events such as the 2008 financial crisis have contributed to increased joblessness around the globe, the shrinking of the middle class (Leicht & Fitzgerald, 2007) and the rise of the "new poor" in America (Cohen, 2010). In contradiction to the overall global decline, the number of Americans in extreme poverty doubled between 1996 and 2011 (Schaeffer & Edin, 2012). This group includes many who never recovered from the financial collapse of 2008. In her book, *Strangers in Their Own Land*, Hochschild (2016: 141) describes the plight of many Americans who no longer believe they can achieve the American Dream:

> for the bottom 90 percent of Americans, the Dream Machine—invisible over the brow of the hill—had stopped due to automation, off-shoring and the growing power of multinationals vis-à-vis their workforces. At the same time, for that 90 percent, competition between white men and everyone else had increased—for jobs, for recognition, and for government funds … In fact, as economist Phillip Longman argues, they are the first generation in American history to experience … lifetime down mobility.

17

Gaps in education and social mobility increasingly separate disadvantaged groups from those who are more privileged.

Overcoming inequality is not simply about creating more jobs but is also inextricably linked to other social, economic, and environmental issues. According to the World Economic Forum (Schwab, 2015: 9), "countries need to embrace an integrated agenda that looks at the problem across the social, economic and environmental dimensions, including access to education, healthcare and resources. Central to these solutions is a basket of interventions that promote equitable access to resources and services, as well as inclusive growth with decent jobs and livelihoods for all people within society." Similarly, The United Nations Post-2015 Development Agenda calls for a new global partnership that pairs eradicating poverty with achieving sustainable development goals. These complex pattern of linkages classify inequality as a wicked problem—the solution to which requires many partners working together. "Significant long-term improvements in many of these complex development problems depend on joint action by many different actors who, together, have the knowledge, resources, and potential for long-term engagement required for sustainable changes" (Brown & Ashman, 1999: 140).

Overall, partnerships are becoming increasingly important vehicles for the reduction of poverty both in the US and worldwide. But to tackle the complexity, a wide array of partners are needed.

> A new global partnership should engage national governments of all countries, local authorities, international organisations, businesses, civil society, foundations and other philanthropists, and people—all sitting at the table to go beyond aid to discuss a truly international framework of policies to achieve sustainable development. It should move beyond . . . state-to-state partnerships between high income and low-income government to be inclusive of more players . . . Partnerships in each thematic area, at global, national and local levels, can assign responsibilities and accountabilities for putting policies and programs in place (Schwab, 2015: 8).

Governments and NGOs have worked tirelessly on problems of poverty for years, but, more recently, businesses and local communities have also joined these efforts.

One partnership type designed specifically to improve the lot of the poor is the base of the pyramid (BoP) approach (London & Hart, 2004; Prahalad, 2004; Hart, 2005; Simanis & Hart, 2008). Early BoP strategies involved businesses designing and marketing products needed by the poor. However, first-generation BoP business strategies for operating in the developing world have been criticized for simply treating the poor as consumers of low-cost corporate products (Simanis & Hart, 2008). Instead, if businesses are to help in alleviating poverty, they need to generate robust sustainable incomes for the poor

(Serafin, 2013). However, many firms that have attempted BoP strategies have had a hard time generating a satisfactory return on their investments.

Those BoP strategies referred to as "second generation" involve the poor as business partners and innovators rather than as consumers. These have a better chance of succeeding because they try to address the underlying conditions creating poverty in the first place (Simanis et al., 2008).

> Second-generation BoP strategy requires an embedded process of co-invention and business co-creation that brings corporations into close, personal business partnership with BoP communities. It moves corporations beyond mere deep listening and into deep dialogue with the poor, resulting in a shared commitment born out of mutual sharing and mutual learning (Simanis & Hart, 2008: 2).

Examples of businesses that have adopted second generation BoP strategies include SC Johnson Company and a Dupont subsidiary called Solae which manufactures soy protein globally.

BoP partnerships face many challenges. As Ruffin and Rivera-Santos (2014) point out, institutional relationships among partners may only be informal with no legal validity. Some "mega-partnerships" such as those targeting agricultural improvements in Africa's growth corridor have been criticized for failing "to ensure that local communities are not disempowered and left behind" as a consequence of global players becoming involved (Oxfam International, 2014). According to Oxfam, the transfer of large areas of land to investors and large agricultural firms sacrifices long-term development goals and "undermines local communities' land rights" (Oxfam International, 2014). In contrast, small-scale partnerships that begin at the local level and expand, such as Grameen Bank, which pioneered micro-credit procedures for the poor, and Honeycare Kenya (described in Chapter 1) may be more effective for empowering the poor and building social capital for the future. These efforts can more easily create the conditions that support successful NGO–business partnerships in developing countries, which include: developing a deep understanding of the cultural context and conditions in which the partnership is operating and creating sufficient infrastructure to support the fledgling business in that context (Dahan et al., 2010: 336–8).

In the US, partnerships may provide some solutions to improving the economic well-being of many Americans. Public–private partnerships for constructing roads, bridges, and similar infrastructure projects offer one prospect for increasing employment opportunities. One example is a partnership between the State of Indiana and three private firms to construct and then operate a new bridge across the Ohio River from southern Indiana to northern Kentucky. Funding for the project will come from the state, with the private partners also contributing and bearing the responsibility for the project's long-term debt.[3] Other public–private partnerships are needed for providing retraining programs for workers from declining industries (like coal and steel) to acquire new technologically oriented skills needed by industries of the future such as healthcare, green energy, and service-oriented firms.

The Growing Importance of Health in the Economy

Maintaining healthy populations and providing needed healthcare present different challenges in different contexts but all are intertwined with economics. Although not uniformly true for individual countries, the average percentage of GDP attributable to healthcare expenditures per capita rose from 8.5 percent to 9.8 percent between 1996 and 2014 (World Bank, 2014). In developed economies, the capacity and financial viability of healthcare systems are increasingly strained by aging populations, while in emerging economies, lack of funding and infrastructure hinders the development of comprehensive healthcare systems (Schwab, 2015). Once again, partnerships are often the solution in the absence of governmental resources.

In lower and middle economic countries, fighting infectious diseases such as malaria continues to be an important agenda. A partnership approach to this challenge is supported by the Bill and Melinda Gates Foundation, which in 2003 announced its Grand Challenges in Global Health initiative contributing $200 million to the Foundation for the National Institutes of Health for research to eradicate disease in developing countries (http:// www.gatesfoundation.org/Media-Center/Press-Releases/2003/10/14-Grand-Challenges-in-Global-Health). The initiative, itself an NGO-government partnership, was designed to foster healthcare partnerships that bring "creative attention to solving the enormous health problems of the developing world." The Gates Foundation noted at the time that few research efforts were targeted toward solving the health problems of the poorest two billion people on earth, and there had been no systematic effort to identify and fund the most critical scientific challenges in global health. Since then, the Gates Foundation has spent tens of billions of US dollars to partner with researchers, government, and NGOs to develop and distribute vaccines and drugs to fight HIV, polio, malaria, and tuberculosis. It has also partnered in Bangladesh, Burkina Faso, Ethiopia, and India to ensure that poor children in these areas receive proper nutrition through the age of two.

Growing attention to improving health globally along with increased integration of healthcare services has created countless opportunities for collaborative partnerships to form (Reay & Hinings, 2009; Remond, 2014; McDonnell et al., 2009). In Denmark, a nationally mandated partnership among regional hospital networks, general practitioners, and municipalities was launched to develop nation-wide coherence in treatment of patients with type 2 diabetes.

Although the program aimed to make healthcare more multidisciplinary, multisectoral, and integrated, it fell short of achieving the more collaborative goals to which it aspired because of its top–down, bureaucratic orientation (Waldorff et al., 2014). Researchers evaluating US healthcare partnerships between businesses (which provided manufacturing, marketing, and distribution skills) and public health agencies (who provided funding, data gathering, and analysis) noted, "private–public alliances are challenging, and developing them takes time and resources, but aspects of these alliances can capitalize on partners' strengths, counteract weaknesses, and build collaborations that produce better outcomes than otherwise possible" (McDonnell et al., 2009: 1).

Although developed economies have enjoyed some success with healthcare partnerships, on a global scale health partnerships have a more checkered pattern of success. On the positive side, the "Paris Declaration on Aid Effectiveness," agreed to in 2005 by the "High Level Forum on Aid Effectiveness," in which more than 100 donor and recipient countries participated, developed guidelines for how effective global health partnerships should work and criteria for evaluating them (http://www.oecd.org/dac/effec). Three criteria in particular were established for effective partnerships. These included having a clear structure with well-defined responsibilities for each partner, effective process management, and a commitment to capacity building within the respective participating country. One early adopter of these principles was The Global Alliance for Vaccines and Immunization (GAVI Alliance). The Alliance's success in increasing immunization rates and reducing mortality rates for children in participating countries has been attributed to its adherence to the Paris principles (Lu et al., 2006; Ulbert, 2008). On the other hand, many global health partnerships working to eradicate disease in poorer countries have struggled to be successful. A program in Mali called the Integrated Neglected Tropical Disease (NRD) Initiative is illustrative. While the program successfully dispensed targeted medicines to the population, it did so at the expense of regular healthcare delivery by diverting healthcare workers from routine services to the new campaign. An evaluation of the initiative argued for a more comprehensive approach because noting: "disease-specific interventions implemented as parallel activities in fragile health services may further weaken their responsiveness to community needs, especially when several GHIs operate simultaneously" (Cavalli et al., 2010). GHIs have also been criticized because of their lack of transparency and legitimacy, lack of national government involvement in PPPs and power disparities between drug company partners, NGOs, and the communities who are supposed to be served (Asante & Zwi, 2007). We will explore the issues of effective partnership design, the need to balance power, and effectiveness in collaborative governance in Chapters 5, 7, and 9 respectively.

Environmental Degradation including Climate Change, Water Crises, and the Need for Sustainability

Concerns about the natural environment such as increased stress on water systems, deforestation, and increases in pollution in developing countries and the oceans continue to create the need for collective action both locally and globally to ensure the sustainability of our planetary resources. At the local level, the need to find collaborative ways to balance resource extraction, recreation, and wildlife preservation often brings parties into conflict (Brown, 2002; Gray, 2004; Gray & Purdy, 2014), although a growing body of work also documents collaborative efforts to address environmental and sustainability conflicts (Brown, 2002; Bryan, 2004; Dukes et al., 2000; Emerson et al., 2012; Glasbergen et al., 2007; Gray & Wondolleck, 2013; Ostrom, 2015; Margerum, 2016; Wondolleck & Yaffee, 2000).

On the local level, partnerships to enhance sustainability are cropping up all over the world (Dienhart & Ludescher, 2010; Geddes, 2008; Glasbergen et al., 2007). One area, in particular, in which such local partnerships play a key role is implementation of Agenda 21. This agreement, forged at the Earth Summit in Rio de Janiero in 1992, refers to "a comprehensive plan to be taken globally, nationally and locally by organizations of the United Nations System, governments and major groups in every area in which human impacts on the environment" occur (https://sustainabledevelopment.un.org/outcomedocuments/agenda21). At the local level, participatory, multi-stakeholder processes to implement Agenda 21 are underway across the globe. The plans are designed to target local priorities for sustainable development. A 2012 survey found that at least 10,000 of these partnerships had been formed globally and that many now direct their focus to climate change or biodiversity planning (ICLEI, 2012).

While no longer novel, collaborative partnerships for addressing natural resource problems continue to be essential to address a myriad of environmental concerns, including logging, agricultural pollution, lack of biodiversity, forest management, endangered species issues, and many problems related to water. Despite their growing use, natural resource alliances often face limitations including insufficient conceptual models (Margerum, 2016), inadequate structuring of implementation (Clarke, 2014), poor leadership (Bryson et al., 2006; Gray, 2007), mishandled representation and unwillingness of some parties to participate (Bryan, 2004; Gray, 2004), and failure to address critical process issues. We explore these issues and how partnerships can address them in Chapters 5, 6, and 7.

Partnerships for enhancing sustainability have also burgeoned in the last several years (Glasbergen et al., 2007; Gray & Stites, 2013). These partnerships typically join businesses and NGOs to enhance corporate sustainability efforts and range in scope from simple two-partner alliances to multistakeholder initiatives like the Forest Stewardship Council, the Soya Roundtable, and the UN Global Compact, which involves fifty top corporations and leading NGOs These multistakeholder initiatives often perform a regulatory or standard-setting function in the absence of an overarching global government (Glasbergen, 2007; Khagram, 2006; Newell, 2001; Pattberg, 2007). We discuss the rise and management of sustainability partnerships in Chapter 8. While partnering to solve local environmental problems is of crucial importance, scaling up such partnerships to regional, national, and global levels adds layers of complexity and setbacks diminishing the possibility of successfully developing collaborative solutions. This is only too evident in the difficulties encountered in reaching international agreements about ivory poaching, conflict diamonds, and climate change mitigation (Ansari et al., 2013). We specifically address problems of scaling up collaborative partnerships in Chapter 10.

Rise in Identity Conflicts across the Globe and Increased Global Migration

According to Held (2007), shifts in economic demands and environmental degradation associated with globalization have propelled migration and mass movements worldwide. The rise of globalization has enhanced the well-being of some countries and threatened that of others (especially, but not exclusively, smaller, less powerful ones), raising uncertainty about their place in a global world. In response to these challenges and fueled by the desire to regain control over their lives and their environment, a "widespread surge of powerful expressions of collective identity" has emerged (Castells, 1997: 2). This upsurge of identity power is also manifest in an increasing number of transnational social movements rooted in identity positions (e.g., sexuality, religion, ethnicity, nationality) (Thomlinson, 2003). Many identity conflicts are rooted in faith differences in which "religion becomes fused with violent expressions of social aspirations, personal pride, and movements for political change" (Juergensmeyer, 2003: 10).

Appadurai (2006) offers one explanation for why these identity conflicts arise. He argues that the threat of the erosion of national sovereignty and, in effect, a meaningful place in the world for one's people, forces majority members of a nation to unleash their national anxiety on minorities within their own state. These minorities, in effect, become the scapegoats for the majority's inability to protect their nation from a loss of identity and a diminished place in the world.

> Minorities are the major site for displacing the anxieties of many states about their own minority or marginality (real or imagined) in a world of a few megastates, of unruly economic flows and compromised sovereignties. Minorities, in a word, are

23

metaphors and reminders of the betrayal of the classical national project. And it is this betrayal . . . that underwrites the worldwide impulse to extrude or to eliminate minorities (Appadurai, 2006: 43).

Other factors about minorities also contribute to arguments favoring their extinction. They are already typically deemed socially inferior, stigmatized because they are economically inferior, religious deviants, illegal immigrants, criminals or otherwise nonproductive members of society. For the privileged, the presence of minorities blurs the boundaries of what constitutes the state. Minorities may also be "carriers of unwanted memories of the acts of violence that produced existing states" in the first place (Appadurai, 2006: 42). Additionally, some states have sought to expand their influence by "non-political means" which further contributes to "flows of migrant labor from one nation to another" (Hall, 2006: 17).

Partnerships to deal with this increase in identity conflicts may be focused on peacemaking activities within war-torn states or on helping to resettle refugees in the communities to which they immigrate. Because of resulting mass migrations, refugee problems have become paramount. Some 20 million of the 65 million people who have been displaced are currently living in refugee status. Partnerships range from local community efforts to global ones led by the UN Refugee Agency (UNHCR). One recent example of a local partnership to assist refugees was recently created between Westpac, a bank-ing giant, and Thrive, a charity working with refugees in Australia. Westpac provides the funding to support Thrive's provision of educational assistance, mentoring, and business-start-up loans as well as refugee settlement services offered by two other partners (Caneva, 2016). Another local partnership in North Carolina, called the Refugee Community Partnership has constructed a network of community volunteers to help refugees on a number of issues including serving as bridges to needed community services, assisting youth with educational needs, and providing food though an arrangement with local farmers.

In Europe, where 1.3 million refugees have arrived from the Middle East, a partnership called The Regional Refugee and Migrant Response Plan was launched in 2015 when refugees started pouring into Europe (http://www.unhcr.org/en-us/news/press/2017/1/5880b1474/unhcr-iom-partners-launch-new-plan-respond-europes-refugee-migrant-situation.html). The partnership, intended to complement governmental responses to refugees, includes UNHCR, the International Organization for Migration (IOM) and 72 other within country partners. The priorities of the program, designed to help 340,000 refugees in 2017, include ensuring safe asylum and protection for them and especially for women and children and children who arrive without their parents. The plan intends to improve the efficiency and coordination of refugee processing while ensuring dignified migration management through-out Europe and Turkey. It also seeks to provide safer alternative routes and support for survivors of sexual and gender-based violence. UNHCR partners with other UN agencies, NGOs, international bodies, and universities to address the plight of refugees around the world through a wide array of programs. For example, another UNHCR partnership (with the International Detention Coalition) addresses detention issues by improving detention conditions, increasing monitoring and searching for alternatives to refugee camps. On a smaller, more local scale but nonetheless important, a partnership among churches and church members, called The Refugee Highway Program (RHP), facilitates local and European-wide ministries among refugees and asylum seekers. Their work includes community education about the plight of refu-gees, aiding in resettlement, helping asylum seekers to connect to churches, and advocacy for them to the EU.

Increase in Violent Weather Events

The increase in violent weather events triggered by climate change is a prob-lem that affects every continent. It is exemplified by the Philippines being deluged with the world's strongest storm, severe drought in central Africa, Brazil, and Australia, massive flooding in Pakistan, and the widest tornado ever seen in the US (Schwab, 2015). According to the Intergovernmental Commission on Climate Change (Field et al. 2012), new research based on computer modeling techniques provides evidence linking climate change and increases in severe heat waves.

Like the other global issues we've identified, partnerships have a role to play in addressing this issue. While the WEF argues the solution lies in improving resilience before disaster hits (Schwab, 2015), partnerships among govern-ments, businesses, NGOs, and communities are needed both before and in the aftermath of disasters. For example, partnerships designed to improve preparedness include advertising and educational campaigns and partner-ships like the National Infrastructure Protection Plan (NIPP) that takes steps to enhance protection of critical infrastructure such as powerlines, bridges, and highways. Another partnership called Stop, Think and Connect assists businesses and individuals to increase cybersecurity (http://stopthinkconnect. org). Coordination between the Church of the Jesus Christ of the Latter Day Saints and Davis County, Utah enables use of church facilities as shelters in the event of storms (FEMA, 2015). Partnerships can enhance response by stockpiling resources in advance of a disaster and by building effective com-munication networks to prepare for severe events. And, partnerships are essential for rebuilding efforts in the aftermath of severe weather events. For example, the Dutch Relief Alliance is a partnership of Dutch and global NGOS

25

with the Dutch Ministry of Foreign Affairs that has provided disaster relief responses fifteen times in 2015 and 2016, with special emphasis on responses in conflict countries (http://www.zoa-international.com/dutch-relief-alliance-2015-2017).

Inability of Governments to Respond

Beyond the usual challenges of corruption and political deadlock (Schwab, 2016), governments are finding that the complex interdependencies that are characteristic of many problems exceed their capacity to respond, both in scope and in scale. This forces them to turn to other stakeholders (business, communities, and NGOs) to garner the needed resources and expertise to meet the challenges of governing and the need for innovation (Ansell & Gash, 2008; Sørensen & Torfing, 2011).

> In sharp contrast to the routinized and collaborative innovation practices in the private sector, the public sector is commonly associated with rule-bound, bureau-cratic silos characterized by red tape, inertia and stalemate. As such, a key part of the neoliberal critique of the public sector has been to blame it for not being sufficiently dynamic and innovative (Sørensen & Torfing, 2011: 846).

Efforts to correct this problem such as deregulation, privatization, contracting out, and reliance on strategic management principles (Sørensen & Torfing, 2011) are increasingly being replaced by national efforts "to enhance innovation in public services and regulation" (Sørensen & Torfing, 2011: 846). Further, the concept of deliberative democracy has advanced the idea that collaborative solutions are needed to ensure governments can satisfy their mandates. Deliberative democracy (Dryzek 2010; Fishkin, 2011) has been defined as "a form of government in which free and equal citizens and their representatives justify decisions in a process in which they give one another reasons that are mutually acceptable and generally accessible, with the aim of reaching decisions that are binding on all at present but open to challenge in the future" (Gutman & Thompson, 2002: 3–7).

Worldwide, the ability of governments to govern is challenged by inequality and persistent joblessness and other problems identified above. Consequently, the role, responsibility, and even legitimacy of governments is increasingly being called into question, often by transnational social movements (Batliwala & Brown, 2006; Held, 2007). In 2015, the World Economic Forum (Schwab, 2015: 7) reported that "We are at a critical fork in the road, a period of decision that will dictate the health and viability of our civilization for decades to come."

In light of these contextual factors driving the formation of multisector partnerships, potential partners have many different motivations to link up with partners from other sectors. In the next section we explore motivations for different kinds of partners to pursue collaborative alliances with partners from other sectors.

Partners' Motivations for Joining Cross-Sector Partnerships

Understanding differences in partners' motivations is important because these differences can produce a mismatch within the partnership and lead to difficulties in working together if motivations are not aligned or complementary. Additionally, when partners have different motivations, different types of partnerships may be needed. Both business and NGO motivations for forming partnerships, can be classified into four main categories: legitimacy-oriented, competency-oriented, resource-oriented, and society-oriented motivations. We define each below and then examine how each applies to business and NGOs respectively.

Legitimacy oriented motivations refer to an organization's desire for social acceptance and are based on its conformance to societal norms and expectations (Brown, 2008). Legitimacy is "a generalized perception or assumption that the actions of an entity are desirable, proper, or appropriate within some socially constructed system of norms, values, beliefs, and definitions" (Suchman, 1995: 574). Legitimacy is important for organizations because without it, organizations will have difficulty acquiring critical resources such as talent, information, and public trust needed for long-term, sustained success. When businesses and NGOs form partnerships, both strive to gain or preserve their legitimacy in the public eye. Legitimacy can be sought either proactively to build acceptance and trust, or reactively to counter or repair threats to acceptance and trust.

Competency-oriented motivations refer to acquiring the necessary skills and knowledge "to coordinate diverse production skills and integrate multiple streams of technologies" (Prahalad & Hamel, 1990: 82). Because businesses and NGOs have very different knowledge, skills, and capabilities, sharing these competencies is an important motivator for both types of organizations. In particular, businesses can often complement NGOs with their "vast resources, an ability to get things done, and readily measurable results," whereas NGOs "are struggling for daily survival, working slowly on more complex problems, and do good works in ways that often cannot be measured" (Kramer & Kania, 2006: 20).

Resource-oriented motivations refer to garnering assets, including financial and social capital. A major hurdle in addressing social and environmental problems is having "access to the right capital at the right time" (Balderston, 2012: 24). Both partners can bring social capital to the table through their network connections. Leveraging these complementary resources motivates both businesses and NGOs to partner in order to share the risks and reduce the costs of acquiring these resources separately.

Both businesses and NGOs may also have broader *society-oriented motivations* for partnering. These motivations are designed to make changes to how society deals with the issues that the partnership is addressing, ostensibly to benefit the common good.

Business Motivations for Partnering

Some stakeholders view businesses as the proverbial "root of evil" with regard to social and environmental maladies, and businesses and NGOs are frequently thought to have opposing sides on issues. From this perspective, "businesses are viewed as purely self-serving, pursuing profit in ways that are inherently destructive to human culture, well-being, and the environment," whereas NGOs are viewed as "altruistic, charged with identifying and solving the world's problems, and acting as public watchdogs to raise the alarm about the evils of business" (Kramer & Kania, 2006: 20). Because of these perceptions and because of campaigns by NGOs and shareholders that target business for its shortfalls, some business motivations to partner may initially be largely reactive. However, many businesses have shifted from being predominantly reactive to external pressure to adopting more proactive motivations for partnering (Laasonen et al., 2012). Sometimes business motivations are purely philanthropic, but they can also go well beyond philanthropy blending both social and financial interests (Emerson, 2003). The problem is that it is difficult to measure social interests because we lack an effective calculus to account for the social value that many corporations now generate (Emerson, 2003).

> What is required is a unifying framework that expands the definition of invest-ment and return beyond the historic one of finance and toward a new definition capable of holding a broader understanding of value than that most frequently reflected in traditionally endorsed financial operating ratios. In truth, the core nature of investment and returns is not a trade off between social and financial interest but rather the pursuit of an embedded value proposition composed of both (Emerson, 2003: 38).

Proponents of this view argue that there is a wide array of social value being created in market transactions that will only be adequately accounted for with the development of proper metrics (Emerson, 2003; Moore, 2014).[4] Nonethe-less, businesses join partnerships for a variety of different motives. Table 2.1 summarizes business motivations for partnering.

Legitimacy-Oriented Motivations. Firms proactively motivated by legitimacy use partnerships to help them build a reputation, image, and brand for social

Table 2.1 Business motivations for partnering

Legitimacy-oriented	Resource-oriented	Competency-oriented	Society-oriented
Proactive	**Proactive**	**Proactive**	**Proactive**
Build reputation, image and branding	Gain access to networks	Gain expertise	Influence policy development
Build the social license to operate	Build capacity	Leverage heterogeneous knowledge	**Reactive**
Avoid confrontation	Create innovative products and markets	Identify issues and trends	Respond to stakeholder and shareholder activism regarding local problems
Attract and retain employees	Secure monetary funds	**Reactive**	
Reactive	Share risk	Grow awareness of complex social problems	
Save face			

and environmental responsibility; attract and retain employees; and build the social license to operate. "By becoming part of a partnership that promotes sustainable development, companies have an opportunity to present a 'good global citizen' side to their operations and may be able to bolster their public image" (LaFrance & Lehmann, 2005: 219). Businesses also use partnerships to help them attract and retain employees whose values align with company values. Through association with a social and/or environmental NGO, firms can avoid confrontation by preempting stakeholder attacks. Partnerships with NGOs can also help firms to build community relationships and manage social conflicts. Partnerships can also emerge from reactive legitimacy motivations, such as saving face after a firm has received negative publicity. In the aftermath of such a conflict, a partnership with an NGO can signify that the firm is taking actions to rectify the concerns raised. Realization that businesses can complement NGO efforts has led to an increase in both breadth and depth of business–NGO partnerships (Rondinelli & London, 2003: 62).

Competency-Oriented Motivations. While legitimacy-oriented motivations are primarily reactive, proactive competency-oriented motivations for businesses to partner include gaining important contextual expertise from NGOs, leveraging synergies based on the different knowledge of the two organizations and identifying emerging issues and trends that are important to stakeholders. A particular competency of NGOs that businesses may seek is expertise in measuring broad or long-term outcomes rather than short-term outputs (Plantz et al., 1997). For example, NGOs measure the impact of their efforts on hunger and homelessness rather than the number of free meals served or shelter beds provided. Recognizing the value of the differential perspectives and expertise that nonbusiness partners can provide, businesses are increasingly eager to take advantage of these differential lenses to gain insight into the complex social and environmental problems they face.

Resource-Oriented Motivations. By engaging in partnerships with NGOs, businesses can use their unique resources to help to solve social and environmental issues. At the same time, they may also reap economic benefits such as improving the marketability or profitability of their existing products or developing innovative new products or markets they might not have envisioned without their partners' help. A key resource that businesses can gain from working with NGOs, for example, is social capital and access to community and volunteer networks that NGOs have already built (Dahan et al., 2010). We have already noted the importance of establishing deep connections with communities in BoP partnerships, for example, but developing this kind of connection to communities is crucial for healthcare, refugee, and environmental partnerships as well.

Society-Oriented Motivations. Businesses may proactively seek to partner as they consider how creating value for society (Emerson, 2003) will shape the future context in which they operate. Often societal benefits go hand in hand with financial ones such as when businesses introduce sustainable practices into their supply chains. Businesses may value the prospect of influencing policy development and shaping legislation that may eventually affect the firm (Esteves & Barclay, 2011; Kolk, 2014; Reed & Reed, 2009). By becoming involved in shaping policy, businesses are able to coopt legislation to minimize its adverse effect on the firm or industry. In a more reactive way, businesses are motivated to address societal issues in order to respond to stakeholder activism. These motivations may stem from the nature of the business itself or from executives' and employees' visions for social responsibility.

NGO Motivations for Partnering

Nongovernmental organizations, commonly referred to as NGOs, are not-for-profit organizations independent of business and government "whose stated purpose is the promotion of environmental and/or social goals rather than the achievement or protection of economic power in the marketplace or political power through the electoral process" (Bendell, 2000: 16). NGOs can be categorized in terms of how they interact with businesses. NGOs use various tactics to promote social and environmental goals, from radical confrontation to a more moderate influence on business activities (Ählström & Sjöström, 2005; Argenti, 2004). For example, Greenpeace and Global Exchange often develop public campaigns to expose controversial business practices, such as Greenpeace's attack on Shell regarding the disposal of the Brent Spar, an oil storage buoy in the North Sea. Other NGOs, such as the Rainforest Action Network and the Environmental Defense Fund, seek to identify and pursue objectives that are complementary to businesses interests.

The public often ranks NGOs higher than governments as environmental stewards. Because NGOs often take a confrontational stance they function as ethical watchdogs for governments and capitalist societies (Nalinakumari & MacLean, 2005). However, in recent years, as a result of globalization processes and scarce resources (Loza, 2004: 299), relationships between businesses and NGOs have dramatically shifted from "gadflies into allies" (Yaziji, 2004: 110), that is, from a generally confrontational stance to a more cooperative posture (Kourula & Halme, 2008; Rondinelli & London, 2003). For example, even Greenpeace, which has often been viewed as a confrontational NGO that won't accept money from businesses, has engaged in partnerships with select firms (Ählström & Sjöström, 2005; Hartman & Stafford, 2006). Table 2.2, NGO Motivations for Partnering, summarizes why NGOs join partnerships.

Legitimacy-Oriented Motivations. Like business, NGOs can have a proactive legitimacy-oriented motivation for partnering, such as boosting their reputations, images, and branding. NGOs also see partnerships as a way to maximize their sphere of impact and garner wider support by acting in accordance with their core missions. Partnerships with firms can help NGOs become more prominent actors because partnerships can extend the NGO's reach and capabilities. NGOs are also motivated to engage in partnerships as a reactive response to funders' demands to become more business-like. NGO funders increasingly demand accountability for NGOs' resources and outcomes; therefore, much like businesses, NGOs require performance legitimacy (Brown,

Table 2.2 NGO motivations for partnering

Legitimacy-oriented	Resource-oriented	Competency-oriented	Society-oriented
Proactive	**Proactive**	**Proactive**	**Proactive**
Build reputation, image and branding	Gain access to networks	Gain expertise	Influence policy development
Build the social license to operate	Build capacity	Leverage heterogeneous knowledge	**Reactive**
Avoid confrontation	Create innovative products and markets	Identify issues and trends	Respond to stakeholder and shareholder activism regarding local problems
Attract and retain employees	Secure monetary funds	**Reactive**	
Reactive	Share risk	Grow awareness of complex social problems	
Save face			

31

2008; Holzer, 2008; Lee, 2011). By partnering, NGOs and businesses can each fulfill many of their legitimacy-oriented motivations.

Competency-Oriented Motivations. The main competency-oriented motivation for NGOs is the proactive acquisition of technical and managerial skills that are complementary to the NGO's own skill base. By combining their differing competencies, "partnerships have been a way to expand capabilities beyond what the organization's own resource base permits" (Sagawa & Segal, 2000: 108).

Resource-Oriented Motivations. Whereas businesses often have deep financial pockets, NGOs often lack the necessary funds to address social and environmental issues. Thus, NGOs can directly or indirectly garner resources to advance their societal missions by partnering with business. As funding by government and philanthropic foundations has become more restrictive in some contexts, nonprofit organizations have sought to increase their earned income through the sale of goods and services, sometimes in conjunction with partnerships. NGOs can also gain access to other businesses and political networks through their partners' contacts.

Society-Oriented Motivations. NGOs are proactively interested in partnering in order to increase public awareness of issues and to induce positive changes in businesses, industries, and society. NGOs that choose confrontational strategies do so to increase general awareness of an issue and to coerce a business to change. Confrontational NGOs may choose their targets based on a variety of criteria, including businesses with prominent brand names, more consequential impacts, and larger size (Hendry, 2006; Yaziji & Doh, 2009). Similarly, NGOs often choose to target front-running companies, because "working with trendsetters gives maximum leverage, because the changes they make ripple through their supply chains and cause competitors to follow suit" (Yarnold, 2007: 23). The ways that NGOs partner with businesses can range from "co-leading projects to solve specific social or environmental problems, to joint marketing, to education activities" (Ählström & Sjöström, 2005: 237). NGOs may sometimes even work with some of the "worst" companies to help address the NGO's core social and/or environmental mission.

Although NGO engagement with business may seem to have shifted from pressuring to partnering, "it is very likely that many NGOs who do engage in collaboration with business corporations still see themselves as adversaries, considering their collaboration as an arena for legitimate disagreement and negotiation" (Laasonen et al., 2012: 538). In many ways, once NGOs are "close" to firm operations, they may be able to better achieve their goals by focusing on practical solutions to social and environmental issues—as in the landmark partnership between McDonald's and the Environmental Defense Fund regarding sustainable food packaging materials.

Intended Purposes of Cross-Sector Partnerships

Two important bases on which partnerships can be distinguished have been identified: (1) the perceived starting conditions from which the partners are pursuing a partnership and (2) the nature of the desired outcomes (Gray, 1996). The perceived starting conditions may be based on a shared perception that an opportunity exists that neither potential partner could capitalize on alone. Alternatively, potential partners may start from a position of conflict—that is, they have conflicting views about how a problem should be defined and addressed, but often these stakeholders have different and even competing views about the nature of the problem itself in addition to differing views about what to do about it (Trist, 1983; Gray, 1989). Partnerships may also differ with respect to the outcomes the partners desire to achieve, ranging from simple information sharing to formulating (and enacting) joint agreements (Kolk, 2014). By cross-referencing the perceived starting conditions and types of outcomes, four distinct intended purposes of partnerships can be identified as shown in Table 2.3.

Partnerships designed to *create a shared vision* occur when the starting conditions are viewed as opportunities and partners simply seek to share information with each other. These may be one-time events or extended relationships. For example, the Global Reporting Initiative provides information and offers guidelines for sustainable development practices. Partnerships perceived as opportunities that have desired outcomes to reach joint agreements and action

Table 2.3 Purposes of partnerships

		INTENDED PURPOSE	
		Information sharing	Action
MOTIVE FOR PARTNERING	Opportunity	Create a shared vision	Design and implement a shared strategy
	Conflict	Open a dialogue	Negotiate a settlement

plans are referred to *as designing and implementing a shared strategy*. When partnerships originate from conflict and partners desire an exchange of information, we refer to these as *opening a dialogue*. As with creating a shared vision, these partnerships may be short-lived or continue for months or even years. For example, the Responsible Business Forum holds an annual conference to support dialogue among businesses, NGOs, and governments on sustainability and environmental practices (http://www.responsiblebusiness.com/). Similarly, dialogues have been held to find common ground among disputants in the debate over abortion (LeBaron & Carstarphan, 1997; Public Conversation Project, 1999) and others have pursued joint research and learning on sustainable food production (Glasbergen, 2007). In these dialogues, differences are explored, but no decisions are made. When parties in conflict convene to try to reach an agreement about how to settle their dispute, these kinds of partnerships are called *negotiated settlements*. These types of partnerships may be temporary or produce long-term cooperation around implementation of the agreements that are reached to provide a new governance system for the field.

Opportunities abound for shared public–private-nonprofit partnerships rooted in opportunities. As noted earlier these can enhance education, improve health, create jobs, advance technology, and serve other community interests. However, even when pursuing noble goals, partners may disagree on the exact nature of the desired goal, or differ in their views of how the goal is to be accomplished (Huxham & Vangen, 2005). In Chapter 6 we explore many reasons for conflict among partners and propose a variety of interventions designed to help partners work through their conflicts to enhance chances of success in their alliance.

As we also identified earlier in this chapter, many pressing problems in the world today are rooted in conflicts over resources, rights, and values, yet our chances of making headway on these problems necessitate partnerships among the very parties that are in conflict with each other. An example of a partnership spawned by social movement activism that provoked conflict is evident in the environmental justice movement. Concerns about environmental justice arose in disadvantaged communities in the US (largely African American) that were located near brownfields that left these communities exposed to disproportionately high levels of toxic chemicals. In Chattanooga, TN, for example, protests by two such communities, coupled with strong principles promoting community activism and community visioning processes throughout the city, eventually turned the conflict into a dialogue among industry, city officials, and residents, and the federal government that ended up generating action to clean-up a Superfund site in the affected area (Elliott et al., 2003).

While partnerships cannot be substitutes for needed government actions or vehicles that simply add to corporate coffers without improving communities, they can offer creative means of tackling the most pressing problems the world faces today if they are organized to reflect a wide array of stakeholder's concerns and balance potential power disparities among those who participate. In the rest of the book, we look more deeply at what it takes to create and manage partnerships that have the greatest chances of realizing the joint aims of partners who undertake them.

Notes

1. According to the World Bank, a person is considered to live in extreme poverty if he or she is living on less than $1.90 per day based on 2011 US dollars.
2. These statistics were calculated using the absolute gini index. Other economists using other indices have reached different conclusions.
3. https://www.americanprogress.org/issues/economy/reports/2014/12/08/102515/public-private-partnerships/ (accessed July 22, 2017).
4. Other organizations that have constructed such metrics include the Global Reporting Initiative, The Aspen Institute and The International Network on Sustainability Indicators. See Emerson (2003).

3

An Institutional Lens on Multistakeholder Partnerships

In this chapter we conceptualize partnerships as new forms of organizing that arise in response to changing conditions within institutional fields. An institutional field is comprised of institutions and networks of organizations that together constitute recognizable areas of life (DiMaggio & Powell, 1983). Fields are evolving and often contentious social orders with sets of common understandings about the purposes, relationships, and rules of interaction (Fligstein & McAdam, 2011). However, fields can also experience "episodes of contention" or periods "of emergent, sustained contentious interaction," characterized by "a shared sense of uncertainty/crisis regarding the rules and power relations governing the field" (Fligstein & McAdam, 2011: 21). These changes in fields give rise to problems, opportunities, and conflicts that single field members (even incumbents) may often be hard pressed to handle on their own. For example, campaigns by NGOs that expose firms' unsustainable practices (de Bakker et al., 2013) can cause firms to rethink their strategies. An example of such disruption in the wood products industry occurred in 2005–6 when Greenpeace and ForestEthics targeted Kimberly Clark and Victoria's Secret with "do not buy" campaigns for sourcing unsustainable Canadian Boreal old growth pulp in their products (Kleenex) or advertising (Victoria's Secret catalogues) (Berman, 2011; Riddell, 2014). This not only forced the firms to change their sourcing strategy but contributed to negotiation of the Canadian Boreal Forest Agreement between twenty-one forest companies and nine environmental NGOs in 2010. (See Chapter 10 for further discussion of this partnership.)

As we outlined in Chapter 2, we face many contested issues as a global society for which no clear path forward is readily apparent. This creates opportunities and even the necessity for partnerships to emerge that bring together multiple groups and organizations within these contested fields. "Contested meanings of globalization, development, sustainability, security, human rights, democracy, and governance are part of the genesis and constitution of these (partnership) arrangements, as well as their evolving dynamics and effects" (Khagram, 2017).

To understand the increasing number and variety of partnerships, we draw on institutional theory to provide a new range of tools to understand how and when partnerships develop and a conceptual framework for diagnosing their effectiveness.

Partnerships as Negotiated Orders

Partnerships have previously been conceptualized as negotiated orders—institutionalized thought structures among networks of organizations (Warren et al., 1974). As Gray (1989: 229) observed, "Collectively establishing an agreement that satisfies multiple stakeholders involves considerable negotiation." Trist (1983) referred to this as a process of appreciation in which stakeholders are evaluating current norms and practices associated with an issue of problem (e.g., homelessness) in terms of what is possible and desirable for the future. Partnering also involves gaining a deeper appreciation for how other stakeholders view the issues and for their visions of the future. Collaborating, therefore, involves a joint process of appreciation (Vickers, 1965): appraising the limits of the current institutional arrangements, agreeing on a process for how to renegotiate them, and then searching for a convergent (Feyerherm, 1995) negotiated order for the field in the future.

The negotiated order of a field can be described in terms of its "logic." Logics describe the material practices of a field, that is, what is done and how it is done, and the symbolic meanings of a field, or what matters and why. More specifically, a logic is a set of organizing principles that govern the selection of technologies, define what kinds of actors are authorized to make claims, shape and constrain the behavioral possibilities of actors, and specify criteria for effectiveness and efficiency (Friedland & Alford, 1991). Much scholarly work has shown that shifts in logics are the sources of change in fields. For example, the field of healthcare has gradually shifted from a care logic to an economic one (Scott et al., 2000), and new logics replaced previous ones in publishing (Thornton, 2004) and in French gastronomy (Rao et al., 2003). However, in some fields, competing logics exist in an uneasy alliance (Dunn & Jones, 2010; Marquis & Lounsbury, 2007; Purdy & Gray, 2009; Reay & Hinings, 2009). To capture these variations, some scholars have classified institutional fields according to their level of coherence, that is, "the extent to which dominant institutional logics are able to provide sufficient guidance to the behavior of actors in the field (Rein & Stott, 2009)" (Vurro, Dacin & Perrini, 2010: 44). Fields with high levels of coherence are relatively stable because conflict among different logics is low and actors see fit to conform to the prevailing norms (Vurro et al., 2010).

A field's coherence and negotiated order are not guaranteed to last over time, however. Coherent fields, especially those with strong boundaries, may eventually become isolated and out of step with wider societal expectations (Seo & Creed, 2002; Zietsma & Lawrence, 2010). When this happens, the organizations comprising the field may lose legitimacy in the wider society. Social movements may introduce new frames (Armstrong, 2005; Schneiberg & Soule, 2005) that challenge the dominant logic among field actors (Anand & Watson, 2004). Frames are "shared conceptions that constitute the nature of social reality" (Scott, 2003: 880). Existing logics may be questioned or challenged in the face of new environmental conditions that generate new ways of understanding reality. In these cases, the field becomes open to new logics and new configurations among its constituent organizations, and new rules of the game may be negotiated.

When field coherence is low, actors have greater latitude to try to shape the prevailing logics in their own interests. In these circumstances, actors can engage in interactive framing, creating field change from the bottom-up (Gray et al., 2015; Dewulf et al., 2009). Logics develop over time through framing processes in which a few actors develop shared understandings of issues that then become amplified and ritualized, gradually spread throughout organizations and/or fields (Gray et al., 2015) and eventually become instantiated as logics. Actors who come from a common background usually take for granted their shared frame, as when government actors frame a problem around policy making, or business people frame a problem using an economic lens. These shared frames can be highly localized, as in when groups of businesses in close competition adopt frames that are distinct from those shared by other strategic groups of businesses (Porac et al., 1989). However, when field-level actors adopt different frames, "fields becomes the center of debates in which competing interests negotiate over issue interpretation" (Hoffman, 1999: 351). One strategy for managing the tensions that result from low field coherence is for field-level actors to form collaborative partnerships. For example, Reay and Hinings (2009) described how physicians and government-sponsored Regional Health Authorities formed partnerships to address the need for innovative healthcare delivery. Similarly, the field of recycling emerged from partnerships between environmentalists—who viewed it as a way to reduce waste and conserve resources, waste management companies—for whom recycling was a potential revenue stream, and government agencies—who were charged with reducing pollution and managing limited landfill capacity (Lounsbury et al., 2003). Consequently, because of this partnership, recycling shifted from a fringe to a mainstream activity in the US through a change in the underlying field frame governing how waste was managed. Waste recycling programs were an outgrowth of this partnering that synergized differing frames into a merged field frame that satisfied business, environmental, and governmental interests.

Recent conflicts between environmentally oriented NGOs and business over sustainability provide other good examples of the emergence of partnerships in contested fields. NGOs have long been at the forefront of campaigns urging businesses to adopt more sustainable practices. Recently this has generated a wide array of partnerships in which businesses and NGOs share resources and competencies to promote more sustainable business practices (Gray & Stites, 2013). Firms have reached out to NGOs as partners because the latter often have expertise as well as societal legitimacy sought by businesses. NGOs profit from getting access to resources to pursue their objectives. "By becoming part of a partnership that promotes sustainable development, companies have an opportunity to present a 'good global citizen' side to their operations and may be able to bolster their public image" (LaFrance & Lehmann, 2005: 219). Some prominent examples include Foron's collaboration with Greenpeace to build a hydrofluorocarbon-free refrigerator and Rabobank's partnership with World Wildlife Fund for Nature (van Huijstee and Glasbergen, 2010b) to promote green banking (which we present in more detail in Chapter 4). These partnerships have spawned the emerging field of business sustainability and transformed how sourcing decisions are made, new products are developed and fledgling new industries (Lounsbury et al., 2003) and innovative governance structures (Ansell & Torfing, 2014; Innes & Booher, 2010) develop.

As we described in Chapter 2, institutional change can generate opportunities as well as conflicts that then spur the development of collaborative partnerships. For example, changing beliefs about the strategic value of employees as well as public expectations for social responsibility have created opportunities for corporations to pursue new approaches to employee engagement and reputation enhancement in collaboration with nonprofit organizations. One partnership emerging from these field-level changes is nonprofit CityYear's collaboration with Timberland apparel, which yielded a clothing line to generate income for CityYear (Dees & Elias, 1996) and significant employee, brand, and reputational enhancements for Timberland (Austin & Elias, 1996). Another example is UMSI, a partnership between pharmaceutical firm Merck and nonprofit United Negro College Fund that provides scholarships and mentoring for African Americans seeking advanced degrees in science and engineering, while generating a larger pool of minority graduates and prospective employees who may spark valuable new innovations (Mervis, 1999).

To summarize our argument so far, changes in organizational fields can create conditions favorable to collaborative partnership formation—either to capitalize on emergent opportunities or to address the conflicts among stakeholders over what the field should be. In either case, stakeholders try to negotiate a new field-level frame (and its associated norms and practices) to govern the field (Ansari et al., 2013). Consequently, partnerships can become the vehicles by which organizations team up to jointly exploit new opportunities or to search for ways to reconcile competing logics and frames. Partnerships are a social space in which frames are negotiated, offering the potential for new frames to amplify and create new field-level settlements (Ansari et al., 2013; Fligstein & McAdam, 2012; Rao & Kenney, 2008). However, not all partnerships succeed. When field level conflicts persist and become intractable (Lewicki et al., 2003), they may destroy the potential for partnership (Gray, 2004), leaving the field riddled by conflicting logics that may coexist indefinitely (McPherson & Sauder, 2013; Purdy & Gray, 2009; Reay & Hinings, 2009).

From Frames to Institutions: An Interactional View

Next we look more closely at the processes through which nascent meanings that emerge in incoherent, or what Brown (1980) calls underorganized, fields may eventually become institutionalized, and we use this as a lens for understanding how both partnerships and fields institutionalize over time. Institutionalization can be conceptualized in terms of emerging alignments in actors' frames about the field as well as with respect to their interactions, goals, and practices. The role of building shared interpretations or shared meanings is a fundamental tenant of institutional processes. This involves explicating the "dynamics of meaning in the process" of institutionalization (Zilber, 2008: 164)—that is, the micro-processes associated with the unfolding of meaning over time, particularly through communication. As Zilber further explains... "studies of meanings must explore the dynamics and micro-processes of theorizing, translation, and discourse, and... explicitly articulate their implications for our understanding of the social construction of institutions and the institutional order."

Bottom-up Approaches to Meaning Making

Various studies have explored meaning making in institutional theorizing and how interpretations can reshape institutions and affect institutional change and maintenance (e.g., Barley & Tolbert, 1997; Thornton et al., 2012), but only a few have offered a detailed bottom–up explanation for meaning making (cf., Phillips et al., 2000b; Zilber, 2008). Moreover, studies of institutional meaning-making have used a confusing welter of terms (e.g., frames, schemas, scripts, texts, vocabularies) that has prevented a clear understanding of how micro-level meanings become institutionalized over time (Purdy et al., 2017). For example, frames are either theorized as the means for translating institutional logics from the societal to the field level (Thornton et al., 2012) or as strategic devices to change fields through social movements (Benford & Snow, 2000). In both cases, the resultant emphasis is on top–down processes that have been decoupled from their moorings in localized social interaction (Barley, 2008; Hallett & Ventresca, 2006).

We adopt an interactional framing approach (Collins, 2004; Dewulf et al., 2009; Goffman, 1967, 1974) to theorize about how micro-level meaning making can develop from the bottom up into institutionalized collective meanings over time. The "interactional" view of framing has its origin in symbolic interactionism (Blumer, 1969) emphasizing the use of symbols to create meaning during interactions. This view is consistent with the cultural-cognitive aspect of institutions which Scott (2003: 880) conceptualized as "the frames through which meaning is made." Specifically, frames are the interpretations that actors construct to make sense of everyday interactions drawing on frame repertoires available in the wider culture. Framing constitutes meaning making and action-taking by enabling actors to "locate, perceive, identify and label" occurrences and renders "what would otherwise be a meaningless aspect of the scene into something meaningful" (Goffman, 1974: 21). The consequence of framing is that "some aspects of a perceived reality" become "more salient in a communicating text, in such a way as to promote a particular problem definition, causal interpretation, moral evaluation, and/or treatment recommendation" (Entman, 1993: 52). For example, when we observe a person running down a sidewalk toward a train station we could entertain many different frames about this activity; for example, we could conclude they are rushing to catch a train or fleeing capture after robbing a store.

An interactional view argues that frames only exist within and are sustained through encounters among actors. Unless frames are "produced and reproduced in interaction" (Poole et al., 1985: 86), they cannot be sustained. If frames are shared and reinforced, as opposed to remaining fluid and divergent, they can begin to take root in fields and even amplify in scope, regularity, and emotional intensity—processes that serve to institutionalize frames as broader systems of collective meaning among actors that eventually may become taken-for-granted cultural conventions (Gray et al., 2015). Thus, "institutional structure does not exist in spite of, or outside, the encounters of day-to-day life but is implicated in those very encounters" (Giddens, 1998: 69).

During interactions actors can uphold frames already in use resulting in frame solidarity, modify extant frames, or depart from them all together. Snow and his colleagues (1986) refer to these processes as "micro-mobilization" tasks that either leave frames intact or add a "re-keying" that modifies the frame to some extent (Goffman, 1974). Frame breaks occur when subsequent actors depart from the frames in use and offer alternative conceptions instead. Frame breaks may also emerge when suppressed institutional contradictions emerge that are often accompanied by strong emotional reactions to prevailing frames (Creed et al., 2010; Seo & Creed, 2002). As interaction proceeds, rekeyings become laminated on top of each other affording actors a variety of frame choices with which to interpret their experiences. These rekeyings may produce negligible changes in meaning when translated, be deemed acceptable as a modification, or generate wholesale frame conflict (Kaplan, 2008; Lewicki et al., 2003) if some actors resist their introduction. Thus, current meanings are either reinforced, modified, or challenged as frames pile up during interactions.

Consequently, the framing perspective also recognizes that multiple and competing frames may be in play simultaneously within a field (Lewicki et al., 2003; McPherson & Sauder, 2013), explaining how competing frames may be held in tension among actors within a field and may or may not be reconciled at various points in time to achieve conformity. This notion extends existing models of institutional change that view change as a settlement process and presuppose resolution of differing meanings (e.g., Rao & Kenney, 2008), even if only temporarily. Thus, some frames and framings become widely shared and others fail to influence collective meanings outside the immediate actors who introduced them.

Amplification via Scope

Amplification of meaning can occur as frames are extended to and adopted by other networks of actors so that eventually the meanings are more widely held and move from the micro to the meso level. Actors often participate in multiple networks and may share the frames they use in one network with associates in another. When there is a high degree of network overlap, actors may feel compelled to conform and to make others conform (Collins, 2004). However, more diverse, non-redundant networks increase the potential for greater diffusion of a frame. Figure 3.1[1] depicts how similar and conflictual meanings may amplify across different analytical levels (Murray, 2010; Purdy & Gray, 2009). It suggests how laminations and their accompanying formulas—rules for the interrelationships of frame layers (Diehl & McFarland, 2010)—can enable micro-level interactions to extend from their creators to larger groups and become more institutionalized through amplification. In referring to levels, we use *micro* to refer to dyadic or small group meanings, *meso* to refer to organizational meanings, *macro* to capture cross-organizational and field-level meanings, and *societal* to refer to meanings that span fields.

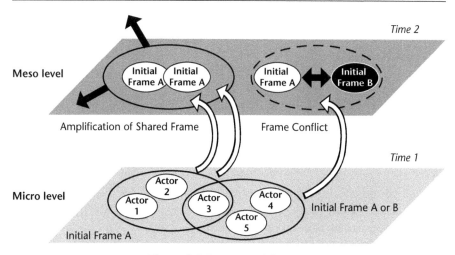

Figure 3.1 Frame amplification

In Figure 3.1 Actor 3 belongs to two networks. If Actor 3 shares frame A with Actors 1 and 2 and persuades Actors 4 and 5 to adopt frame A also, frame A diffuses. Amplification of the shared frame is likely to continue through additional networks and spread throughout an organization or even an entire field if justifications embedded in discursive narratives and shared accounts are available, emphasizing the compatibility of new frames with extant practices and values of the new adopters (Gondo & Amis, 2013; Green, 2004).

On the other hand, frame conflict is more likely if actors in overlapping networks already hold frames that differ from the emergent one (Gray, 2004; Lewicki et al., 2003). Thus, if Actors 4 and 5 in Figure 3.1 adopt frame B instead of A, this rekeying would produce what Goffman (1974) calls a frame break. If adherents of frames A and B each attempt to make their frame resonate to gain more followers, the ensuing frame conflict may amplify to the meso level to become a full-fledged "framing contest" (Kaplan, 2008); thus, a micro-level difference of frames between two people could eventually replicate itself at the organizational level. In dense networks with many triadic relationships (in which there are reciprocal ties among three network members), negative interpretations of others more easily diffuse and solidify these differences in framing (Labianca et al., 1998). Thus, shared frames can amplify to the meso (or organizational) level.

A similar depiction could be used to describe how meanings amplify from the meso to the macro (or field) level. Social movement organizations (meso level) deliberately promote such amplification processes by advancing frames designed to appeal to or put pressure on specific organizational targets. If these targets adopt the new frame, it garners greater legitimacy (Green, 2004) and,

43

in so doing, ramps up pressure on other targets to do the same, moving the field toward wholesale adoption of the emergent frame (Rao et al., 2003; Strang & Soule, 1998).

Similarly, frame breaks can amplify from the micro to the macro level as competing groups gain more members and efforts to construct common field frames go awry. When the competing frames persist, field conflicts may end in ceasefires (Meyer & Höllerer, 2010) or agreements to disagree (Purdy & Gray, 2009), turn into political battles resolved when powerful elites coercively impose dominant logics, or leave fields in states of perpetual conflict (Hajer, 2003; Pache & Santos, 2010). For example, Murray's study of patenting at the science–commerce boundary showed how hybrid fields "can be produced through the pursuit of differentiation . . . and are maintained in productive tension rather than through easy coexistence" (2010: 346). We pursue the issue of frame amplification and levels more thoroughly in Chapter 10.

The Evolution of Goals, Norms, and Practices within Fields

When a consistent set of micro-level actors interact, the intensity and durability of shared meanings can amplify through frequent and regular use, eventually granting to this meaning a normative force within the group that comes to confer both moral and practical legitimacy on the interpretations (Suchman, 1995). Eventually, through repeated use the meanings become typifications—that is, they come to be taken for granted (Berger and Luckmann, 1966) and invoked without deliberate attention. When networks are fluid (i.e., many different individuals are joining and leaving), however, typification is less likely. In more stable networks, micro-level interaction rituals become institutionalized at the meso (or macro) levels through repetition and eventual routinization of practices.

Eventually, as frames amplify and solidify and are re-enacted by actors over time, they develop into routines and may eventually become accepted as cultural practices or conventions. A routine is "a repetitive, recognizable pattern of interdependent actions involving multiple actors" (Feldman & Pentland, 2003: 96; Parmigiani & Howard-Grenville, 2011). Practices represent the recognition and acceptance of sets of routines (Whittington, 2006). Practices don't belong to individuals but have a recognized social component; they have been accepted and carry normative legitimacy within a community (Zietsma & Lawrence, 2010).

While routines are frequently conceptualized as stable and enduring patterns that comprise organizational structures and create the means by which work is accomplished (Cyert & March, 1963), recent conceptualizations view routines as in flux and subject to change (Dionysiou & Tsoukas, 2013; Feldman, 2000; Feldman & Pentland, 2003; Parmigiani & Howard-Grenville, 2011).

This conceptualization argues that "routines are dynamic processes involving interdependent actors whose agency makes a difference in how routines are enacted" (Dionysiou & Tsoukas, 2013: 183). It is this more fluid account that fits our purposes here. In particular, we view collaboration as the process of negotiating a common set of both norms and routines that will govern future interactions among the participating stakeholders but are subject to revision as stakeholders continually renegotiate their relationship over time. Thus, collaboration involves the negotiation of new meanings, routines, and practices, trial and error enactment of these and the ongoing appraisal of their efficacy for regulating subsequent interactions among stakeholders within a field. "As experience with joint activity accumulates, each participant abstracts and generalizes... from understandings and actions that have been jointly, intersubjectively established" (Dionysiou & Tsoukas, 2013: 191).

In addition to developing routines and practices to enact joint interpretations, some routines may take on a ritualistic character that binds stakeholders together as they develop a shared emotional commitment to them. As Collins notes, an interaction ritual "involves focusing attention on the same activity... and it has a shared emotional focus, which builds up as the ritual successfully proceeds" (Collins, 2004: 112). Shared emotions (which Durkheim (1912/1965) referred to as collective effervescence) can be rekindled and intensified through joint rituals. The power inherent in rituals lies in their ability to generate emotional contagion or to construct a collective mood within a group (Hatfield et al., 1993) which has been shown to influence the levels of cooperation, the degree of conflict, and the overall performance of the group (Barsade, 2002). The generation of emotional contagion is what propels rituals to eventually institutionalize, but the levels of emotion associated with rituals need not be dramatic; they can simply refer to "long-lasting, underlying tones or moods that permeate social life" and become taken-for-granted interpretations embodied in corresponding symbols and cultural practices (Collins, 2004: 106). The effect of rituals is to develop both individual commitment to the meanings and practices and to establish boundaries that help solidify group-level identification (Collins, 2004; Hardy et al., 2005). Once a ritual is instantiated within a group or organization or field, it appears to exist outside of the interaction, that is, it is reified or objectified (Tolbert & Zucker, 1996) and "merely reflects macrostructure" in contrast to the more fluid interaction rituals from which it emerged (Collins, 2004: 7).

However, actors can also import negative emotional residue from previous encounters into partnerships linking them across time and space. That is, emotions and emotion-laden cognitions generated in previous interactions set up the conditions for current and subsequent interactions and can reignite past cleavages among stakeholders who have historically been in conflict

(Gray, 2004) if their current interactions are not carefully managed (Gray & Wondolleck, 2013) ultimately rendering conflicts more intractable (Lewicki et al., 2003). For example, in a conflict over levels of recreational usage within Voyageurs National Park, resolution was elusive as wise-use activists, environmentalists, and park officials became mired in frozen frames for over forty years (Gray, 2004). Not only do such conflicts persist over time, but they can become part of each opposing group's collective memory that is passed on from generation to generation, as in the Israeli–Palestinian conflict (Barthel, 1996). Thus, emotional energizing plays a key role in the amplification and persistence of meanings and practices and, depending on where boundaries are drawn (Zietsma & Lawrence, 2010), can either promote or impede broadly accepted institutionalized meanings and practices from gaining wider acceptance within a field.

Summary

Our conceptualization of partnerships as new forms of organizing that arise in response to changes within institutional fields reveals interactive framing as an important tool for understanding the emergence of collaborative partnerships. Overall, a bottom–up theory of interactional framing helps us to understand the relationship between partnerships, meaning, and institution building because it unpacks the steps by which interactive framing may (or may not) lead to institutional change in fields. An essential part of the collaborative process is exploring the initial frames that actors bring to the partnerships and how these are enacted through dialogue (Innes & Booher, 2003). If potential partners seek to understand the basis of the others' frames and search for and craft collective interpretations where possible, these may create the foundations on which new collective routines, rituals, and practices for the field may emerge. Just as important, however, our theory explicates how these outcomes may be impeded if powerful competing frames arise or are rekindled to disrupt accepted systems of interpretation within fields (Creed et al., 2010; Fiss & Hirsch, 2005; Snow et al., 1986). Thus, theorizing about framing and framing mechanisms can account for both maintenance and change within fields and provides insights into when and why these differential outcomes occur, making it more possible for actors to forecast and understand whether or not and why their change efforts may prove successful. Our model emphasizes the recursive aspects of institutional change and helps to explain why some institutional changes may unfold quickly while others may take decades, e.g., acceptance of climate change as a commons (Ansari et al., 2013). In sum, we show how partnerships can shape institutional fields through a structurationist cycle of framing, action, reframing, and institutionalization over time. Thus, it allows for both the possibility that partnerships may foster the emergence of new fields (Lounsbury et al., 2003) and the possibility that fields in conflict may not always achieve collective mind (Weick & Roberts, 1993) or reach settlements (Rao & Kenney, 2008) and may instead remain in flux and tension for extended periods (Meyer & Höllerer, 2010; Purdy & Gray, 2009).

Note

1. Figure originally appeared in Gray, Purdy & Ansari (2015). Used with permission.

4

Three Diverse Examples of Multistakeholder Partnerships

Case #1: Rabobank and NGOs

In the early 2000s, as sustainability became an increasingly important issue for corporations, the number of partnerships between business and NGOs began to increase (Gray & Stites, 2013). Although they were initially strange bedfellows, both businesses and NGOs often found value in these alliances, particularly when they allowed reputational advantages for business and offered NGOs needed resources for conducting or expanding their missions (Austin & Seitanidi, 2012). Not all such partnerships were characterized by initially complementary goals, however, as more combative NGOs using more confrontational tactics (Bosso, 1995) challenged businesses by exposing their non-sustainable practices. This case describes a series of interactions among a single organization and two NGOs who used contrasting strategies—one collaborative and the other combative—to move the bank toward more sustainable practices.

Rabobank, the second largest bank in the Netherlands in terms of total assets, is comprised of 174 independent local banks as well as many specialized international units and subsidiaries in forty countries, all organized centrally by Rabobank Nederland. The banks were founded on cooperative principles but are sustained by private investing. Traditionally strong in the food and agriculture sectors within the Netherlands, the bank is also globally known for its investments in food and agribusiness financing. The bank prided itself on having a strong sustainability orientation and in 2006 was considered the most progressive of Dutch mainstream banks (van Huijstee & Glasbergen, 2010b).

Partnership with World Wildlife Fund for Nature Netherlands

As part of its sustainability efforts, in 2006 Rabobank teamed up with a nature conservancy NGO, the World Wildlife Fund for Nature Netherlands (abbreviated WFN in Dutch) to launch a climate-neutral credit card. As a global organization, the World Wildlife Fund had thirty offices around the world. Within the Netherlands, WFN identified itself as an engager (Bosso, 1995) reporting on its website in 2008 that, "In all its projects, WNF looks for collaboration with other parties, for example governments, companies, local communities and partner organizations" (cited in van Huijstee & Glasbergen, 2010b: 6). This strategy was consistent with World Wildlife Fund globally which has historically been involved in many business–NGO partnerships.

When WFN approached Rabobank in 2006 about launching a green credit card, the project appealed to the bank. According to van Huijstee and Glasbergen (2010b: 601), the proposal was appealing to the bank for several reasons: "the rising importance of climate change as an issue, the firm intention of Rabobank's climate expert to develop a climate-neutral consumer product, and the results of a research report concluding that consumers did not perceive Rabobank as a credible source of climate-related communication." They also viewed WFN as a credible partner and the project as one that could enhance the firm's overall reputation.

In order to develop a green credit card, the partners had to address two issues: (1) the footprint calculation method (to determine the emissions associated with consumer purchases) and (2) the compensation method (how the footprint would be offset). For the former, they settled on an existing footprint calculation tool; for the latter, they agreed to buy international clean development mechanism (CDM) credits. However, the partners' preferences regarding whether to adopt the Gold Standard label diverged. The WFN pushed for the Gold Standard because it "guarantees that the existence of the CDM project is sustainable, advantageous to the host country, and genuinely results in a reduction of CO_2" (van Huijstee & Glasbergen, 2010b: 602), but this choice resulted in greater costs for Rabobank. For WNF, however, the partnership's credibility depended on "maximum transparency and integrity of compensation, making these essential and non-negotiable issues" (van Huijstee & Glasbergen, 2010b: 602). Ultimately, Rabobank acquiesced to WFN's preference reasoning that the reputational gains to the bank from offering the card were worth the extra expense.

Concurrent with these efforts, WWF UK (WFN's British partner) released a report in 2006 that compared the sustainability performance of thirty signatories of the Equator Principles, including Rabobank.[1] The report challenged all major Dutch banks over their investments in nonsustainable industries. Given this pressure and pressure from competitors seeking CSR visibility (Van Huijstee & Glasbergen, 2010a), Rabobank proposed making work on its investment policy part of its partnership with WFN, who gladly agreed. Together the two organizations agreed on five components of their partnership (Van Huijstee & Glasbergen, 2010b: 603–4):

1. a communications program;
2. collaboration on CSR in Rabobank's investment policies;
3. product collaboration regarding a credit card with CO_2 compensation;
4. product collaboration regarding investment funds;
5. possible future collaboration on markets.

Partnership with Friends of the Earth

During approximately the same time period in 2006, Friends of the Earth Netherlands (FoEN) launched a campaign called *Banks: Save the Climate.* FoEN called out Rabobank and three other Dutch banks because of their large carbon footprints stemming from nonsustainable global investments in soy and palm oil (van Huijstee & Glasbergen, 2010a). In a departure from its usual combative strategy, FoEN signaled it was "prepared to engage in a constructive dialogue with banks willing to create climate-friendly products and policies and demonstrate the feasibility of the alternative practice FoEN demanded" (Van Huijstee & Glasbergen, 2010b: 605). Consequently, unlike its competitors who resisted pressure from FoEN, Rabobank begun to explore with the NGO how it could credibly assess the sustainability of its portfolio and was able to link these efforts with its partnership with WFN as well. As a result of its interactions with these two NGOs, Rabobank reappraised its investment portfolio and modified its investments in accord with the criteria the partnerships produced. This involved shedding some unacceptable investments and frustrating some customers while enhancing its CSR reputation to become the best among all major Dutch banks. Figure 4.1 provides a schematic of the steps in Rabobank's partnerships with the two NGOs.

Questions about Collaborating Raised in This Case

1. What benefits are derived for business and NGO partners respectively from partnering with each other?
2. How do different NGO strategies for encouraging (provoking) firms to engage in CSR affect the partnerships that emerge?
3. What do partnerships look like from the vantage point (level of analysis) of the focal firm trying to engage in CSR?
4. What factors influence the ability of corporations to effect CSR-related or sustainability related change in the larger fields in which they are operating?
5. How/why do firms and NGOs address conflicts in their value orientations and assessment criteria for judging the success of partnerships?

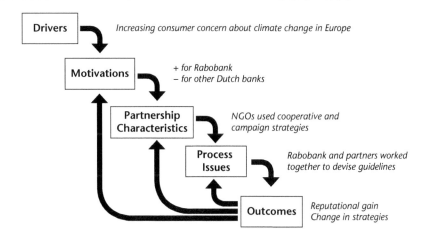

Figure 4.1 Rabobank and NGOs partnership

Case #2: US Hydroelectric Licensing Rules

Hydroelectricity is the largest source of renewable energy in the United States, providing about 7 percent of the total electricity generated (National Hydropower Association, 2016). While hydroelectricity is a clean, renewable energy source, hydroelectric dams have significant environmental and social impacts. Hydroelectric dams change the course and flow of a river, affecting fish migration, plant and animal life, the water supply, land use, and communities in the river's watershed. How a dam affects these areas is dictated by the terms of a license granted by an agency of the US government, which must balance the demand for electricity with public and environmental interests. Licenses have a long-lasting and widespread impact; the terms of a license remain in effect for 30–50 years, and about 1,600 hydroelectric dams are governed by such licenses (Federal Energy Regulatory Commission, 2004).

In the late 1990s, the federal agency responsible for licensing hydroelectric projects sought to revise the process by which dams were relicensed. Recent advances in environmental science, new environmental regulations, and increased stakeholder concern about the impacts of hydroelectric dams had converged to make the relicensing process lengthy and expensive, averaging ten years and $10 million USD in costs (Swiger & Burns, 1998). Licenses must include terms that satisfy the sometimes-conflicting regulatory requirements of national, state, and tribal governments—hydropower is the second most regulated of all electricity generation sources in the US, after nuclear power. In addition, environmental activists argued that federal regulators should use the licensing process to make hydroelectric projects more

51

environmentally friendly (Kriz, 1993). Thus license requirements typically reduced the generating capacity of a dam by 8 percent (National Hydropower Association, 1999), creating challenges for dam owners who were concerned about economic viability as deregulation of electric power had created increased competition and uncertainty in the industry.

Initial Attempts. In 1997, complaints from the hydropower industry association spurred the Federal Energy Regulatory Commission (FERC) to introduce an alternative process for relicensing that relied on stakeholder collaboration to negotiate license terms, speeding up relicensing by about one year on average with lower costs. However, some participants found the collaboration process burdensome and some processes required judicial interventions to determine jurisdictional issues, set precedents, or overcome impasses.

In the winter of 1998, FERC formed the Interagency Task Force that included members from the Departments of the Interior, Commerce, Agriculture and Energy, the Environmental Protection Agency, and the Council on Environmental Quality. The task force's goal was to make the hydroelectric licensing process more effective and efficient through administrative reform without revising the entire licensing process. The group issued seven reports before concluding its work in late 2000. At about the same time, the Electric Power Research Institute formed a committee called the National Review Group (NRG), which began as a consortium of hydroelectric project owners, but soon expanded to include conservation groups and federal agency representatives. After a series of eight meetings, the group published the *Hydro Relicensing Forum Preferred Practices* Guidebook in 2000.

Industry representatives continued to insist on the need for licensing reform (Swiger & Grant, 2004). In December 2000, the National Hydropower Association concluded that "procedural reform, no matter how far reaching and well meaning, will not be enough to correct the structural flaws in the licensing process and the role of the Departments in that process" (Comments of the National Hydropower Association, 2000). A team of federal agencies began drafting possible changes to the licensing process, while at the same time, the National Review Group also began developing a set of recommendations for a new licensing process, which it conveyed to FERC in 2002.

Collaborative Efforts. In September 2002, FERC announced an effort to completely revise the hydroelectric licensing process (the process is summarized in Figure 4.2). The agency recognized that a collaborative partnership would be needed to effectively balance the demands of the nation's energy supply, environmental sustainability, regulatory requirements, and the public interest. A conventional process for rewriting federal rules would involve the agency issuing a public notice, drafting revised rules, inviting public comment on the proposed rules, and finalizing the rules in conjunction with feedback.

HYDRO RULEMAKING SCHEDULE

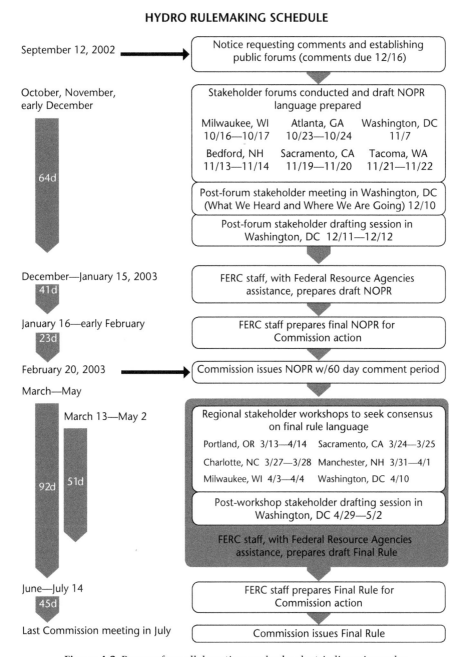

Figure 4.2 Process for collaboration on hydroelectric licensing rules

FERC instead sought extensive input and involvement from stakeholders to help craft its revisions to the hydroelectric licensing rules.

Because FERC holds statutory authority for hydroelectric licenses, it served as designer and convener of the collaboration process that would rewrite the rules for relicensing. The process involved a series of face-to-face public meetings held in cities proximate to hydroelectric dams in the northeast, southeast, upper midwest, northwest, and southwest United States. FERC's public notice about changes to hydroelectric licensing provided an explicit framing of the issues to be considered in the collaborative process. It posed a series of nine questions, beginning with "is there a need for a new licensing process?," that identified issues related to the roles of states, Native American tribes, scientific studies, time frames, and dispute resolution. FERC also included two proposals for a new licensing process, one that had been developed by the Interagency Hydropower Committee (IHC) comprised of federal agencies, and one that had been developed by the National Review Group (NRG), comprised primarily of dam owners.

The Meeting Process. Over the next two months, FERC held eleven meetings in six locations throughout the US that were attended by representatives from the primary stakeholder groups: hydroelectric project owners, federal agencies, state agencies, tribal governments, and conservation organizations. Five of these meetings were specifically designated as Tribal Forums that provided preferential opportunities for input from recognized Native American tribes, which govern as sovereign states that oversee territory and treaty rights. Members of the public were welcome at tribal forums and tribal representatives were welcome at public forums.

Each session was hosted by a panel of four to seven members representing FERC and its federal agency partners at the Departments of Commerce, Agriculture and the Interior. Most sessions also included one or more members of the NRG on the panel. Each meeting consisted of an introduction of the proceedings by FERC staff followed by presentations of the IHC and the NRG licensing process proposals. A two-hour period for formal public comment was followed by a two-hour period for open discussion, and each session concluded with a FERC representative summarizing the next steps in the process. A court reporter captured comments verbatim so that complete transcripts could be produced.

Attendance at each meeting ranged from one person to over sixty people. Federal agencies and state agencies were represented in the meeting by their employees. Organizations that own hydroelectric dams, which include private enterprises, cities, and quasi-governmental agencies, typically sent employees to the meetings and some included consultants and/or attorneys in their delegation. NGOs were usually represented by employees and volunteer supporters. Tribes variously sent elders, elected leaders, and/or nonmember experts they employed (such as fish biologists who help manage fisheries, or attorneys who assist with monitoring treaties). Individual members of the public also participated including landowners, elected officials and citizens from communities near dams, and professionals such as scientists and attorneys who provide services during the licensing process.

Stakeholder Input.[2] Meetings permitted stakeholders to voice their perspectives. Dam owners were interested in a licensing process that would reduce the time and costs of licensing, as under the traditional process "relicensing costs will consume one to two years of revenues." Owners also sought greater technical clarity about licensing requirements and processes: "[The process] needs to encourage the use of neutral, objective decision criteria for assessing ideas, making decisions and resolving disputes. The way it works now is every time we have a problem, we have to invent the process to solve the problem or solve the dispute." Industry representatives also questioned the authority of various organizations to impose license conditions and sought to limit the ability of other stakeholders to reopen aspects of the license on which agreement had been reached. Some conflicting interests were evident within this group based on the differing interests of small hydroproject owners versus large hydroproject owners. The dominant view presented was that of the large hydroproject owners, particularly through the words and actions of industry associations.

Federal agencies sought to ensure that the process would reinforce their authority to solicit information during the licensing process and to place mandatory conditions upon the license. They were also interested in demonstrating responsiveness to the interests of key stakeholders. These agencies had successfully formed a coalition with FERC prior to the collaborative process in the interest of administrative reform, and that coalition remained intact throughout the collaborative process. Federal agencies presented a united front and represented themselves as members of the IHC rather than advancing the particular interests of their agencies. One federal agency employee noted, "I think that one of the greatest benefits we are seeing so far has just been an overall development of a good cooperative working relationship between the agencies...half the challenge is just getting the responsible parties in the agencies, to work closely together towards a common end, which is an efficient licensing process that reaches quality decisions." State agencies expressed one dominant interest: that federal agencies and the licensing process recognize their authority to impose conditions or restrictions on licenses.

Like state agencies, the tribes sought recognition of their decision-making authority and ultimately, of their status as sovereign nations. A tribal leader commented, "FERC has not articulated how it considers and incorporates its trust responsibility to protect and enhance tribal resources including fishery and culture resources that are impacted by dams." Tribes sought stronger personal relationships with FERC staff rather than interactions through legal filings and expressed concern that the coalition of federal agencies excluded tribes from important decisions. Tribal government leaders also sought recognition of the cultural and spiritual value of the natural resources affected by licensing, and the incongruence of the rule of law with the natural world: "The river to us is a living body. It speaks to us. We pray to it. So we don't make a law to govern it; we make a law to be cooperative with our relatives in the universe." Finally, tribes sought a longer time period for the licensing process: "We are naturally concerned with any reform that purports to shorten or expedite the process, as we tend to believe that such changes are designed to benefit the applicant at the expense of the tribes and other stakeholders." Short deadlines made it difficult for resource-constrained tribes to respond in a timely way to a huge volume of filings. In contrast, conservation groups sought a process that would be both speedy and thorough to create maximum protection for natural resources. They also emphasized the need for a process that facilitates citizen and NGO involvement in the licensing process.

Crafting an Agreement. After reviewing comments from the meetings as well as written comments from others not present, FERC reported its findings at a stakeholder meeting held in Washington, DC. This was followed on the next day by a session in which sixty-one stakeholders assisted in drafting new proposed rules. In February 2003, FERC issued its proposed rules and held another series of eleven meetings at different cities around the US to solicit feedback. Six of these meetings were designated as public workshops and five were designated as tribal workshops. The goal of the workshops was to try to reach consensus on the final language that would govern the licensing process. For these workshops, FERC produced a "yellow book," which included an agenda, copies of presentations, and a redlined version of the regulation that allowed comparison between the existing and proposed regulation. Within this structured framework, time was devoted to issue identification and interactive discussion of the issues that were most important to those present at each meeting.

The conclusion of the collaborative partnership process was a four-day drafting session in Washington, DC, referred to as "hydro hell week," to finalize the language of the rules for a new licensing process. The drafting session included multiple breakout groups to address specific aspects of licensing and a group to address tribal consultation. These groups were tasked with proposing solutions to complex issues that had arisen in the course of the collaborative process. This process focused on problem solving by the participants rather than by FERC. A FERC representative noted that "it's one thing to read somebody's comment letter, but it's another thing to actually hear them explain themselves, hear them talk, hear them react to other people and what they say. That, to me, is the most valuable part, just listening to the way you've developed your recommendations. So that has been extremely valuable to us at FERC staff in putting this rule together."

Integrated Licensing Process. On July 23, 2003, FERC adopted its new process for licensing of hydropower projects. The new licensing approach, known as the Integrated Licensing Process (ILP), emphasizes better coordination within FERC and across federal agencies, with clearer schedules for all activities. A tribal liaison was appointed within FERC to serve as a point of information and contact. The new guidelines provide for formal dispute resolution by referral to a three-member dispute resolution panel that includes FERC staff, a representative of the referring tribe or agency, and an independent third-party expert.

The new process also includes public participation early in the licensing process and better coordination with state water quality certification processes. The integrated licensing process became the default process in 2005 but use of the previous traditional and alternative processes is permitted with Commission approval.

FERC conducted evaluations of the new integrated licensing process in 2006 and 2010 through interviews, teleconferences, and regional meetings. The new process has improved the tone and speed of the licensing process. The tensions regarding time were not resolved in that the increased speed of the process benefitted by dam owners and the natural resources that NGOs sought to protect, but created higher demands on tribes, federal and state agencies, and the public.

Questions about Collaborating Raised in This Case

1. How do the parties differ in terms of how they are represented in the collaboration (e.g., number of representatives, support or compensation available for participants, use of agents to represent a party)?
2. How does having multiple avenues for participation, which here included written comment, regional meetings, and national meetings, affect the nature of representation and participation in the collaboration?
3. What does collaboration look like from the perspective of the convenor, FERC? How might the partnership look different if it had been convened by a nonregulatory group such as the NRG coalition?
4. How might a collaborative process that results in new regulations written by participants yield changes in the broader field of hydroelectric power?

5. What was the impact of designing a process that gave special status to one group (Native American tribes) on the collaboration?
6. How does a collaboration that occurs within a well-established, high-level governance context differ from a collaboration outside such a context?

Case #3: Mesá de Diálogo y Consenso

Yanococha gold mine, owned by the US Newmont Mining Corporation began operating near Cajamarca, Peru in 1993. However, the mine became the object of protests by local community members because of lack of transparency in its land purchases, unsafe practices, and eventually environmental contamination. After numerous unsuccessful protests, in June 1999, an indigenous people's organization, Federation of Female *Rondas Campesinas* of Northern Peru (FEROCAFENOP) appealed to the International Finance Corporation (IFC) on behalf of local residents asking the IFC to intercede on the community's behalf, but initially this, too, yielded no change. The IFC is part of the World Bank Group and owns a 5 percent share in Yanococha. It provided loans to the mine in 1993, 1994, and 1999. In May 2000 FEROCAFENOP representatives joined a campaign organized by the US-based NGO, Project Underground, and traveled to Colorado to attend Newmont Mining Corporation's annual shareholders' meeting. Project Underground had served as a voice critical of Yanococha in a 1999 report alleging water contamination and other negative environmental and social impacts. A subsequent visit by the IFC to Cajamarca to meet with FEROCAFENOP and other local stakeholders also produced no immediate change. While the IFC became increasingly concerned, Yanococha did nothing to respond to the community.

In July 2000 the IFC's Office of the Compliance Advisor/Ombudsman (hereafter referred to as CAO) took notice of the situation after a disastrous toxic spill occurred the month before. A truck contracted by Yanococha released 151 kilograms of mercury along 40 kilometers of a road in Cajamarca. The spill affected three towns—Choropampa, Magdalene, and San Juan—and exposed hundreds of community members to mercury poisoning when they tried to clean it up without proper protection. Shortly thereafter, the CAO convened an independent commission to investigate the mercury spill. The independent commission's report was critical of Yanococha and its contractor that had transported the mercury, Ransa Commercial, claiming that their reaction to the spill was slow and inadequate. The report also criticized the Ministry of Health for being ill-equipped to handle the cleanup and care for victims. The report stated that

The companies did not apply international standards to the handling and transport of hazardous materials, and that monitoring and audit systems failed to identify these shortcomings. Underlying causes identified by the commission included inadequate governmental and company policies on hazardous waste management and weak oversight of mine operations (Building Consensus, Monograph 1, 2007: 5).

This was followed in early 2001 by two community organizations (Frente de Defensa de Choropampa and FEROCAFENOP) filing separate formal complaints with the CAO. The first complaint criticized Yanococha for an insufficient response to the people's health needs, for not implementing the Commission's recommendations and "undermining community cohesion through coercion" (Building Consensus, Monograph 1, 2007: 7). The second complaint was broader, citing adverse environmental and social impacts and failure to comply with IFC policies.

The CAO's Response and the Formation of the Mesá

In July 2001, the CAO traveled to Cajamarca to conduct its first assessment. Its first report was published in August based on interviews with 40 Cajamarchan stakeholders. These interviews showed that trust between the community and the mine was exceedingly low and uncovered a host of unresolved issues including how to deal with the long-term health effects of the mercury spill, polluted air and water, environmental damage from the spill, repression of those who spoke against the mine, unfair treatment of landowners, no attempts to consult the community on plans for the mine, corruption of the regional and national governments, adverse social impacts and no follow-through on promises for public works (Building Consensus, Monograph 1, 2007: 10). The interviews also persuaded the CAO that a roundtable dialogue was a preferable approach to take moving forward rather than a fact-finding or compliance audit "that would issue specific findings on the past actions of the company, the complainants and IFC" (Building Consensus, Monograph 1, 2007: 9). The decision was explained this way:

An audit might have responded more succinctly to some specific allegations in the FEROCAFENOP complaint concerning the company's non-compliance with the IFC's regulations. However, the CAO's wide-ranging conversations with local stakeholders indicated that the potential for conflicts between the community and mine was the central concern, overriding issues specific to the IFC—at least in the beginning stages of the dialogue (Building Consensus, Monograph 1, 2007: 9).

To test the community's readiness for a dialogue, the CAO convened a series of three workshops in September and three more in November 2001. Roughly 65 participants attended these workshops about half of which were representatives from stakeholder groups and the other half were unaffiliated citizens.

The assessment and the workshops revealed that stakeholders differed in their beliefs about the utility of a dialogue. While many agreed that lines of communication between the community and mine needed to be improved, others preferred that the mine be held accountable for its past wrongdoing—something the dialogue could not accomplish on its own. Additionally, not all executives within Yanococha believed that a dialogue was a useful endeavor, particularly because of past community protests and threats against the company. Nonetheless, a few executives agreed to participate in the dialogue, called the Mesá de Diálogo y Consenso.

Although the CAO envisioned an open and inclusive discussion among all stakeholders, not all that were invited agreed to participate. Some NGOs insisted that Yanococha be held accountable for the damage it had caused. Others declined to participate because they believed the table was tipped in Yanococha's favor or that the CAO, because of its affiliation with IFC, could not be neutral despite the fact that four mediators with no connections to the mine or the community were hired by the CAO. A local farmers' group expressed concerns about the mine's effects on water and plant life and demanded that Yanococha: (1) create conservation programs for the local flora and fauna; (2) conduct new environmental impact surveys of the water and soil; and (3) establish educational and health programs for the local residents (BBC News Online, March 15, 2002). Still others simply did not trust the company or other stakeholders who were participating in the dialogue and believed they would be tainted by affiliating with the mine and lose credibility within the Cajamarchan community. In the words of those who opposed the Mesá,

> The [dialogue process] proposal avoided the issue of Choropampa explicitly. We wanted the mine to be held strictly to fixing the problem. It was not time for conflict mediation and discussion of less urgent issues. The mine is very good at talking about its good deeds. We were sick of their talk. We wanted to know when will they do something that the people need, and they were not discussing this in earnest at the Mesá (Building Consensus, Monograph 1, 2007: 15).

Despite these serious objections, many other stakeholders believed that dialogue was the best way to address the corrosive relationship between the community and the mine and to address the power differential that existed. The assessment report had found that the mine dominated all aspects of Cajamarchan life and that stakeholders believed they had no say in decisions the mine made that affected their lives. The Mesá offered these people a voice for the first time, and they believed the Mesá would "level the playing field between the mine and the community" (Building Consensus, Monograph 1, 2007: 15). Some stakeholders also hoped to gain status or leverage with Yanococha by participating in the Mesá. The question of IFC's participation was also debated since it was a shareholder in the mine and a development institution. However, "the IFC preferred that Yanococha interact directly with community members on issues of conflict, with the CAO serving as mediator, and IFC pursuing on a separate track its technical capacity-building programs with local government and the company" (Building Consensus, Monograph 1, 2007: 24). Project Underground, however, was not seated as a representative and later produced a report critical of the Mesá (discussed below).

In the end, the list of initial stakeholders who participated in the Mesá included:

- Minera Yanococha
- FEROCAPHENOP
- CORECAMIC (Regional Coordinator of Watersheds affected by mining in Cajamarcha)
- ASPADERUC (Association for the Rural Development of Cajamarcha)
- CARE (Cooperative for Assistance and Relief Everywhere)
- ITDG (Intermediate Technology Development Group)
- Chamber of Commerce of Cajamarcha
- ADEFOR (Civil Association for Forest Development)
- National University of Cajamarcha
- Private University of Antonio Guillermo Urrello
- Vicary of Ecumenical Solidarit
- MEM (Peruvian Ministry of Energy and Mines)
- SEDACAJ (Sanitary System Provider of Cajamarcha)
- Mayors of Choropampa, Magdelena and San Juan
- Mayors of small towns in La Encañada and Baños del Inca.

Governance of the Mesá and Training of Participants

Each stakeholder seated at the Mesá was assigned one vote in the subsequent proceedings. However, FEROCAFENOP believed they deserved a larger voice because they had filed one of the original complaints with the CAO and represented the largest group of community members. Others stringently objected to this level of representation for FEROCAFENOP. In the end, the leadership of the Mesá decided on equal voting rights for all stakeholder groups. Nonetheless, FEROCAFENOP was well represented at the meetings so its members received a lot of air time during the deliberations as did ACEPAMY (Association of Smaller Population Centers), which represented 12 rural communities that the mine affected. As the CAO report on the Mesá explained, "It was clear that some level of distinction among participants was needed. The facilitator decided that the centrality of each group to the discussion would depend on its stake in the mine-related conflicts and the size of its representation base" (Building Consensus, Monograph 1, 2007: 23).

The initial meetings of the Mesá were designed as training sessions to help the participants learn how to dialogue with each other and to overcome some of the class, race, and gender differences and trust issues among the participating organizations that had existed for centuries. The training was also intended to give the participants a different means of communicating than their usual approach—trying to outshout one another—and to level the playing field at the negotiating table so that less powerful voices such as those of women could be heard. One of the ground rules invoked by the facilitators for these sessions was that no issues related to Yanococha would be discussed. This angered some participants, but the facilitators held to this rule. Others believed too much time was spent in the training sessions, leaving less time for discussion of the real issues facing the community.

In spite of these objections, over time a series of procedures were agreed to for the Mesá's operation, and a leadership committee (Comité Directivo, that eventually became the Board of the Mesá) was formed to take responsibility for the evolution of the dialogue.[3] This involved negotiating a set of protocols to lay out the Mesá's mission, objectives, governance structure, and rules of conduct (Building Consensus, Monograph 1, 2007: 22) that were first agreed to in January 2002 and then finalized and ratified by the Mesá General Assembly by February 2003.

During this process, however, a disagreement arose over how to prioritize the Mesá's goals. "Although some Mesá member groups preferred that the Mesá focus on creating a space for dialogue, others saw more value in directly overseeing the mine, and advocated focused discussion on Cerro Quilish" (Building Consensus, Monograph 1, 2007: 22). Revelations that Yanococha had plans to construct a new mine on a hill called Cerro Quilish, just outside Cajamarca, had fueled further mistrust of the mine by the community. Fearing severe adverse impact to the region's water supply, the municipal government of Cajamarca had declared Cerro Quilish a protected area, which the mine proceeded to contest in court. Consequently, the Comité decided that the topic of Cerro Quilish was "off the table" until the court had rendered its decision.

Ultimately, the Mesá's mission was defined as "prevention and resolution of conflicts between the public and private sectors of civil society and Yanococha" (Building Consensus, Monograph 1, 2007: 23). More specific objectives were also stated:

- addressing the conflicts in a framework of good faith, respect, cooperation, and tolerance, looking for solutions through consensus that satisfy the interest and needs of the parties;

- promoting and spreading the mechanisms of prevention of conflict through dialogue and active participation, with the objective of maintaining harmony into the future;
- supporting actions that have as their purpose the improvement and preservation of the environment and respect of individual differences, poverty alleviation, and care for cultural patrimony; and
- promoting the development and socioeconomic potential of the region and managing its resources in a sustainable manner (Building Consensus, Monograph 1, 2007: 23).

In addition to establishing formal objectives, the Mesá eventually agreed upon a coordinating committee (Comité) whose role was to co-organize and convene the meetings, advise the facilitators about the content of the meetings, propose working groups, tasks, and sustainability strategies, and represent the Mesá to the wider community. Representation issues surfaced again, however, when FEROCAFENOP insisted they should have two seats on the Comité. Although in violation of its own protocols, the Comité eventually allowed both FEROCAFENOP and CORECAMIC to participate to ensure indigenous peoples' voices were represented.

The Water Study

Because the mine's impact on water quality and quantity was a highly contested issue requiring immediate attention, the Mesá's first action was to commission an independent water study. Residents had repeatedly expressed concerns about these issues, and questioned whether the independence of a study could be assured. Using criteria established by the Mesá to ensure the researchers' neutrality, they commissioned a US-based environmental consulting firm, Stratus Consulting, Inc., to conduct it. Yanococha feared the firm had environmental leanings because of its previous testimony against a mine in Washington State, but eventually reluctantly acquiesced to the choice of Stratus. Still other issues about neutrality arose over who would pay for the study. Ultimately, to prevent Yanococha from undue influence on the study, the mining company deposited funds into an account that was administered by the CAO (Building Consensus, Monograph 2, 2007: 5).

Several additional challenges needed to be addressed in designing and conducting the study. One involved gaining access to data from the mine itself including baseline information and water samples. The mine refused to allow water sampling on mine property, but "provided data from discharge compliance points on mine property that are part of Yanococha's required monitoring and reporting" (Building Consensus, Monograph 2, 2007: 5).

A second challenge involved determining how to design the study to address residents' complaints. Ultimately, two questions guided the data collection: One that addressed water quantity and its impacts on the potable water supply for Cajamarca and the rural areas and another that investigated changes in water quality and its possible effects on health and aquatic life. A third challenge involved hiring of a trusted local coordinator for the study. This need was met by a Cajamarca resident with a degree in water management from a US university. Fourth, determining what standards and guidelines to use to assess levels of water quality and quantity required considerable ongoing deliberation by the Mesá. Eventually they cobbled together a set of standards that included criteria from Peru, the World Health Organization, the US EPA and the State of Nevada depending on the issue (e.g., drinking water vs. water for agricultural use). A fifth challenge was ensuring that Yanococha did not compromise the integrity of the data collection. FEROCAFENOP proposed that community observers (called *veedores*) could observe collection of all water samples. According to a Mesá Comité member, "It was the only way the study would have legitimacy in the eyes of the town" (Building Consensus, Monograph 2, 2007: 10). At more distant sampling sites, mayors were notified when samples were to be taken and local residents were invited to accompany the Stratus team. However, participation rates by *veedores* varied and communication between *veedores* and communities was sporadic, which led to uneven information distribution and some community accusations that the *veedores* had been coopted. Overall, despite these setbacks, the CAO reported that "the agreements reached on these issues, as well as the participatory process through which they were attained, enhanced the study's legitimacy and relevance to Mesá members and local communities" (Building Consensus, Monograph 2, 2007: 9).

The results of the study became available in October 2003. A concise summary of the findings includes the following points:[4] First, the mine has altered water quality and water quantity in some locations and at some times. Second, changes in water quantity and quality are greatest close to the mine boundary and diminish with distance downstream from the mine. Third, the quantity of water available for the City of Cajamarca has not been reduced by the mine. Fourth, the water quality changes caused by the mine are not serious enough to pose imminent short-term danger of illness or death to people, livestock, or crops, including to people who drink the water in the City of Cajamarca. Fifth, international water quality standards for drinking, livestock, and crops have been exceeded in some locations, posing a danger to aquatic life in some locations. This is a concern for the long term and may require future improvements by the mine for locations close to the mine property. Sixth, overall, mining operations have not reduced the amount of water available for people at the present time although some streams have either decreased or increased flows due to mining operations.

The fact that the study's findings validated some of the observations of local communities about the water quality and quantity impacts of Yanococha's operations increased their overall trust of the study. A national government official also noted, "The work of the Mesá in terms of gaining local trust in the data is unique in Peru and worth emulating."

Among the suggestions based on the study's findings were continued participatory monitoring of surface water, erosion control, and sediment management, treatment or replacement of affected rural drinking water sources, assessment of water use at locations of potential concern, and continued involvement by the Mesá to "foster dialogue, consensus, trust, and transparency between the mine and the community" (Letter from Stratus Consulting to Mesá Comité, 2003). However, communication of the results of the study to the community also posed challenges for the Mesá and the Stratus Consultants. To help translate the scientific results for members of the community, Stratus held a number of demonstrations at the Mesá in which it reviewed basic concepts such as PH, porosity, and the effects of sustained vs. intermittent exposure to hazards.

Ongoing Monitoring, Reporting and Implementing of Solutions. The next step in the Mesá's work was to design a program for continued monitoring of the water affected by Yanococha and to do this in a way that was complementary to other institutions that were also monitoring water. The Mesá's program, designed by a technical working group and rolled out in June 2004, was intended to supplement rather than duplicate the programs operated by these other institutions. This meant that the Mesá would "focus on quality control statistical analysis, and synthesis of all data collected by participating institutions, building local capacity and increasing participation in data analysis, and communication of monitoring results to local communities" (Building Consensus, Monograph 3, 2007: 6). Funding for the first phase of this program was provided by the CAO, and the technical team consisted of three Peruvians, one technical expert from the US and continued oversight by the *veedores*, although maintaining a network of committed volunteers posed continual challenges, especially as monitoring expanded beyond the original study areas. Eventually, the technical working group evolved into the Technical Commission with participation from many water-related public institutions including some not originally in the Mesá and also Yanococha. Because of its outreach to so many communities, the Mesá received praise for its efforts, especially in the distribution of the results to local communities that previously had never had credible data about the quality of their water.

Although the ongoing results of monitoring in 2004–5 were similar to the earlier ones, problems arose when local groups reinterpreted the results in attempts to gain political advantage for their communities—a practice that fueled dissension within the Mesá between Yanococha and the Technical Commission along with disagreements over the application of international vs. Peruvian standards to the data. Additionally, because the Mesá lacked formal recognition as an institution and had little leverage over the mine, remedies to correct the water problems in communities with exceedances were not forthcoming. In the end, neither the mine nor government agencies within Peru took steps to provide remediation, even though the December 2005 monitoring report outlined specific recommendations for doing so. "Indeed, despite periodic requests from the Mesá for updates from Yanococha on the implementation of recommendations, the Mesá did not establish a systematic approach for holding Yanococha accountable and measuring outcomes" (Building Consensus, Monograph 3, 2007: 19).

Evaluation of the Mesá and Withdrawal of the CAO. As part of its planned phase-out from the Mesá, in February 2005, the CAO commissioned an evaluation of the Mesá that was conducted by four experts in environmental management and conflict mediation. The evaluation team interviewed seventy people, offered findings about the Mesá's work and recommended that the organization choose between two strategic pathways for the future: One of these would stress the Mesá's role as a forum for conflict resolution; the other would refocus the Mesá as an organization for studying the environmental impact of the mine's activities using a participatory methodology. In a workshop in May and June 2005, the CAO facilitated a strategic planning workshop to consider these options. Ultimately, the Mesá opted for an approach that merged the two objectives. In the fall of 2005, however, the group was unable to agree on new leadership. Without this and the continued backing of the CAO, the organization failed to move forward.

In its final report, the CAO concluded:

the Mesá was hampered by an absence of strong Mesá leadership and clear commitment from Yanococha to fully support Mesá processes. Also absent was active encouragement and involvement of IFC, which in some ways minimized the Mesá's importance as a venue for constructive dialogue and participation . . . As a result, maintaining a group of participants that represented a broad sector of Cajamarcan society proved difficult, and the Mesá was not able to fully develop the potential of its technical work. Despite a strong local demand for continuation of the Mesá's participatory water monitoring program, these institutional shortcomings prevented the Mesá's successful transition to independence from the CAO (Building Consensus, Monograph 3, 2007: 40).

POSTSCRIPT

Interestingly, Newmont Mining attempted to open another mine, Conga, in Cajamarcha in 2011. This project, which would have destroyed four Andean lakes, received considerable pushback from residents of the Cajamarcha region (Conga No Va, 2015). Consequently, in its April 2016 filing with the Securities and Exchange Commission, the company removed the Conga from its reserve statement (Sampat, 2016).

Questions about Collaborating Raised in This Case

1. How does this case illustrate the challenges of defining the scope and the scale of a collaboration, both at the time of initial convening and as collaboration continues over time?
2. In what ways was the collaboration affected by the emergence of new conflicts about the process of dialogue?
3. In what ways was the collaboration affected by the emergence of new conflicts linked to the substance of the problem (environmental issues)?
4. What kind of power was available to the potential participants?
5. How did the availability of other avenues for recourse (such as judicial) affect participation in the collaboration?
6. How did the lack of involvement by superordinate governance systems (national or global) affect the Mesá?

Notes

1. World Wildlife Fund UK and Banktrack (2006).
2. All the quotes in this section were derived from the public transcripts of the licensing meetings.
3. Members of the Comité included representatives from the Municipality of Cajamarca, Yanococha, the National Public Library, FEROCAFENOP, ACEPAMY, SEDACAJ, and the Cajamarcan Chamber of Commerce.
4. A more detailed summary of the report can be found in CAO, Monograph 2, 2007, Appendix B, pp. 36–45. Recommendations based on the study can be found in Appendix C of the same document, pp. 36–53.

5

Designing Multistakeholder Partnerships

Partnerships are born of diversity and require capitalizing on that diversity to achieve joint ends. "Collaborating is a process through which parties who see different aspects of a problem can constructively resolve their differences and search for solutions that go beyond their own limited vision of what is possible" (Gray, 1989: 5). However, working across organizational boundaries is neither easy nor straightforward. Simply agreeing to work together does not automatically ensure success. Achieving collaboration has been compared to becoming multivoiced or polyphonic (after music of the same name that emphasizes the equitable juxtaposition of multiple melodies) (Bouwen & Steyaert, 1999). This means "generating an appreciation for the diversity of viewpoints that multiple parties bring to a problem (or opportunity) and, at the same time, corralling and channeling this diversity into problem solutions that all parties can accept" (Gray & Schruijer, 2010: 122–3). In this chapter we offer frameworks to help partnership designers understand how collaborations evolve over time and how they are influenced by elements such as political maneuvering or covert power brokering (Hardy & Phillips, 1998), environmental exigencies (Denis et al., 2001; Sharfman et al., 1991), and serendipity (Huxham & Vangen 2005). We then identify concrete actions that can be taken by those who are organizing and participating in cross-sector partnerships to enhance their likelihood of success.

Actors seeking to engage in interorganizational partnerships face the often-daunting prospect of trying to integrate their diverse perspectives and goals, which are frequently misaligned or competing. The complexity and challenges of initiating and maintaining such partnerships have been chronicled extensively (Faulkner & de Rond, 2000; Gray, 1995; Gray & Clyman, 2003; Gray & Schruijer, 2010; Hardy & Phillips, 1998; Huxham & Vangen, 2000b; Koppenjan & Klijn, 2004; McCaffrey et al., 1995; Vansina et al., 1998; Wondolleck & Yaffee, 2000). One important finding from this stream of research is that while partners initially may be intrigued about proposed alliances, they often lose interest when the desired benefits are not quickly realized.

Despite believing they are pursuing a common goal, partners often find they espouse diverse aims that provoke difficult-to-reconcile conflicts (Gray & Purdy, 2014; Huxham & Vangen, 2005). Consequently, many partnerships succumb to collaborative inertia; that is, they experience slow progress or truncate their efforts without any tangible outcomes (Huxham & Vangen, 2004).

A host of factors have been identified that contribute to the potential for collaborative inertia, including mistrust, framing, identity, process, and power struggles. In a study of a business/education collaboration in New York City, for example, several factors including differences in organizational cultures of the participants, histories of misunderstanding and the erosion of trust among parties, cultural differences, and institutional disincentives posed obstacles to successful collaboration (Gray, 1995). Also, when parties frame the issues or the reasons for their interdependencies through different lenses, the quality of their agreement diminishes (Curseu & Schruijer, 2005), and sometimes the potential for finding any areas of agreement disappears completely (Lewicki et al., 2003). Additionally, partnerships require the construction of new identities (Hardy et al., 2005; Koot et al., 2003) that often live in tension with past affiliations. In some cases, partners may refuse to team up in the first place or exit the partnership rather than compromise their identity if its loss proves too threatening (Beech & Huxham, 2003; Gray, 2004; Rothman, 1997). For example, the merger between a service delivery and a teaching hospital ended in divorce after two years when neither would compromise their core mission. Even when partners freely join up, another major impediment to success is the absence of process skills among the partners (Wondolleck, 1985). Sometimes psychodynamic factors also arise in the subconscious work of the group that derail collaborative efforts (even when the parties are well intentioned about working together) (Gray & Schruijer, 2010; Vansina, 2000). Finally, at a more systemic level, institutional forces and power differences create imposing obstacles to success (Denis et al., 2001; Gray 1995; Hardy & Phillips, 1998; Himmelman, 1995; Purdy, 2012).

In response to this body of research, we address the questions "To what extent can partners proactively design successful alliances?" and "How can collaborative inertia be prevented?" In our view, partners *can* intervene to steer partnerships in positive directions. As Berger and his colleagues (2004: 61) suggested, "Many of the problems . . . are predictable and can be preempted or at least mitigated if they are anticipated and dealt with appropriately." Toward this end, we consider a variety of interventions to improve the quality and the likelihood of partnership success. These interventions involve deliberate actions taken by an alliance partner or partners, with or without a third party neutral, to influence the formation, design, or process of interaction among alliance partners. Interventions can originate from three sources: (1) they can be initiated by the partners themselves; (2) they can be imposed by others who have authority or leverage over the alliance (such as government agencies or resource providers); or (3) the partners can invite neutral third parties to offer assistance. Whatever their origin, these interventions have the potential to improve interorganizational partnerships if they are done skillfully.

This chapter unfolds as follows. First, we offer a life-cycle model of the issues that partnerships face as they evolve. The model is not intended to be prescriptive but rather to provide a heuristic for conceptualizing partnership evolution over time that can help to ensure the utilization of effective and timely interventions. Next we explore factors that motivate and block collaborative efforts at each of four phases in the partnership's evolution. The model conceives of the intervener's role in Lewin's (1951) terms as either decreasing the restraining forces or increasing the motivating forces that influence partnership success. Third, we propose a number of critical tasks that interveners can undertake to shift these forces in positive directions. These eight tasks offer a framework for organizing an array of more specific intervention activities. For each task, we review the theoretical premises undergirding it and outline specific intervention techniques that can accomplish the task. We then appraise each intervention technique and its usefulness for intervening in different phases of cross-sector partnerships. Many of these interventions have their roots in the organizational development, social ecology, and conflict resolution or mediation literatures, but have evolved and been adapted to meet the needs of specific partnerships in specific contexts. Additionally, the interventions have been tested and refined through practical application in numerous contexts, often using action research (Elden and Chisholm, 1993; Lewin, 1951) and mediation methodologies (Herman, 2005; Moore, 2014; Winslade & Monk, 2000) and thereby reflect the best of theory-to-practice wisdom because they have been vetted in real world partnerships.

A Life-Cycle Model of Partnership Evolution

Just as we envision institutional fields as in flux, we also see partnerships as shifting and transforming over time. Some are short-lived; others become institutionalized and some eventually transform into ongoing organizations, such as the Applegate Partnership and Watershed Council in Oregon, which has existed for over 25 years (Rolle, 2002). For analytic purposes it is useful to conceptualize partnerships as potentially moving through phases in a life cycle, from inception to eventual institutionalization (see Figure 5.1). Not all partnerships follow a linear progression though the life-cycle model, however; some move more cyclically, repeating phases as new projects are undertaken, new parties join, leadership changes, implementation efforts founder or

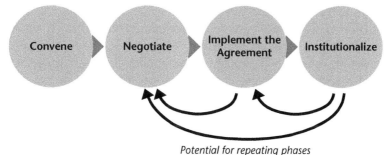

Potential for repeating phases

Figure 5.1 Phases of partnership formation

external resources or mandates unexpectedly shift. As Rolle (2002) notes, progress in partnerships may best be measured as a series of successes and failures so we indicate the possibility of repeating phases in Figure 5.1.

The first phase we refer to as "convening." As in any negotiation or before taking any plan of action, preparations are needed. Initiators must assess who the partners should be and how ready potential partners are to engage in deliberations and to consider taking joint actions. As we noted in Chapter 2, the convening phase can arise because the potential partners share a common goal or because a conflict has arisen among them. In the first case, one or more of the potential partners themselves may serve as "convener(s)" and invite others to the table. This occurred in the Rabobank case (see Chapter 4) when World Wildlife Fund and Rabobank saw a joint opportunity to work on a green credit card. On the other hand, Rabobank's partnership with Friends of the Earth Netherlands (FoEN) began as a conflict with FoEN challenging all Dutch banks about problems with their sustainability portfolios. If the conflict is severe, a neutral third party may be needed as a convener. This occurred in the Mesá case when the CAO[1] stepped in to bring various stakeholders into dialogue with the mine (see Chapter 4).

The second phase in the life cycle involves *negotiation* in the broadest sense of the term. Once parties agree to partner, they need to identify the interests they bring to the table, build a joint base of information about the problem, and share their preferred solutions. Ideally during this phase, partners become aware of the values underlying their partner's concerns and begin to identify and appreciate a sense of common purpose or direction. Hence, this phase has also been called direction setting (Gray, 1989; McCann, 1983). Depending on the scope and complexity of the problem, this phase can last a few days, several months or even many years. And, while it can proceed smoothly, more than likely it will be contentious at some point during the process (see Chapter 6). Ideally, this phase produces a preliminary agreement among the partners that may need further modification during phase three.

The third phase involves *implementing the agreement*. At this point, additional negotiations may be needed among the partners or with others (such as those in the negotiators' home organizations) whose efforts are needed to put the agreement into practice. It may also require modifying the partners' existing organizations and/or creating entirely new organizational arrangements to carry out the agreement(s) the partners reached.

Depending on the duration and capabilities needed for implementation, a fourth phase that we call *institutionalizing* may also be required. During this phase, the partnership agreement takes on a life of its own either by permanently altering practices within one or more of the original partners' organizations or by constructing an independent organization to carry on the partnership's objectives. Institutionalizing was illustrated in the hydroelectric relicensing case (Chapter 4) when FERC adopted a new set of rules for the licensing process. This phase may also include efforts to scale up the scope of the partnership or to replicate the original partnership in other venues although it is likely that these new efforts would need to revisit some, if not all, of the earlier phases since new partners will be involved and potentially new problems may arise.

Motivating and Restraining Forces on Partnerships

In Table 5.1 we present a model of factors that either drive or restrain partnership formation. At the strategic level for each partner factors such as the need for resources, opportunities for economies of scale, interdependence on other organizations, and the prospect of enhanced knowledge generation all serve as driving forces, particularly when prospective partners share a common goal or purpose for partnering. When partnerships arise out of conflict, a hurting stalemate—when continuing an impasse is judged worse than searching for an agreement (Touval & Zartman, 1985)—may offer a powerful motivator for

Table 5.1 Driving and restraining forces for partnership formation

	Driving forces	Restraining forces
Organizational partner level	Need for resources Interdependence Economies of scale Knowledge generation Hurting stalemate	Limited vision Perceived loss of control Fear of damaging reputation Differing views of value of partnering
Institutional/societal level	Government incentives Legal/regulatory mandate Public crisis New opportunity	History of mistrust Cultural/religious differences Institutional disincentives Power differences

forming a collaborative partnership. Institutional and societal driving forces may come from government incentives to collaborate, legal or regulatory mandates, or shifting societal conditions (such as a natural disaster or crisis).

Restraining forces at the partner level, on the other hand, may emerge if partners have a limited or zero-sum vision of the prospects of teaming up, fear that they will lose control over their affairs, worry about their reputation or fear loss of constituent support from partnering or are plagued with conflicting internal factions who can't agree on the value of partnering. Partnering may also be impeded at the institutional and societal level if there is a long-standing history of conflict, animosity, and mistrust among the potential partners. Cultural or religious differences may also stand in the way. Finally, large power differentials pose formidable barriers to partnership formation.

Critical Tasks of Interveners

To advocate intervention implies that interorganizational relations are at least partly malleable and can be intentionally or strategically designed, managed, or guided towards someone's desired ends. While theories of interorganizational relations (IOR) may not agree about the extent of control that interveners can exercise (Faulkner & De Rond, 2000), most attribute some agency to the parties involved. If alliance partners are not totally at the mercy of exogenous forces, then, through intervention, individuals can exert leverage over how they themselves and their partners are interacting. The tasks that interveners take to assist partners in working more effectively have been described in a variety of ways. Generally, interveners serve as matchmakers (Gray & Yan, 1997) or conveners (Carlson, 1999; Dorado, 2005), who bring partners together, design experts who help partners structure their interactions, and process consultants who can play practical roles that include facilitators, mediators, recorders, educators, and advocates (Strauss, 1999). While it is possible the same person(s) may perform more than one of these functions, it is neither necessary nor likely, especially if the partnership has many parties and continues over an extended period of time. Eight interventions to enhance partnerships are presented in Table 5.2 along with the phase of partnership formation for which they are most suited and some general conditions for their use. We describe each phase in detail next.

Convening

Identifying and Attracting Partners. Whomever serves in a convening or boundary spanning (Isbell, 2012) role, needs a broad understanding of the problem and the ability to rally those potential partners with a stake in it.

Table 5.2 Interventions to enhance partnerships

Intervention task	Description	Useful in phase	Specific techniques	Conditions of use
Convening	Facilitating partners' need for organizing and recruiting appropriate stakeholders and gaining commitment to partnership	1	Inviting partners Feasibility assessment Determining representation	Intervener is neutral, legitimate and has clout; representational issues are addressed
Managing the process	Defining and managing the process of partners' interactions	All, but 2 especially	Defining the problem Establishing ground rules Agenda setting Information exchange processes	Partners recognize need for process help; transparency is assured
Visioning	Appreciative work that explores need for partnering and identifies an ideal future for the field	1 and 4	Shared strategy maps Search conferences	Need to get everyone on board with future directions for the field; enables search for common ground without solving conflicts
Large-group interventions	Testing ideas and gaining views of large numbers of stakeholders	2 and 3	Town meetings	Need for widespread input to gain insight and/ or test preliminary agreements
Conflict handling	Assistance to partners in working through conflicts and disagreements	All, but 2 especially	Mediation Interest-based negotiation Consensus building Trust building Perspective taking Translating Reframing	Mediator is perceived as neutral; time and effort may be needed to ensure the table is level and to build trust and work through disagreements
Action research	Partners study their process to enhance learning; PAR: Some partners mobilize to gain voice & promote partnership	1 or 2	Double loop learning Appreciative inquiry Participatory action research(PAR)	Need to build commitment to partnering process, jumpstart a flagging process or enhance understanding of differing views; build voice and access for less powerful partners
Gaining buy-in back home	Ensuring that constituents are on board with partnership agreements and gaining their feedback	1 or 2	Dealing with two-table problem Formal ratification	Formal or informal representatives need to gain input from and eventual commitment to agreements from back-home constituents

Institution building	Promoting the establishment of norms to govern implementation of agreement and constructing new organization as needed	3 & 4	Structuring Replicating	Need to internalize changes within partner organizations; need for separate, ongoing organization to execute agreement; desire to replicate partnership in other venues

Convening has its origins in social ecology theory (Trist, 1983). The primary tasks of conveners are to assess whether a partnership is feasible and to identify and motivate potential partners to participate (Carlson, 1999). Conveners have the ability to see the potential benefits of collaboration in hazy fields where the future is complex, volatile, and unpredictable (Dorado, 2005), such as those fields plagued by what we have referred to earlier as wicked problems (see Chapter 2). In addition to seeing collaborative advantage more clearly, successful convening involves not only recognizing who has a stake in the issue, but also having sufficient influence to attract or persuade these stakeholders to join a collaborative alliance. A convener may or may not be a potential partner themselves, but he/she requires convening power, that is, the ability to induce others to participate. "Convening power may derive from holding a formal office, from a long-standing reputation of trust with several stakeholders, or from experiences and reputation as an unbiased expert on the problem" (Gray, 1989: 71).

While any partner can propose a collective appreciation for the others, this task is usually performed by someone who knows the issues, has legitimacy (in the eyes of other stakeholders), is viewed as neutral, and has enough political clout to frame the collaborative vision in a way that others cannot ignore. For example, in a dispute between snowmobilers, other citizens, and state park officials over maintenance of snowmobile trails, park officials needed to solicit the help of neutral third parties to construct a collaborative table because park officials themselves were too deeply embedded in the conflict to be seen as neutral conveners on their own (Purdy & Gray, 1994). According to Bryson and Crosby (1992: 33), conveners "need to understand the social, political and economic 'givens' in a situation as well as the relevant people involved." Conveners are sometimes the same individuals who initially appreciate the potential for partnerships in the first place; however, depending on their legitimacy and clout, different conveners may be needed to test the feasibility and assist in the launch of a potential collaborative alliance.

Assessing Feasibility. Conveners also need to be able to assess the readiness of potential partners to work together. This activity, called feasibility assessment,

75

involves determining whether the potential partners (or disputants) have the requisite motivations to form a partnership. Stakeholder groups will also be making their own decisions about whether or not to embark on a collaborative process, weighing such factors as whether:

- the formulation of the problem includes their interests;
- the partnership has the potential to produce positive outcomes;
- the partnership can produce better outcomes than other alternatives (such as protest or litigation);
- the playing field is level enough to generate a fair agreement;
- participation will enhance or tarnish their reputation; and
- they believe other potential partners are legitimate stakeholders.

Stakeholders are viewed as legitimate when potential partners believe they have the right and capacity to influence the issue or problem under consideration. "Legitimacy involves perceptions of entitlement. People believe they are entitled to participate when they will be impacted by the decisions taken. Collaboration presumes that their voice is also critical to arriving at a comprehensive and fair resolution of a problem" (Gray, 1989: 122).

If the feasibility judgment is affirmative, conveners may also need to persuade reluctant partners of the value of joining in. This may include helping some to weigh the consequences of not being at the table, such as loss of voice in shaping future responses to the problem. In some cases, conveners also strive to level the negotiating table if there is an imbalance of power among those with a stake in the problem. If critical stakeholders withhold participation, however, a convener may also advise against going forward with the partnership.

Determining Representation. The convener should also oversee the selection of partnership members. Unlike governmental bodies, partnerships are not typically "representative" in the sense that those participating are elected by a constituency. Nonetheless, it is important that there is balance among the various stakeholders who are affected by the issues. While some alliances may have unlimited voluntary representation, in most, each group with a stake is granted a single seat at the table. Representation in partnerships, then, involves decisions about who can participate in an alliance and for whom they can speak. Determining who represents that group's views is an important step. In some cases, for example, the group's legitimate leader may not be the best representative for a successful partnership if that person cannot work effectively with others to search for a solution (Gray & Hay, 1986). The degree to which representation needs to be circumscribed and will differ depending on the purpose of the partnership, but alliances often falter because representational issues, such as how inclusive the group of participants will be and who has "authority" to act on behalf of the collaborative group, were neglected during initial discussions (Carlson, 1999). When partnerships are convened primarily for information exchange, decisions about who should be included to ensure availability of needed information is critical, but including parties with redundant information may not be necessary. Replication is helpful, however, to preserve organizational memory should the original representative need to leave for any reason (Gray, 1995). Also, groups engaged primarily in information exchange may not need firm decision rules. For example, social service agencies collaborating to keep track of common clients or promote client referrals may want wide and open-ended representation whereas a policy-making partnership should have explicit criteria about stakeholder representation and decision-making guidelines. However, "being representative of" is not the same as "representing" (Carlson, 1999: 186). When there are too many stakeholders to effectively participate in consensus decision making, the larger group can be asked to select a smaller group to represent them (Carlson, 1999). Process designs (discussed below) can also distinguish participation levels between those parties that only provide input and others with decision-making authority. If the group will be assembled for considerable time and has decision-making authority, having alternate representatives could also be useful to ensure continuity in the partnership should those originally appointed leave for personal or professional reasons.

Ineffective resolution of representational issues can cause collaborations to fail. When a US federal agency tried to organize ten local partnerships to address issues related to the spotted owl controversy in the US Pacific Northwest, the agency didn't enlist community members in each location in issue identification or selection of partnership representatives, but instead made decisions unilaterally (Carlson, 1999). Consequently, participants "were concerned . . . about the federal government's motives, the balance of power at the table, and the availability of resources to enable all groups to participate on an equal footing" (KenCairn, 1997, cited in Carlson, 1999: 173). Ensuring psychological safety in the ensuing discussion and reaching agreement upfront about decision authority and ownership of outcomes can prevent later withdrawal by participants (Carpenter, 1999), misunderstandings, and accusations of failure to negotiate in good faith (Bingham, 1986). Such accusations and attendant mistrust often derail negotiations when parties later announce they don't have the authority to make decisions. On the other hand, in a study of over one hundred mediated environmental negotiations in which agreements were reached, Bingham (1986) observed that when representatives had the authority to implement decisions, the likelihood that agreements were implemented significantly increased.

In place-based conflicts, elected officials can often serve effectively as conveners (Carlson, 2007), but other "respected leaders, by virtue of the credibility and social capital they have built in their communities, regions, or states, also have the power to convene" (Carlson, 2007: 29). In some cases it may be necessary to have multiple conveners to balance the diverse perspectives. These "initiating committees" are small groups comprised of "people with the credibility to convince others that something can and must be done" (Chrislip & Larson, 1994: 87). Conveners may also be mediators who work with the partners in subsequent phases of the collaboration, but this is not a necessary, nor always desirable, condition for a convener. It is essential, however, that "other stakeholders believe the convener has the legitimate authority to organize the (problem) domain" (Gray, 1989: 71).

If the convener's neutrality is in doubt, other potential partners may question his/her credibility and refuse to participate or even try to subvert the partnership's formation (Gray, 1989). For example, when two university professors tried to convene a forum on nuclear power, their efforts were sabotaged "when the university's president contemporaneously agreed to serve on the board of the local power company, which operated two nuclear reactors. Environmental groups used this event to discredit the conveners and...dissuade a funding agency from supporting the project" (Gray, 1989: 72). Finally, however the convener is chosen, the process needs to be transparent just as the process of identifying and inviting stakeholders needs to be.

Managing the Process

Process intervention makes a critical distinction between the content (or task work) of the partnership (e.g., providing better healthcare in disadvantaged communities) and the process (or interaction among the partners) (Schein, 1978). Paying attention to the phases in which collaboration unfolds (Gray 1989; McCann 1983; Ring & Van de Ven, 1994), to how meetings among the partners are conducted, and the patterns of interactions occurring over time, constitute important tasks for process designers (Gray, 1989; Schuman, 1996; 2006). Explicit consideration of the principles by which the deliberations will be conducted and decisions will be undertaken can mean the difference between a well-managed process and one in which various parties feel "used" by others.

Process interventions have their roots in the action research/organization development tradition informed by Lewin's (1951) early work, but are also informed by the Tavistock tradition of group dynamics (Bion, 1961) as well as by more recent work on group facilitation (Schuman, 1996; 2006), communication (Lewis et al., 2010) and negotiations (Fisher et al., 1991). The group dynamics approach argues that individual behavior is highly influenced by group membership and the notion that understanding dynamics at the group and intergroup levels is essential for intervening to facilitate partners' relations. For example, groups often divert from the task of joint problem solving to address members' underlying anxieties and needs (such as concerns about belonging, influence, and dependence versus independence (Bion, 1961)). Attention to process dynamics helps groups address these underlying anxieties and redirect their attention to the task of building the partnership.

Interveners engaged in process design assume responsibility for thinking through and executing a design for how the parties will interact and gaining commitment to the process from them. It is often easier to get partners to agree on a fair process for managing their interactions than on immediate solutions to the problem under consideration (Potapchuk & Polk, 1993). However, when conflict does occur over the process, it can foreshadow impending substantive conflicts. Not all collaborators have or think they even need a process designer, but someone with knowledge of meeting design and group dynamics can help to ensure the parties' interactions are constructive and to avoid classic pitfalls that can derail even well-intended partnerships. Process designers can advise partners and encourage discussion among them about the principles governing representation within the partnership, expectations regarding participation, decision-making processes, ownership of and responsibility for outcomes, power sharing, and interactions with constituents, the media, and with the larger community in which the partnership is occurring.

Mistrust of the process, and the anxiety associated with it, also arises when participants have differing conceptions about what will happen. Tensions can arise because partners have different ideas about the issues and about how to collaborate and alliance partners differ in the degree of process knowledge they want to exercise (Huxham, 1996). "Conferring with the parties about what is going to happen next and who is going to do it ensures that expectations are not mismatched and that the parties retain ownership of everything that happens" (Gray, 1989: 266). Still, since collaborating frequently involves coordinating in the face of ambiguity (Huxham & Vangen, 2000a), even the most careful designs can go awry because of environmental exigencies, unwitting behavior by participants, or deliberate power plays (Hardy & Phillips, 1998). For example, in a cross-sectoral partnership designed to create back-office jobs in New York City, within a six-month period after an agreement was reached, several key members left to start new jobs. In this situation, a useful "process" remedy would have been to ensure redundancy of representation so that institutional memory of the agreements is not lost when key partners leave the process. While this remedy might have prevented collapse of the partnership, in reality, increasing the number of partners may reduce the group's ability to work together effectively unless more time can be contributed and/or other designs such as subgrouping can be used.

Schuman (1996: 128–9) identified three types of process: cognitive (dealing with the information, values, beliefs, and ideas of partners; social (concerned with interpersonal interactions and communication); and political (focus on shifts of influence and resources). Many cross-stakeholder partnerships proceed without explicit attention to any of these processes by which the stakeholders interact including those that evolve very organically over time (Cropper & Palmer, 2008), and conveners and partners frequently underestimate the critical role of process in ensuring successful collaboration (Patton, 1981; Wondolleck, 1985).

Defining the Problem and Its Scope. An important process task that needs attention during phase 1 of any partnership involves defining and setting the scope of the problem or issue under consideration. Determining the scope of the problem is critical because where the boundaries of the problem are drawn will determine, at least in part, who should participate in the deliberations and whether and how the initial deliberations will proceed. For example, in the Mesá case, an early decision was taken to exclude those issues that addressed the mine's culpability in conjunction with the mercury spill because this was being adjudicated in the courts. Establishing this restriction on the Mesá's agenda resulted in the refusal of some indigenous groups to join the dialogue. The permeability of the boundaries of the process can also make a difference (Zietsma & Lawrence, 2010).

Establishing Ground Rules. Reaching agreement about how partners will interact with each other is another vital process intervention, especially in cases in which partners are wary or unsure about the utility of teaming up. Ground rules can remove some uncertainty for the participants and lessen the likelihood of misunderstandings. They can set the tone for the meetings and signal to partners how the proceedings may differ from conventional processes (such as public hearings, legal proceedings, etc.). Ground rules should not be imposed by leaders of the partnership, but, instead, agreement on the ground rules should involve all the partners, should precede discussion of substantive issues, and can provide everyone with an initial sense of confidence in their ability to reach agreements. Sufficient time should be allocated for discussion of the ground rules, however, because often preferences about ground rules can foreshadow some of the deeper differences that may surface among partners later in the deliberations. Establishing ground rules often helps to resolve "shape of the table" and other procedural issues (such as those which initially stalled the beginning of the Paris Peace Talks to end the Vietnam War). Useful ground rules would address, among other things, issues of representation, speaking order, how

---

TYPICAL ISSUES COVERED IN GROUND RULES

Note: This is adapted from Gray (1989), p. 78.

- What is the role of representatives?
  - Do they represent the views of a constituency?
  - Do they have authority to take binding action on behalf of their constituency?
  - Can alternates serve in a representative's place?
- Is there a deadline for the negotiations?
  - What is the timetable for the meetings?
  - What happens if a timely agreement is not reached?
- How will confidential information be handled?
- How will media publicity be handled?
  - Who will speak to members of the press on behalf of the partnership?
  - When and in what form will information be released?
  - What information will be kept confidential?
- Will parties receive compensation and/or reimbursement for expenses for their participation?
- How will a record of the proceedings be kept?
  - What will be recorded? By whom?
  - Who will have access to it?
- How will consensus be determined?
  - Must all parties reach agreement on all issues before decisions are presented to sponsors or others?
- How will partners treat each other during deliberations?

---

conversations with the media will be handled, what the decision rules are for reaching agreements, and how partners should comport themselves during meetings.

An example of how ground rules can be useful and how they are enforced can be found in the archives of the National Coal Policy Project in the US. Ground rules for those negotiations among environmentalists, coal producers, and coal consumers over regulations for coal mining included prohibitions against impugning the motivations of other partners "lightly." When one participant was called out for violating this ground rule by directly attacking the motives of another during the proceedings, he facetiously pointed that the ground rules prohibited impugning others' motives "lightly" but that he was doing it "seriously." This remark turned an anxious moment into a light-hearted one, and allowed the negotiations to continue without further incident. Empowering the partners to enforce their own ground rules gives them a considerable sense of responsibility for the proceedings and serves as an effective enforcement tool. Depending on the context in which the partnership is formed, some ground rules may be prescribed by statute such as whether the deliberations must be open to the public. US federal rule-making processes are governed by the Administrative Procedure Act (5 U.S.C. Sub-chapter 2) that sets the guidelines under which agencies can invite stakeholders to participate in rule-making proceedings. A fundamental provision of the APA prohibits government officials from delegating authority for rule-making to these invited stakeholders whose role can only be consultative. The hydroelectric relicensing case (Chapter 4) offers one illustration about how rules for licensing power plants were rewritten in consultation with key stakeholders.

Agenda Setting.[2] Another process intervention involves setting the agenda for how substantive issues will be addressed. Agenda setting must be handled carefully to ensure that all partners believe their interests are being taken into account as the deliberations commence. "The agenda is often the object of intense debate since some parties will work hard to add or delete issues of special concern" (Susskind & Madigan, 1984: 185). This part of process design needs to consider how partners will share interests, how trade-offs among preferred approaches will be handled, and whether issues will be handled in plenary sessions or broken out for subgroups to consider. Often it is advantageous to create subgroups or task forces if the number of issues under consideration is large or the number of stakeholders exceeds the twelve-to-fifteen-member limit for effective group functioning. Organizing into task forces allows the group to address several issues simultaneously. Ensuring diversity of viewpoints in the subgroups is also critical as subgroups submit their findings and recommendations back to the plenary for modification and approval.

Exchanging Information among Partners. An important ingredient in building a consensus is reaching agreement on the facts supporting the problem definition and the proposed solutions. However, partners do not always have all the information they need to take decisions on the issues they are considering. Often partners are knowledgeable about different aspects of the problem, but sometimes they directly disagree on what the facts are. In such cases, the process needs to create opportunities for gaining relevant data in as impartial a manner as possible. Mutually examining relevant data can help the partners to develop a common basis for discussion and to discuss specific elements of discrimination between shared, opposing, and differing interests.

Procedural suggestions for addressing disagreements over facts can often effectively be handled by joint information search in which participants travel to sites where data can be collected together to ensure its authenticity and veracity. Another approach for dealing with controversial issues is impaneling experts to offer testimony to the partners collectively and allowing for public questioning of them. Choosing the panel of experts may itself be contentious, but, if the parties collectively query each other's experts, they can often gain a more subtle appreciation of the "factual" bases for their own differences. Additionally, they can narrow the range of issues in contention by permitting the experts to stipulate some fundamental areas of agreement among themselves, or they come to realize that pushing for a specific technical outcome is unnecessary as long as monitoring of progress is assured. Sometimes, by proving the technical issues in depth, the parties are able to set or agree on broad parameters that address their most significant areas of interest and to relegate to technical experts the details of these technical issues. Both of these processes, site visits, and expert panels, are especially useful for handling complex problems involving scientific terminology, mathematical or economic projections, perceptions of risk, and large quantities of data. In addition, use of computerized processes to facilitate collaborative information sharing may be useful in cases where participants are widely distributed and cannot easily meet face to face or when a large volume of information needs to be gathered and compiled for use by the negotiators (Kaplan & Fry, 2006).

Visioning Processes[3]

A useful intervention for launching a new partnership is that of visioning, which involves constructing a joint image or map of the problem or issue the partners intend to tackle that can guide their work together. Visioning processes have their origins in the notion of appreciation introduced by Vickers (1965) and adopted by social ecology theorists such as Fred and Merryln Emery (Emery & Emery, 1977) and Eric Trist (1983). Appreciative processes were designed to counteract the potentially unanticipated and maladaptive consequences that occur in fields when highly interdependent stakeholders fail to coordinate their actions (Emery & Emery, 1977). The process of appreciation enables stakeholders to develop common knowledge about the field and about how their interdependencies affect the problem of interest. Effective intervention can help reduce field level turbulence by encouraging partners to adopt a system-level perspective and develop an understanding of how each one's actions influence choices and outcomes available to their partners. Such knowledge then facilitates the design of collaborative partnerships to enable correlated responses (Trist, 1983).

Shared Strategy Maps. Several visioning techniques have been developed and used successfully to build appreciation among cross-sector partners. One appreciative technique involves the construction of shared strategy maps (Bryson & Finn, 1995; Eden, 1989). This process involves querying each partner and constructing a cognitive map of their views on the issue or problem. Then individual maps are combined into a computerized composite map that reflects the perspectives of all the partners. The composite map becomes the basis for discussion, revision, and hopefully agreement about desired future directions. This mapping process facilitated identification of a common vision and mission for 45 stakeholders in a school district as part of a wider strategic planning process (Bryson & Finn, 1995).

Search Conferences. Another visioning process that has been widely used is the search conference. Visioning has been explained as "a process in which people build consensus on a description of their preferred future—the set of conditions they want to see realized over time" (Moore et al., 1999). Two critical early steps in search conference process promote system-wide learning about the problem/issue by (1) focusing participants' attention on their mutual aspirations for the future and (2) identifying broad contextual influences and current and anticipated trends that impinge upon the problem area (Emery & Emery, 1977; Emery & Purser, 1996; Weisbord & Janoff, 2000). These steps encourage the partners to build a common interpretation of the various factors governing their interactions and help them to understand how each one's actions influence their partners' outcomes. Often the realizations produced through such analyses break down barriers among potential collaborators and promote awareness of their common plight. As Weisbord and Janoff (2005:80) note, "a short, intense, whole system meeting enables something not available in any other way: A gestalt of the whole in all participants that dramatically improves their relationship to their work and their co-workers." By identifying ideal future states, the process facilitates finding common ground that may be less possible when focusing solely on the present. The success of such designs "can be explained at least partially by social network theory, in that such forums enable the creation of networks and strong ties between networks of actors" (Tenkasi & Chesmore, 2003: 297). For example, search conferences can reorient the centrality and influence patterns of actors within a collaborative group or even an entire field (Clarke, 2005: 43).

Large Group Interventions

In some collaborative settings it is desirable to involve large numbers of participants in the process to ensure diversity of viewpoints and widespread support for agreements that are reached. In these large-scale interventions sponsors may employ interveners to assist with the convening function and to design and conduct a large-scale system intervention (Bryson & Anderson, 2000; Bunker & Albans, 1997, 2006). Particularly on public issues when incorporating the viewpoints of a wide array of participants is desired (as in a deliberative democracy project), process facilitators can bring both the technological expertise and the process skills to assist in convening and managing the process.

Using what they refer to as the 21st Century Town Meeting, America*Speaks* successfully convened a citizen engagement effort in which 4,500 New York residents, representing the city's demographic diversity, offered reactions to the initial site plans for the design of the World Trade Center memorial (Lukensmeyer & Brigham, 2005). The participants met in face-to-face facilitated round-table dialogues and used simultaneous voting via electronic keypads to test for group consensus on the major issues. The consensus recommendations informed the next phase of planning for the project (Lukensmeyer & Brigham, 2005). For more depth on large group process methods, see Bunker and Albans (2006).

Conflict Handling

Interventions designed to address and resolve conflict often distinguish successful from failed partnerships. The task of conflict handling is critical to partnership success because unresolved conflicts can negatively impact performance (Gray & Purdy, 2014; Gray & Schruijer, 2010; Steensma & Lyles, 2000) and contribute to collaborative inertia (Huxham & Vangen, 2004). There can be:

> significant challenges, including overcoming turf and territoriality issues, identifying and addressing differences in organizational norms and procedures, expanding communication both within and across organizations, coping with tensions concerning organizational autonomy and differential power relations
>
> (Takahashi & Smutny, 2002, p. 167).

These kinds of problems can be exacerbated when the number of partners is large, partners are distributed geographically and historical animosities among partners are imported into partnerships.

Negotiating from Interests. While there are many approaches available for resolving conflicts effectively, we focus here on interest-based negotiation. Interested based negotiation (Fisher et al., 1991) is premised on the idea that disputants typically focus on positions that routinely lead to stalemate or suboptimal agreements rather than interests. Positions are parties' preconceived ideas about how the problem should be solved. It is easy for partners to get locked into their own positions. Interests, on the other hand, refer to negotiators' fundamental needs without specifying how they will be met. Hence, they are aspirations rather than demands. Another premise of position bargaining is that if the parties' positions are incompatible, then their interests are as well (Fisher et al., 1991). However, this may not be the case as it is often possible to find trade-offs at the level of interests that were not apparent when only positions were considered. In searching for such tradeoffs, disputants look for ways to satisfy each partner's interests by trading off what is important to one for something that is costless or only has small costs for another (Fisher et al., 1991). Counter to traditional bargaining in which gains for one imply losses for another, negotiators search for differing interests that enable a win–win solution.

A good case in point is illustrated by deliberations among loggers and environmentalists in New South Wales, Australia (Brown, 2002). Initially these groups believed they held opposing positions about what was needed to satisfy what they believed were differing interests—the need to clear-cut old growth forests for the loggers and the desire to prevent destruction of old growth forests through more sustainable logging practices for the environmentalists. After carefully exploring their actual needs, however, it became clear that loggers' future projections for softwood (that could more easily be regenerated in a shorter time) would soon exceed their desire to harvest the old growth forests. This made it possible to agree on a phased plan that restricted future damage to old growth forests while still providing sufficient timber to harvest. Finding tradeoffs like this is the goal of interest-based negotiation.

Talking at the level of interests rather than positions also takes some of the heat out of the negotiations because it is difficult to argue with what someone needs to make a deal work. Additionally, positions often mask true interests. Disputants often make incorrect assumptions about what is really important to the other parties. When these assumptions are debunked, negotiation space opens up and hidden trade-offs can become apparent. Finding tradeoffs is also aided by creativity. For example, trading off current needs for future ones can also interject flexibility in finding integrative solutions (Lax & Sebenius, 1986). In cases where trade-offs among interests are truly constrained (zero-sum games), compromise rather than collaboration may be the only solution possible. When disputes have a history of intractability (Lewicki et al., 2003), levels of mistrust among partners are high, and/or issues are especially contentious, enlisting the services of a mediator to initiate an interest-based dialogue may not only be prudent but necessary to assist the parties in finding common ground.

Mediation. Mediation is a dispute resolution process in which a third-party neutral helps disputants to jointly educate each other about the issues and interests involved in the dispute and to design and possibly implement a solution (Moore, 2014). "The goal of formal mediation is to change a competitive conflict to a cooperative interaction characterized by a) effective communication, b) less obstruction, c) orderly discussion, d) confidence in one's ideas coupled with support for the ideas and concerns of other participants, and e) coordinated efforts to resolve the conflict" (Deutsch, 2000: 25). Mediation models typically embrace notions of interest-based negotiation, which has proven effective for finding integrative solutions in a host of different contexts (Fisher et al., 1991). Mediation has also proven effective in numerous countries and a variety of different cultural contexts. Mediators are typically third parties who themselves are not invested in the substantive issues the partners are trying to negotiate. In some cases of partnership conflict, partners skilled in conflict-handling may be able to apply the same techniques used by mediators to reconcile differences within their own partnership.

The advantages of mediation over other forms of dispute resolution (e.g., negotiation, arbitration, litigation) are: (1) the parties are treated with respect, their personal worth is confirmed, and they experience psychological success and are more willing to accept change (Argyris, 1970); (2) the process is voluntary (which ensures a sense of personal control over one's participation); and (3) the parties themselves, who are the most knowledgeable about their own needs relative to the issues under consideration, design and select alternative courses of action (rather than having solutions imposed by a judge or arbitrator). First and foremost, mediators try to ensure that effective communication is occurring among partners (Gray, 2008). They can be enlisted to help with process design and establishing ground rules, facilitate disclosure of interests and construction of alternative solutions as partners strive to understand and integrate their differing perspectives on the problem or issue to promote win–win solutions (Gray, 2005; Moore, 2014; Susskind, 1999). Once agreements are reached, mediators can help partners garner buy-in from their home organizations.

Consensus Building. Mediators also facilitate consensus-building (a process that can be used with or without a mediator). In consensus-building, partners strive for solutions that satisfy all parties. Since unanimity is rarely possible, however, consensus-building utilizes the criteria that all parties can "live with" whatever agreements are reached, even if they were not a partner's first choice for resolving a conflict. The idea is to produce the best possible realistic agreement. Consensus-building often requires considerable trial and error as negotiators try to find the most efficacious trade-offs that optimize potential gains for all involved. The importance of consensus building to partnership success has been well documented (Ansell & Gash, 2008; Baldwin & Ross, 2012; Doelle & Sinclair, 2006; Manring, 2007; Rondinelli & London, 2003; Van de Kerkhof, 2006; Weible et al., 2010). When consensus-building is the desired process, it is best to specify this in the ground rules. This helps to motivate partners to listen carefully to each other's interests and makes it clear that a majority decision on the issues will not suffice. Then, if a partner cannot agree with a potential decision others are willing to support, it is incumbent on that partner to propose an alternative. The alternative should take their own and others' interests into account. The process continues until everyone can agree to support the decision even if it is not their first preference.

Several articles stressed the importance of consensus-based decision making as an important process for decision making among partners. For the policy-making context, consensus-building is thought to have a number of instrumental advantages over formal (nonparticipatory) policy making. Consensus-building reduces conflict, increases compliance, improves policy, prevents litigation and promotes public participation (Susskind and Cruikshank, 1987; Van de Kerkhof, 2006). Because each partner's concerns are given serious consideration in decision making, consensus-based decision making can also contribute to trust building and joint learning.

Trust Building. As just noted, another critical role of mediators is to help to build or restore trust among partners in contexts where trust is absent. Trust issues can arise from the moment parties consider joining forces. Decisions about whether to enter into an alliance with a partner are based on trust levels in past alliances (Gulati, 1995), and many collaborators decry the lack of trust in their partnerships (Vangen & Huxham, 2003). If a history of trust already exists, interveners can reinforce it by asking potential partners to recount instances in which they behaved trust-worthily (Moore, 2014). When partners' relationships are characterized by mistrust, trust must be demonstrated repeatedly to be restored. An iterative process of forming expectations followed by demonstrations of good faith will be necessary to overcome the vulnerability they may feel towards one another (Vangen & Huxham, 2003). "Through increasing the number of promises and congruent actions that reinforce the belief that the commitment will be carried out, negotiators gradually build a relationship of trust" (Moore, 1986: 142). "When business, government and civic leaders attempted to revitalize the city of Newark, New Jersey, community groups refused to begin work on the process design until the business sector demonstrated its commitment to the city" (Strauss 1999: 142). Several concrete short-term projects were identified and completed as a demonstration of good faith before a longer consensus-partnership commenced.

As noted earlier, process interventions that establish clear ground rules also enhance trust if they are actively and evenly enforced by facilitators and participants (Dukes et al., 2000), as do efforts to ensure voice for all parties. Mediators may also elect to conduct preliminary interviews with participants (as part of the feasibility assessment) and then feedback a composite of this information so that parties learn the level of issue consensus and gain a clear understanding of the issues. In situations where the potential for defection from a trusting relationship is perceived to be high, mediators can assist parties to construct contractual provisions that mitigate against breaches of trust and ensure that future interests are protected (Das & Teng, 1998; Ring &

Van de Ven, 1994). This is particularly helpful during implementation when partners may fear that their counterparts will renege on the agreement.

Perspective Taking. When parties harbor ingrained stereotypes about each other and mistrust is long-lived, multiple experiences of matching experience to expectations may be necessary before they begin to trust one another. Research has shown that unless parties spend time within positive interactions with each other (Amir, 1994), they continue to employ stereotypes in their views of each other. Supplanting stereotypes with more realistic appraisals of other stakeholders can be accelerated through joint data-gathering trips (Gray, 1989; Redford, 1987), in which participants share common experiences and get to know each other as individuals, and perspective-taking exercises that enable groups to acknowledge and work past their biased views of each other. These perspective-taking activities encourage parties to reconsider the ways they have framed each other and try on alternative interpretations (McHugh & Stewart, 2012; Tenkasi & Mohrman, 1999).

Translating. Mediators with cultural fluency can serve as translators to facilitate alliances across cultural boundaries. Cultural fluency refers to the capability to "experience from as many angles as possible the multiple levels of meaning, identity, and communication in cultures" (LeBaron, 2003) and is an important skill for bridging cultural conflict within partnerships. One concrete way this can affect collaborative design is in the selection of the ground rules. "Most common ground rules in use today have evolved from a Western tradition that emphasizes efficiency and individuality" (Dukes et al., 2000: 55). If participants hail from non-Western cultures, then sensitivity to selecting ground rules that respect the values inherent in these cultural traditions will go a long way to beginning to reduce stereotypes and engender trust. Designing in rituals that reflect indigenous people's ways of knowing and communicating is one such example of attention to cultural differences.

Reframing. In some situations, even with mediation, some stakeholders are highly resistant to partnering because they hold incompatible frames about the issues. By framing we mean shaping, focusing, and organizing the world around us (Gray, 2003). When parties frame their worlds in ways that cast other stakeholders as their enemies, view them as antithetical to their interests, experience threats to their own identity framing, and/or construe options for overcoming their differences with these others as hopeless, launching a successful partnership will be difficult if not impossible. If an intervener cannot assist parties to reframe their experience (e.g., a trusted visionary creates a plausible argument for partnering) or exogenous factors call attention to unrecognized interdependencies, frames can inhibit parties from even searching for joint interests (Gray 2004; Lewicki et al., 2003).

Action Research

This form of intervening is rooted in the practice of organizational development. It involves designing activities in which participants study themselves, their past and current interactions, and decide on needed changes to the partnership arrangements. While originally designed to guide participatory interventions *within* organizations, organization development processes (diagnosis, feedback, intervention, and evaluation), have also been used in interorganizational systems (Cummings, 1984; Elden & Chisholm, 1993) to facilitate learning among the partners. They stress co-creation of reality by those involved (Reason, 1994), active involvement of partners in shaping the outcomes of or changes to the partnership, and the importance of developing an ongoing learning process among the partners.

Double Loop Learning. Scholars have noted that learning in collaborative partnerships is difficult and often promotes misunderstanding (Hibbert et al., 2016) and is often short-lived (Ferlie et al., 2005). Action research interventions facilitate the involvement of the partners in diagnosing the primary reasons for seeking a partnership and the primary obstacles that may be impeding it. By building this diagnosis jointly, partners can then agree on action steps to take to rectify these limitations. These learning models intervene by trying to instill double loop learning (Argyris et al., 1985; Argyris & Schon, 1978) in which partners observe and reflect on how they learn, and then initiate change in their interactions to facilitate joint learning. These processes require "curiosity driven dialogue" (Hibbert et al., 2016: 36) in which the process of new understanding of the problem emerges from collective interpretation and questioning and from "doing differences" in which the partners learn to reframe their own ideas and make them acceptable to their partners without having to give them up (Dewulf & Bouwen, 2012: 176).

Appreciative Inquiry. Another action research technique is called *appreciative inquiry*. This technique stresses the positive potential inherent in working together (Barrett 1995; Cooperrider & Srivastva, 1987). In this process, participants are encouraged to ask questions about each other's strengths, achievements, visions, and the possibilities each envisions for what they might jointly create. By valuing the positive, rather than emphasizing threats or problems, appreciative inquiry tries to minimize social-psychological resistance to change.

Participatory Action Research. Some forms of action research stress the importance of leveling the playing field among partners when there are substantial power differences. Community empowerment is an express premise of participatory action research interventions (Elden & Levin, 1991; Fals-Borda & Rahman, 1991; Himmelman 1995; Tandon, 1989). This approach "aims to confront the way in which the established and power-holding elements of societies worldwide are favored because they hold a monopoly on the definition and employment of knowledge" (Reason, 1994: 328). Key tasks of interveners in these circumstances are to take preliminary actions to guard against cooptation (Selznick, 1957) and to ensure lower power partners have a legitimate, independent base from which to raise their concerns. For example, interveners may need to mobilize low power groups to present a coherent voice and gain the attention of more powerful parties in order to even launch a partnership when power disparities are large (Gray, 1989). In these circumstances, involving power-bridgers may also be necessary. Power-bridgers can be powerful stakeholders themselves or third parties who have the necessary clout to bridge the gap between low and high power partners. Their primary function is to provide standing for low power partners and to play bridging roles (Westley & Vredenberg, 1991) in the negotiations among partners of differential power. For example, the Catholic Church played this latter role in Ecuador in 1995, using their institutional leverage to garner a role for indigenous people in negotiations over land reforms with the government and the International Development Bank (Treakle, 1998). Once at the table, power-bridgers can help to level power differences by building checks and balances in to the process to prevent cooptation and ensure elite compliance with collaborative agreements. For example, independent watchdogs can be enlisted to oversee the fairness of the proceedings or sanctions agreed upon in advance can be evoked if powerful parties abuse their power during implementation. Powerful parties can voluntarily make themselves dependent on other stakeholders. For example, the partners can stipulate that if any of them fail to comply with the agreement, decisions can revert to traditional enforcement procedures (such as agency enforcement of codes). FERC's extraordinary efforts to reach out to Native Americans in the hydroelectric relicensing case are illustrative of how power-bridging can prove successful. Notably also, the absence of such power-bridgers in the Mesá, may offer another reason for its eventual collapse as a partnership.

Gaining Buy-In Back Home

Negotiating at Two Tables. A typical problem that many partnerships face concerns gaining buy-in to an agreement by members of each partner's organization who are not serving as representatives at the negotiating table. Colosi (1985) refers to this process as the two-table problem, meaning that representatives have two distinct groups with whom they must negotiate. This occurs when negotiators need to ratify their agreement with back-home constituents (Putnam, 1988). Ideally, representatives are constantly reporting back to their back home constituents any progress made at the negotiating table, querying them for any concerns they perceive, and raising the issues that constituents identify in subsequent meetings with partners. But it also involves helping constituents understand the rationale for the trade-offs made at the negotiating table and nuances in the agreement that may not be obvious to those who weren't present (Gray, 1989). In the end, representatives are faced with persuading constituents that they have secured the best deal possible.

Formal Ratification. A key point at which trust is often broken among partners occurs once an agreement is reached, but then one or more partners insist that it be ratified by their constituents. To avoid this disjuncture, the degree to which representatives "require" such a ratification step should be hammered out during the setting of ground rules so that none of the partners are caught by surprise once an agreement is reached. Building in this feedback loop to and from constituents may lengthen the negotiation process a bit, but it can also help partners avoid eleventh hour rejection of potential partnership agreements. In addition, addressing the two-table problem during negotiations can surface back home concerns and workarounds that might disrupt translating the agreement into action. Thus, it can surface and avert potential roadblocks to later implementation of the agreement.

Institution Building

A final intervention task entails institution building. Once partners have reached agreements and decided on follow-up actions to implement them, the new practices, routines, and norms need to be constructed within the field to ensure lasting success (Lawrence et al., 2002). In fact, Osborn and Hagedoorn (1997: 272) have noted that "alliances and networks can be seen as experiments in institution building." Forging new relationships and new ways of working not only requires a cognitive shift but also a shift in routines and practices and may require forging new structural arrangements among partners. If the new practices can be embedded in existing routines and align with prevailing values, they will be easier to institutionalize, but when partners are initiating new fields, the task of norm construction and implementation must accommodate values and practices from diverse partners (Maguire et al., 2004). For example, partners may differ in the degree to which they find formal rules, procedures, and contractual specification advantageous. While under-institutionalization may thwart coordination, over-institutionalizing—by establishing tight boundaries, formal structures, and clearly specified rules and procedures to regulate partners' interactions—may backfire, by curtailing the flexibility needed to incorporate diverse views (Westley & Vredenberg, 1997), reduce partners' ability to learn from each other, cause alliances to revert to pre-alliance power relations, and lead to disappointment when expected outcomes are not realized. The institution building role becomes salient during the implementation and institutionalization phases when agreements reached by the parties need to become routinized and monitored for consistency.

Structuring. Many of the pitfalls that partnerships face in the early phases can resurface in the institutionalization phase. At this phase, the original negotiators may step aside in favor of bringing in more permanent employees to oversee operationalization of the agreements. This may involve institutionalizing new practices within each partner organization and/or forming an entirely new organization to carry out this work. Transferring the insights and historical memory of partners from the earlier phases is also critical to the institutionalization process since new participants may not appreciate delicate or nuanced aspects of the agreement and can intentionally or unwittingly damage trust by giving them short shrift. Ameliorating this setback can be helped by constructing authoritative texts to record the collective understandings that guide the partners' progress over time (Koschmann et al., 2012).

Replicating and Scaling Up. Another important aspect of institutionalization may involve replicating or translating a successful partnership design to a new context or location. This work may involve a corporation transferring practices developed with one partner in a specific venue to different partners in other venues or promoting multiple innovative alliances simultaneously in multiple locations. A critical step in the success of replications is to get buy-in from stakeholders in the new context before proceeding—thus, essentially starting the partnering process over again in phase 1 to ensure that the new partners have an opportunity to include their interests and tailor the partnership to their particular contextual conditions. For example, partnerships that are trying to scale up in base of the pyramid (BoP) contexts often face problems that partnerships in less-poverty-stricken contexts do not. For example, BoPs may not be able to publicize their success without triggering requests from rent-seekers and may face institutional voids that make the usual rules and regulations that support profit-making organizations scarce or non-existent (Chliova & Ringlov, 2017). Many partnerships and socially oriented enterprises are highly embedded, causing them to suffer from founder's syndrome. This is a two-edged sword because the very advantages that accrue to founders who have ties to the local context (Ruffin & Rivera-Santos, 2013) can make it difficult for them to allow others to pursue different strategies in the replications (Ansari et al., 2012; Dorado & Ventresca, 2013). In Chapter 10 we examine issues in scaling up in more detail by considering the many levels at which partnerships can be organized and how one level of organizing influences those above and below it.

Applying the Intervention Techniques

Determining which intervention technique to apply during a partnership's life cycle should be based on the phase of the partnership's development, the extent of mistrust and conflict that characterizes the partners' interactions, the nature of the problem itself (e.g. public policy development, BoP, adaptive resource management, etc.), the complexity of the issues, and the number of participants. While many of the interventions can be adapted for multiple contexts, careful review of the strengths and weaknesses of each technique should be undertaken before selecting one. Convening, of course, corresponds to initial phase of partnership development and offers assistance in ensuring that the right stakeholders join the partnership. Process interventions typically would kick off the negotiation phase, but, in some cases, determining the shape of the table or the scope of the problem and making ground rules may influence whether some stakeholders agree to participate so these issues may need to occur during the convening process. Visioning may be most productive in the negotiating phase, but could also prove useful in institutionalization to help bring new partners on board. Conflict handling may be needed throughout the partnership (as will be seen in Chapter 6), but it is most likely during the negotiation phase. Large group interventions can be useful either during the negotiation phase or during implementation such as to gauge the degree of support for a tentative agreement and to anticipate implementation issues. Institution building could begin during implementation if partners need to change their internal practices or routines to abide by the agreement, but are clearly needed also in the final phase if new formalized networks are required or replication of the agreement in other contexts is sought.

Finally, as we noted earlier, while partners themselves can serve as interveners, many of the techniques described here require considerable knowledge, training, and skill that are best provided by a professional third party. Interveners who are not caught up in the dynamics and concerns central to cross-sector partnerships can prove potentially useful in navigating the minefields that lead to collaborative inertia. Critical to promoting effective collaboration are leaders who can "create a constituency for change that can reach implementable agreements on problems and issues of shared concern" (Chrislip & Larson, 1994: 73). We have argued that process leadership includes a host of activities related to ensuring that the interactions among team members are constructive and productive. Attending to the process dynamics of a partnership demands an especially important set of interpersonal leadership skills that are critical to successful team collaboration. Leadership intervention in the important aspects of team life can prove especially beneficial, because interpersonal tensions generate negative emotions that erode the open exchange of ideas. The vicissitudes of evaluation and re-application for funding can also affect the emotions of team members. At these times, effective leaders need effective communication skills (Lewis et al., 2010) including active listening skills, empathy, and the ability to reorient the team's efforts toward their long-term goals. Finally, while these skills are imperative for negotiating contemporary organizational forms (Heath & Isbell, 2015; Huxham & Vangen, 2000b), it is important to note that partnership leadership need not necessarily be performed by a single leader, but could be handled in a distributed fashion when multiple members within a partnership possess the requisite skills.

In Chapter 6, we delve more deeply into how and why conflict arises within partnerships. We also explore other tools, in addition to mediation, that are helpful for managing conflict productively when it arises.

Notes

1. As we indicated in the case, the CAO may not have had sufficient clout or neutrality to successfully perform this role; nonetheless, they did convene the Mesá.
2. This section drew heavily on material from Gray (1989), pp. 75 and 77.
3. This section drew heavily on material from Gray (1989), pp. 81–3.

6

Conflict in Multistakeholder Partnerships

As we noted in Chapter 2, partnerships may form to tackle joint problems which individual stakeholders are ill-equipped to address on their own. By pooling knowledge and resources, stakeholders may be able to surmount these obstacles together. However, despite a strong commitment to collaborate (Gray, 1989), partners may encounter conflict as they work together. Even when partners agree on goals and a common agenda, conflicts still may arise over the process they will use to search for agreements, over their relationships or about how agreements will be implemented.

For example, watershed partnerships exemplify collaboration that forms around a shared vision—that of protecting and managing natural resources in a watershed (Fan & Zietsma, in press; Wondolleck & Yaffee, 2000). These partnerships bring together state and local government officials, citizens, farmers, and other water users to find ways to ensure water quality and quantity in the watershed. Partners in such situations seek to advance a collective goal that requires ongoing cooperation and agreement among all of them. However, despite their shared goals, reaching agreement about how to achieve and implement them may prove problematic for the partners. Differences in partners' underlying logics, identities, and emotional attachments may emerge, leading to conflicts over how to operationalize agreements in principle. This is especially likely if one party shoulders an inequitable burden of responsibility for implementation, or if agreements restrict some stakeholders more than others (Bidwell & Ryan, 2006). In extreme cases, when conflicts go unresolved, parties may abandon their shared vision and adopt individual strategies that block or reverse the progress the partnership initially made (Sousa & Klyza, 2007).

In a partnership to explore the impacts of MNC's corporate practices on people living in poverty, the giant British-based Unilever and Oxfam (an NGO devoted to poverty reduction) faced some conflicts as they worked together. Clearly these two organizations saw the world differently causing them to engage in "intensive and sometimes difficult debates." During these debates the partners were forced "to recognize their blind spots and rigid preconceptions" and "challenge their respective biases and assumptions" (Senge et al., 2006: 429). Approaching their differences in this way required a spirit of "openness, respect and trust" (Senge et al., 2006: 429) which enabled them to learn a great deal about the problems they were studying together.

In another case, a utility planning to build a hydroelectric power plant in western Mexico sought to collaborate with government and community groups to plan for the project's social, economic, and environmental impacts, which included population growth. Despite community support for the project, conflicts about the scope of the project, compensation to landowners, and ownership rights for natural resources surfaced as the project progressed (Chavez & Bernal, 2008). In such cases, the partnership may fall apart unless the partners can agree upon effective processes (such as those we present later in this chapter and in Chapter 7) for addressing such conflicts when they emerge.

In this chapter we first take a closer look at factors manifesting at the partnership level that generate conflict within partnerships. Then, we examine how and why at least some of these conflicts may have deeper roots within institutional fields or society writ large. Finally, we introduce a number of actions that partners can take to address conflicts that arise as partnerships are forming and as they progress. We now turn our attention to several reasons why conflict within partnerships is not surprising.

Factors Generating Conflict within Partnerships

Many reasons have been identified to account for why conflicts flare up among partners who seek to collaborate. Conflict over values, goals, procedures, roles, and relationships is part of working in partnerships that bridge sectors (Gray, 1989; Castro & Nielsen, 2001; Todd, 2002; Crosby & Bryson, 2005; Rauschmayer & Risse, 2005), For example, partners may refuse to participate if they perceive that their identities, values, reputations, or core missions are or will become jeopardized if they agree to join up (Rothman, 1997; Gray, 2004; Fiol et al., 2009) or if mistrust of another stakeholder simply runs too high to be repaired. For example, mistrust of the US federal government deterred local residents and snowmobilers from signing an agreement after a 16-month mediation to regulate snowmobiling in a forty-year-old conflict over Voyageurs National Park in northern Minnesota (Gray, 2004).

History

Some partnerships emerge only after long-standing conflict has paralyzed a field—sometimes for many years. In such cases, stakeholders cannot see eye to eye but neither one can prevail because each has the capability to prevent the other from accomplishing its individual goals. These conflicts persist until the parties reach a hurting stalemate (Zartman, 2001)—that is, until the pain of not settling the conflict outweighs continuing to battle. Many early collaborations over environmental issues brought together parties who had been at odds for years (in the courts, on the ground, and in the public media). For example, environmentalists and loggers in Quincy, California had engaged in conflicts over clear-cutting of forests for years. The conflict festered and eventually turned violent. Only then were the disputants willing to try to search for common ground (Bryan, 2004). Their collaboration became known as the Quincy Library Group (QLG) because they decided to hold their deliberations in their local library. Their negotiations enabled them to forge an agreement that eventually became the standard practice for the National Forest Service (after much political in-fighting in Washington, DC) (Bryan, 2004). While cases such as the QLG represent success stories, not all such deliberations produce lasting resolutions or develop institutionalized partnerships that can transform conflictual fields even when third-party mediators are brought in to design and assist the process (Gray, 2004; Gray et al., 2007).

Distrust

When historical patterns of interaction among parties have historically been violent and/or social distance among them has been maintained over decades, distrust is inevitable. Distrust has been defined as "confident negative expectations regarding another's conduct," where "conduct refers to words, actions, and decisions (what another says and does and how he or she makes decisions)" (Lewicki et al., 1998: 439). Distrust can stem from fear or attributions of sinister intentions by others and the desire to avoid contact with them (Lewicki et al., 1998). Distrust is exacerbated by limited information flow among groups and enhanced by recurring violence by one group on another (Pruitt & Kim, 2004). Cultivating trust is a critical ingredient in the maintenance of successful collaboration (Sheppard, 1995) regardless of whether the partnership is among cross-functional team members, among strategic alliance partners, within multistakeholder partnerships or even among competitors (Hamel & Prahalad, 1994). Repairing trust, once it is broken, however, requires a lot of work and patience because once a breach of trust occurs, restoring it is a slow process. As Figure 6.1 shows, it may take two or three times as long to restore trust, but even then it is unlikely to be as strong as it was initially. Partners need repeated assurances that their counterparts' words match their actions before they will begin to trust them again. Approaches to overcoming mistrust often need to be designed into initial efforts to collaborate when the history of distrust among parties is bitter or protracted.

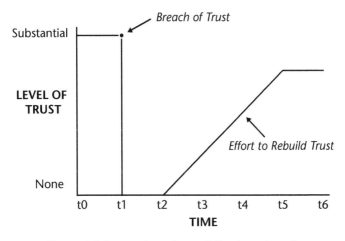

Figure 6.1 Restoration of trust following a breach

Differing Frames

Another reason conflict may ensue is that partners operate with different interpretations or frames about the issues and problems the partnership is designed to address and how to solve them (Lewicki et al., 2003). "We construct frames by sorting and categorizing our experience – weighing new information against previous interpretations" (Gray, 2003: 12). Frames not only shape how partners see the issues but they also influence what actions they are willing to take. For example, partners employ frames to project their identities (e.g., "we are pacifists"), to justify our actions and to convey judgments about others (e.g., "they are treehuggers"). Frames are also used strategically by social movement leaders to mobilize others to take action (Benford & Snow, 2000). "Through framing, we place ourselves in relation to the issues or events thereby taking a stance with respect to them (Taylor, 2000) and placing ourselves in concert with or in opposition to other parties" (Gray, 2007: 225).

Differences in frames are prevalent for natural resource disputes and in partnerships about sustainability issues in which the problems are often ecologically and socially complex (Gray & Wondolleck, 2013). As Rauschmayer and Risse (2005: 656) note, "the existing knowledge that can be used for conflict resolution is multifaceted and often conditional; certain outcomes can be reached by various alternatives, and probabilities may or may not be known; additionally, the information is often incomplete." Thus, the less certain predictions are about future conditions, the greater the likelihood partners may have different frames about the risks and

potential consequences of various future actions. In order to partner successfully, parties may need to consider the calculated risks they are willing to
take to pursue joint actions. To the extent partners' perceptions of risks
and their tolerance for risk-taking differ, conflict is more likely to impede
collaboration.

Even when partners are concerned about the same general problems or
issues (e.g., crime, global warming, or poverty), differences in how they
frame the issues can prevent partnerships from forming or derail ongoing
attempts to collaborate. Partners' institutional affiliations and the leverage
they have to influence the others' actions also shape their frames (e.g., as
"arbiters of the common good" or "as helpless victims") that then affect the
content and outcome of collaborative discussions. "Organizational culture
and preexisting constituent relationships may dictate partnerships' definition
of the problem and the range of preferred alternatives in agency-affiliated
partnerships" (Bidwell & Ryan, 2006). In a study of cross-watershed management partnerships among public agencies, nonprofits and citizen groups:
citizen-based groups framed group achievements in terms of lobbying and
advocacy; agency-based groups identified achievements in terms of launching
sustainability initiatives; and mixed groups defined success as creating a
watershed management plan (Moore & Koontz, 2003). In an effort to deal
with homelessness in Massachusetts, three potential partners initially clashed
in their framing of the problem. One adopted a market frame, another a social
welfare frame and a third, a social control frame. Through deliberations, they
began to enlarge their framing of the issues to incorporate all three perspectives which eventually enabled them to agree on which joint actions to take
(Schon & Rein, 1994).

Conflicts are usually exacerbated when one group attempts to force its
frame on others. In a natural resource management project in Southern
Ecuador government engineers were charged with helping indigenous peoples
to improve their irrigation systems. The engineers conceptualized the problem
in terms of a theoretical flow rate model and could not understand why the
indigenous farmers failed to defer to their expertise, preferring instead to rely
on a practical frame based on years of observation and experience with the
system (Dewulf & Bouwen, 2012). In order to find common ground on a
solution, these partners needed to adopt several conversational techniques
to reframe the issues that included frame incorporation, accommodation, and
reconnection (Dewulf and Bouwen, 2012). In large scale, highly political
disputes, however, these techniques may be insufficient on their own. International negotiations over climate change, for example, are a case in point.
Despite many shifts in parties' frames over a thirty-year period, it is still
questionable whether the parties have reached a lasting agreement for averting global warming (Ansari et al., 2013).

Mandated Collaboration

Some partnerships may emerge because collaboration among the partners is mandated by authorities. Such mandates can occur in the context of regulatory proceedings or adjudication of legal disputes or may be required by certain granting agencies. In such cases, conflicts among the parties may have festered for a long time, and mandates may be the only way to force resistant parties to collaborate. Despite the fact that, by all objective measures these parties' interests would be better served by negotiating than by resisting (Katz, 1993), sometimes only mandated collaboration can bring them to the table. Mandated negotiations may also be necessary when the scope of an issue "extends beyond existing institutional opportunities that might accommodate voluntary engagement" (Gray & Wondolleck, 2013: 463).

There are liabilities in using such a big stick approach though, and some scholars have expressed skepticism about what it can achieve (Rodriguez et al., 2007; Genskow, 2009).

> For example, in mandated negotiations, the parties may collaborate "in name only" just to appear to satisfy the regulatory requirement. Also, local relevance and ownership may be absent (Taylor & Schweitzer, 2005) and thereby reduce parties' overall commitment to collaborate. Parties may also feel constrained to negotiate within narrower parameters (Gray & Wondolleck, 2013: 463).

Mandated collaborations may not reduce conflict if externally imposed deadlines prove too short to successfully work through knotty issues or if agencies with the authority to mandate collaboration are able to exert disproportionate power over the negotiations. In such cases, Hardy and Phillips (1998) assert that compliance, contention, or contestation may occur rather than collaboration, and it is likely that the conflicts will surface again down the road. Some scholars have also questioned the degree of learning that occurs when conflicts are "resolved" through mandated negotiation. Several factors have been found to influence the degree and duration of social learning that occurs (Bouwen, & Taillieu, 2004) including number of partners, quality of the facilitation, length of the process, and use of a standard template (Brummel et al., 2010) with some of these only producing enhanced coordination but no innovative outcomes.

Identity or Value Differences

Identity issues are at the core of much resistance to collaborate and can generate clear obstacles to the search for common ground (Rothman, 1997; Kreiner et al., 2006; Fiol et al., 2009). Two categories of value conflicts are possible, those "that arise over the basis of consensus and those taking place within the basic consensus" (Coser, 1956: 75). When the dispute falls into the first category, "parties believe that no common ends can be discovered so that a compromise can be reached" (Coser, 1956: 75), whereas in the second, parties may have differing values that guide implementation of an agreement. Deep value differences, and disputants' identification with those values, pose the most difficult challenges for collaboration. Differing values may be rooted in religious beliefs, cultural differences, and/or political ideology. For example, disputes over what is considered "sacred" often impede collaboration when Native Americans or First Nations or other indigenous cultures clash with Western values as in current resistance by the Sioux tribe in Nebraska to the Keystone pipeline. Disputes over the "sacred" involve:

> fundamentally different orientations toward land and nature held by Native Americans and many other non-native groups in the U.S. The former exhibit strong reverence for nature which often translates into opposition to proposed projects on public lands and how they are managed (Gray & Wondolleck, 2013: 447).

Because they engender strong emotions and high levels of mistrust, values- and identity-based conflicts often escalate and become intractable (Gray, 2004; Kreiner et al., 2006). Emotions exacerbate the conflict because "people deem expressions of anger more unfair in value conflicts than in interest conflicts" (Harinck & Van Kleef, 2012: 741).

Whether values become a roadblock depends, in part, on the language invoked by disputants (Tetlock et al., 1996) and whether respect for identity differences is built into the partnership proceedings (Rothman, 1997; Elliott et al., 2003). For example, abortion conflicts are heavily values laden, but tools for constructive dialogue on this topic have also been proposed (Baker, 2011; PCP Dialogue Tools, 1999).

Differences in Risk Perceptions

Conflicts among partners can also be fueled by differences in how partners perceive the risks of adopting various actions to deal with the problems the partnership is tackling. In the 1980s research on risk perceptions was spurred by public conflicts over nuclear power. Studies showed that "risk is inherently subjective" (Slovic, 1992: 121), and that technical and lay populations assessed risks differently. Risk perceptions and tolerance also differ based on the perceived benefits of a hazard, whether the perceiver's exposure is voluntary, their familiarity with the hazard and whether they believe they are vulnerable (Baird, 1986). Recent advances in human genomics provide a good example. The promise of human genomics research lies in the potential to cure both common and rare diseases (such as cancer or Alzheimer's or

Hailey-Hailey disease). While largely still unrealized, the prospects of this research require compiling huge databases of human DNA. While many people are ready and willing to make their DNA available, the risks of doing so, to individuals and to society as a whole, are still largely unknown, but privacy concerns pose one potentially important risk. For example, an individual's DNA could be used as a screening device for employment or insurance decisions or even for finding a partner in the future (Berryessa & Cho, 2013). While some people work to publicize these risks, others seem indifferent to them (Briscoe & Gray, 2017). While many types of partnerships (among hospitals, genomics researchers, pharmaceutical companies, investors, disease advocacy groups, and others) are forming to advance the potential of human genomics and personalized medicine, not all players agree on the risks and some seek greater levels of regulation over how genetic data can be gathered, stored, and reused. Finding ways to secure the transfer of genomic data is key to successful personalized medicine.

Resource Constraints

If the solutions to the problems partnerships are addressing are severely constrained, this also can fuel conflicts among partners. Problems with a limited negotiation range present few opportunities for partners to make trades among issues they value differently since no one wants to contribute the scarce resources they control. While assistance from mediators can often help to resolve difficult conflicts among partners, in some cases such assistance is still not enough to overcome truly intractable conflicts (Lewicki et al., 2003). Instead, they may fester for years, leaving parties at odds with each other and fields in a state of flux.

Power Differences

Differences in power among the potential partners can also fuel conflict within partnerships. These differences may manifest in terms of different expectations about what problems the partnership will address, who should participate, and how the process of collaborating will occur. Consequently, while partners may express concern about some of the same issues, their vantage points and expectations about what the collaboration will accomplish may differ depending on the relative degree of power they wield over the issues (Gray & Stites, 2013). These differences were illustrated in a collaboration about the future of refugees analyzed by Lotia and Hardy (2008). These authors noted, "Although these organizations were working on the same overall problem of refugees and their settlement, their divergent views and asymmetrical power relations led them to define the refugee 'problem' in different ways and to advocate for different 'solutions' namely those that reinforced the organization's position in the refugee system" (p. 375). Thus, power differences may exacerbate conflict and lead to stalemate in partnership proceedings. More powerful partners may also engage in collusion by withholding effort and information; this enables them to retain power and avoid exposing potential weaknesses (Gray and Schruijer, 2010).

When partnership conflict is rooted in relative power differences among the partners, this may kindle disagreements over "representational" issues (Gray, 1989; Laws, 1999). That is, partners may dispute which stakeholders should have a legitimate voice in the deliberations and, if technical experts are invited to elucidate key issues, who qualifies as such an expert. "Representational debates may also impact the number and variety of potential partners since, when views are exceedingly different, some groups may seek to exclude others from participating in the collaboration to reduce the diversity of perspectives under consideration or to tip the table in their own favor" (Gray & Purdy, 2014: 213). If some stakeholders perceive that others wield considerably more power than others over who participates or how the agenda is constructed, these potential partners may refuse to join the partnership. If they feel voiceless or outmaneuvered during the proceedings, they may exit the partnership in midstream (Gray, 1989; Hardy & Phillips, 1998; Susskind & Thomas-Larmer, 1999). This was the case in the Mesá de Diálogo when an important indigenous people's group, chose to leave the Mesá. (See the section "Conflict within the Mesá de Diálogo Case" in this chapter and Chapter 7 where we discuss this case more fully.) In another example, Greenpeace withdrew its role as a signatory of the Canadian Boreal Forest Agreement (CBAF), an unprecedented agreement reached in May 2010 among logging companies and environmental groups to adopt sustainable logging operations in Canada's Boreal Forest in order to protect caribou habitat. However, by December 2012, Greenpeace had withdrawn its signature because it believed that the logging companies were dragging their feet in implementing it, or worse, were in direct violation of the agreement. (Myles, 2012). Ultimately, in 2017, the entire agreement collapsed.

Analysis of the Conflicts in Our Three Cases

In this section we revisit the cases presented in Chapter 4 to examine in greater depth the sources and nature of conflict in each. We then consider the relationship between these conflicts and the institutional contexts that are represented in each multistakeholder partnership.

Conflict in the Rabobank Case

To a large extent, the conflicts that arose in this case centered around identity issues and values. One of Rabobank's key motivations for launching the green credit card was to enhance its reputation with consumers, specifically to demonstrate its commitment to green issues such as climate change and sustainability, since the bank was not viewed "as a credible source of climate-related communication" (van Huijstee & Glasbergen, 2010b: 602). This stain on the bank's reputation gave impetus to its teaming up with WFN initially. Once the partnership had formed, at least one other conflict among the partners surfaced—the issue of what level of standards the new card would use to satisfy the need for carbon offsetting. In this conflict, which was value-based for WFN, the NGO prevailed in persuading Rabobank to meet the gold standard requirement for offsetting. Banking on additional reputational gains, the bank acquiesced to the additional expense associated with the higher standards. This trade-off by the partners appeared to be a win/win for both partners, if not financially, at least in terms of their reputations.

However, when FoEN's study of sustainability practices by Dutch banks was released, it again challenged Rabobank's core identity as a reputable bank in the Netherlands. Rabobank's investments in soy and palm oil created negative exposure for the bank because of their large carbon footprints. Once again, spurred by identity and reputational concerns, the bank agreed to partner, this time with both NGOs, to develop criteria to examine its investments and overhaul its portfolio, subsequently securing its first-place reputation for CSR among Dutch banks.

Conflict in the Hydroelectric Relicensing Case

In this case, the US federal agency FERC's initiative to introduce a new process for relicensing of hydroelectric dams was actually born out of conflicts among the various stakeholders involved in licensing these dams. These stakeholders included the dam owners, environmentalists, and state, federal, and tribal governments. The proposed new process that was drafted during this collaboration was, in itself, a response to previous conflicts among these players over how licensing had been handled in the past.

Representational issues stemming from differences in power were central in this case and factored into how FERC designed the process of drafting the new rules. For example, not all stakeholders welcomed others whom FERC invited into the process. Industry representatives did not consider some other participants as legitimate stakeholders for issues in the license that had previously been negotiated. As a result, small hydroproject owners' views may have received less attention than those of large hydroproject owners who held greater sway in trade associations that were active in the process. Similarly, federal agencies' views were well represented and presented a united front because they had coalitional power stemming from the pre-process consultation in which they had engaged while state agencies, on the other hand, fought to ensure that their authority to influence the provisions of a given license in their jurisdiction remained intact.

Tribal governments, who often feel excluded from or given short shrift in US federal proceedings, sought to ensure that they built stronger connections with FERC employees so that they would have avenues for sustained input into future licensing processes. Interestingly, one provision of the final licensing procedure that FERC adopted was to create a special tribal liaison role to address this issue.

An ongoing conflict for tribes in many of their interactions with the US federal government is rooted in the strong cultural and spiritual values they hold about how natural resources should be regulated. These particular types of values conflicts are especially difficult to reconcile because tribal solutions for addressing them conflict with the federal government's emphasis on the rule of law.

Finally, tribes sought a longer time period for the licensing process. Short deadlines made it difficult for resource-constrained tribes to respond in a timely way to the huge volume of filings. In contrast, conservation groups sought a process that would be both speedy and thorough to create maximum protection for natural resources. They also emphasized the need for a process that facilitates citizen and NGO involvement in the licensing process.

Conflict in the Mesá de Diálogo Case

In the Mesá de Diálogo Y Consenso case some indigenous people's groups refused to join the Mesá because they strongly believed the Yamococha mine was not sincere in its efforts to engage with the communities that were adversely affected by its operations. Mistrust of the mine by some indigenous people's groups persisted even after the Mesá was convened. The fact that only some individual employees participated in the Mesá process, rather than an officially designated representative from the company, did little to overcome this mistrust. For many local people, too, the mine's flagrant disregard for their wellbeing and the company's and government's complicity in failing to engage locals in the initial permitting decisions, posed formidable obstacles to reducing mistrust between the mine and the community. This was further exacerbated by the company's lack of transparency in its dealings with the Mesá. Although the Mesá opened up a chance to gradually ameliorate distrust, it seems clear that the less than good faith efforts by the mine prevented this from happening. We discuss power differences that were also apparent in this case in Chapter 7.

How Institutional Contexts Shape Conflict among Partners

The characteristics of the partners (e.g. with regard to power differences) or the scope of the problems (e.g. local vs. transnational) may spark conflicts, generate dynamics that make conflicts difficult to resolve, or impair the partnership's ability to achieve resolution. Impediments such as those we just discussed can often be acknowledged by the participants and possibly mitigated by mutual agreements about interaction processes and decision-making procedures. We discuss this approach later in this chapter. When fundamental differences between stakeholders are more difficult to reconcile, however, it is useful to understand the broader contextual dynamics operating within the field as a whole and to search for barriers that may exist at a deeper, more institutionalized level. We identify several field level characteristics that may influence the level of conflict among partners.

Nature of the Field Itself

We already suggested in Chapter 3 that partnerships are likely to form in fields that are experiencing some turmoil. Field level conflicts are rooted in efforts by various stakeholders to control the field: to shape the overarching logics that prevail and the rules operating in the field, to govern or regulate other stakeholders' actions and to gain or retain power over the field's resources.

Logics. As we mentioned in Chapter 3, the level of coherence within a field refers to the extent that a given institutional logic guides the behavior of all actors within a field (Vurro et al., 2009). Institutional logics are "the socially constructed, historical patterns of material practices, assumptions, values, beliefs, and rules by which individuals produce and reproduce their material subsistence, organize time and space, and provide meaning to their social reality" (Thornton and Ocasio, 1999: 804). Some logics are associated with sectors—e.g., public, private, and non-profit—that can be used to classify the roles of organizations and actors (Bowker & Star, 1999). Other logics are rooted in religion, the nuclear family, and the conduct of democracy (Friedland & Alford, 1991).

Institutional logics provide a template for interpreting events, creating meaning, and experiencing a sense of identity among those who share them (Friedland & Alford, 1991). The bureaucratic state logic, for example, includes a hierarchical system, highly defined roles and interactions governed by rules all intended to increase efficiency through specialization, and to ensure fairness through oversight and consistency in applying the rules (Weber, 1947). In contrast, the private sector operates by a market logic in which actors engage in voluntary transactions to generate wealth. That logic is predicated on economic rationality linked to supply and demand and stresses benefits to individuals or organizations (Friedland and Alford, 1991). The logic associated with the non-profit or third sector emphasizes social and community benefits (Thornton et al., 2012). This community logic stresses universal rights and shared concerns designed to advance the common good of communities (Etzioni, 2004)—concerns that aren't addressed by either the market or the governmental logic (Kaghan & Purdy, 2012).

When logics are shared, they are largely invisible, guiding actions without debate among members of a field. Challenges to prevailing logics can emerge from within a field (Rao et al., 2003; Thornton, 2004; Zilber, 2002) or from outside it, for example, when new technology threatens the viability of extant logics (Lounsbury et al., 2003) or when the prevailing logic is challenged by a new social movement (Armstrong, 2005; Doh, 2003; Rao et al., 2000). Such movements challenge the extant norms and practices—deeming them immoral or unjust—and thereby calling their legitimacy into question (Benford & Snow, 2000; Zald, 1999). For example, AIDS advocates forced changes in healthcare delivery and triggered many new partnerships within the healthcare field as a result (Maguire et al., 2004). Field level logics may also conflict when two fields intersect and a new field emerges in the interstices or overlapping spaces connecting them (Dorado, 2005; Morrill & Owen-Smith, 1998; Purdy & Gray, 2009).

No matter what the source, when logics are challenged, conflict will likely ensue within a field pitting proponents of the new logic against the defenders of the old. As Wooten and Hoffman (2008: 139–40) observe,

> While field constituents' actions may be initially conducted in opposition to one another... protracted institutional engagement can yield a gradual merging of interests with a concurrent alternation in the structure of the field itself. However, until that happens, the field is not a collective of isomorphic actors, but an intertwined constellation of actors who hold differing perspectives and competing logics with regard to their individual and collective purpose (McCarthy & Zald, 1977).

Such battles may unfold in myriad ways and are likely to induce radical change within fields (Reay & Hinings, 2005). Such change occurs when the old logic is supplanted by a new one (Rao et al., 2003; Thornton, 2004), hybrid or blended logics emerge (Battilana & Dorado, 2010), different logics are invoked locally on a contingency basis producing a kind of mutual coexistence (Fan & Zietsma, in press; McPherson & Sauder, 2013; Purdy & Gray, 2009), or protracted conflict persists within uneasy alliances within the field (Dunn & Jones, 2010; Marquis & Lounsbury, 2007; Purdy & Gray, 2009). It is against this backdrop of competing logics that partnerships are often born and conflicts among partners need to be understood because these underlying logics can explain the source of conflict among potential partners.

> These logics affect many aspects of the partnership, from the way problem domains are interpreted to how information is presented and analyzed to preferred solutions for addressing the domain. For example, private sector participants may assume that a cost/benefit approach is the most appropriate approach to evaluating a problem, while public sector participants may interpret the problem in terms of rights and fairness, and a nonprofit sector participant may primarily consider the collective impacts of the partnership on those served by it and how they match up with deeper values such as decency and well-being
>
> (Gray & Purdy, 2014: 214).

While logics comprise enduring assumptions and practices, frames operate at a more tactical level and are typically more pliable (Ansari et al., 2013) and can be ascertained through frame elicitation techniques and discussed among the parties (Kaufman & Gray, 2003). Designing processes within partnerships to help partners understand the source of each other's competing frames and their reasons for attachment to them may help partners begin to embrace a broader conception of the problem they are facing and enable them to find a collaborative solution by enlarging their repertoire of frames (Elliott et al., 2003; Fan & Zietsma, in press; Gray, 2007).

Regulatory Structure within the Field. Whether the context is a regulated one or not can also have important implications for the kinds of conflicts that emerge within a partnership and how they are handled. Effective collaboration among multistakeholder partners may be hampered in situations where a governmental participant has regulatory authority linked to the opportunity or problem being addressed. Because governmental organizations have legitimate societal authority for certain decisions and accountability to the public, they may be more likely to assert control and attempt to dominate collaborative partnerships even if the partnership is ostensibly "voluntary." For example, Gazley (2008) found that in noncontractual public–private partnerships, local governments were doing most of the decision making. In describing a national effort to redraft the rules for licensing US hydroelectric projects, Purdy (2012) notes that in addition to legal authority over the final rules, government agencies had human and financial resources that allowed them to set the agenda, determine the meeting locations and schedule, and be well-represented at every meeting. Although the process was designed to maximize public impact on the writing of the rules, nongovernmental and private sector participants lacked the ability to reconfigure the process, and the government ultimately had veto authority over the final decision (Purdy, 2012). The presence of regulations or the inclusion of regulators in a partnership can be particularly problematic if the partnership has been formed to revise, challenge, implement, or create substitutes for regulation (Gray & Purdy, 2014: 211).

Scope and Scale of the Problem or Issue

The sheer scope and/or scale of the perceived problems within a field can engender conflicts among field members. As problems increase in scope and scale, field members face greater difficulty in coordinating their efforts to address them. Increases in the scope of a problem add complexity. As problems increase in scale, more political jurisdictions are implicated (i.e., levels of government within a nation or different governments when the scale transcends national borders). Negotiations over future management of Voyageurs National Park (a body of water on the border of the US and Canada) would increase in both scale and scope if the problem was defined as an international one. Consequently, when the Federal Mediation and Conciliation Service stepped in to mediate this conflict, they restricted the negotiations to only US players leaving any international issues for future negotiations.

Added complexity ensues when field-level conflicts are transnational or global in scale and no legitimate overarching governmental authority has jurisdiction over the nations implicated in the problem (Ansari et al., 2013; Rosenau, 1992). For example, many different organizations all generally aligned with issues such as women's rights or global security (Zald, 1999), but their views may differ culturally and politically. With no regulatory framework or normative conventions for addressing these kinds of problems, no forum for convening the relevant stakeholders and no norms for how the negotiations will be conducted, field conflicts may persist indefinitely. This also means that, "in cases like the Palm Oil Roundtable or the Kyoto Protocol, even if the parties reach a binding agreement, no explicit means of enforcing the agreement exists" (Gray & Purdy, 2014: 212). Forming partnerships to tackle these complex kinds of issues means orchestrating the efforts of hundreds of partners which often makes these alliances unwieldy and subject to dynamics associated with blocking coalitions and with diverse logics and frames rooted in national, cultural, religious as well as sectoral differences (Ansari et al., 2013: Dewulf, & Bouwen, 2012; Nikoloyuk et al., 2010). "Institutional building in the transnational sphere involves multiple actors or groups of actors with mental and action maps originating from quite different institutional contexts" (Djelic & Quack, 2008: 309). This is also true for base of the pyramid strategies that link partners vertically from the local to the national or inter-national level. When these efforts are successful, however, they can trigger shifts in meso-level governance practices (Ruffin & Rivera-Santos, 2014). Wooten and Hoffman (2008: 138) claim this topic deserves additional research to learn "what drives organizations to interact with each other" to engage in field restructuring. We argue that partnerships serve as one vehicle for structuring of fields. Such restructuring may also threaten the underlying power relationships among actors within a field resulting in old coalitions falling apart and new ones coalescing and gaining ascendency (Wooten & Hoffman, 2008). Alternately, if actors cannot reconcile their divergent logics and no convergent logic emerges, field-level conflict may remain protracted (Ansari et al., 2013; Purdy & Gray, 2009). We take up the issue of power in fields in more detail in Chapter 7 and consider how partnerships restructure fields in Chapter 11.

Addressing Conflicts within Partnerships

In Table 2.3 we showed different starting conditions for partnerships. In two of these, partnerships emerged from conflict among potential partners. In Chapter 5 we introduced the role of the mediator as a means of conflict handling and we referred to consensus building as a promising process for handling conflict within partnerships. Here we explore explicit processes that may prove useful for addressing conflict in certain circumstances along with illustrative examples. These are summarized in Table 6.1. Partnerships originating from conflict (listed in the center column of Table 2.3) face unique challenges in shifting their interactions from conflict to collaboration. This may necessitate the use of different tactics than partnerships arising from opportunities (listed in the right column of Table 2.3). In the following paragraphs we discuss in further detail the tactics for managing conflict-based multistakeholder partnerships.

For conflict-rooted partnerships, the use of a *conflict assessment* process may be necessary to determine whether any intervention is possible and might be productive (Susskind & Thomas-Larmer, 1999). For example, public policy mediators use assessment to "(1) understand the history and background of the conflict, (2) determine the relevant parties and their power relationships, (3) glean the positions and, more importantly, the interests and BATNAs of the parties, and (4) diagnose whether or not a consensus-building process is feasible" (Gray, 2007: 238). In addition to these considerations, Gray (2008) has suggested that such assessments should also include how the conflicting parties are framing the dispute in order to deepen and sharpen understanding

Table 6.1 Additional strategies for dealing with conflict

Conflict management strategy	Potential outcomes
Conduct a conflict assessment	• Understand history and background of conflict • Determine relevant parties and power relations • Learn positions, interests, and BATNAs of partners • Diagnose feasibility of consensus-building process • Understand how partners are framing the conflict
Acknowledge critical identities	• Reduce prejudice among partners • Foster a superordinate identity • Reduce need for defensiveness
Identify leaders	• Help partners focus their attention on key issues • Create a sense of urgency • Frame problems in terms of opportunities • Persuade stakeholders to collaborate
Level the playing field	• Increase voice of low power partners • Reduce need for displays of power by partners • Increase trust
Synchronize de-escalation	• Save face of partners • Increase trust • Move toward problem solving
Explore each other's frames	• Overcome misconceptions about partners' interests • Discover shared frames • Find trade-offs • Develop accommodations
Use Shuttle diplomacy	• Diffuse/dampen escalatory tendencies • Keep partnership moving forward • Increase trust

of cognitive and relational impediments to partnership and how they might be overcome.

Once forming a partnership is judged to be feasible, another important tactic for moving parties from contentious behavior to a problem-solving orientation is *acknowledging of the parties' critical identities*. Rather than ignoring or smoothing over their different identities, it may be crucial for potential partners to acknowledge each other's prized and distinctive identities in order to minimize feelings that collaboration may threaten these. In addition, finding ways to create a superordinate shared identity (Fiol et al., 2009) that enables parties to develop a common in-group identity that does not require them to forsake their individual prized identities has been shown to reduce prejudice among groups (Dovidio & Gaertner, 1998) thus enhancing the possibility that the partners will be able to see past their differences in order to collaborate. Gray (2007) has referred to this as frame enlargement since the partners are entertaining a broader conception of their own and their partners' identities.

For example, in a partnership between Oxfam and Unilever to explore how to reduce poverty in Indonesia, the partners encountered major differences stemming from their organizational identities.

> During the Indonesia study process, Oxfam and Unilever entered into intensive and sometimes difficult debates. To move beyond mere transactional exchanges, such projects demand people be willing to open themselves, recognize their blind spots and rigid preconceptions, and enter into a process of genuine mutual influence. Such discussions caused all parties to challenge their respective biases and assumptions. This process was a great source of learning, which would not have occurred without a spirit of openness, respect and trust (Senge et al., 2006: 429).

Consequently, the partners were able to reach an agreement that "eased pressure" because the partners "knew they had a way to manage irreconcilable differences if they arose" (Senge et al., 2006: 426). While these partners did truly wrestle with each other during this partnership; nonetheless, they never reached an impasse that required them to use the formal dispute resolution procedure to which they had agreed up front.

Telling identity stories is a helpful tactic for opening up dialogue when there is a history of intergroup or interorganizational mistrust and partners are deeply wedded to their historical identities. By telling their own story (and engaging other participants as reflective listeners), partners' grievances are personalized and brought into the present. The process enables each partner to establish their own voice in the dialogue and begin to "hear" the other partners' concerns as well. One specific reflective technique to promote deep listening is the Samoan Circle in which heartfelt concerns are heard and acknowledged by all participants. This process is best conducted with a neutral mediator or facilitator who can ensure that important points are responded to and not glossed over.

Another important step in moving from conflict to problem solving is *identifying leaders* who are sufficiently powerful to move a multistakeholder partnership forward. The structure of a situation may dictate leadership, such as in a regulatory context or when participation is mandatory, but leaders can also emerge from the conflict itself; that is, the conflict may emerge as a catalyst for initiating the negotiations. In such cases, battle-worn enemies may become partners to end the conflict (Gray, 1989; Castro & Nielsen, 2001; Bryan, 2004). The National Coal Policy Project and the Quincy Library Group (both mentioned in Chapter 5), grew out of protracted conflicts. In the former, after battling for years in the courts, two leaders (one from coal producing and consuming companies and the other from environmental NGOs) had the vision to see past the conflict and draw parties into partnership (Hay & Gray, 1985). Similarly, leadership emerged in the Quincy case once the parties reached a hurting stalemate (Bryan, 2004). Multistakeholder partnerships rooted in conflict may require such leaders (or a leadership committee) to step forward who have "the ability to focus people's attention and create a sense of urgency, the skill to apply pressure to stakeholders without overwhelming them, the competence to frame issues in a way that presents opportunities as well as difficulties, and the strength to mediate conflict among stakeholders" (Kania & Kramer, 2011, p. 40).

Third parties can also help to level the playing field when power differences exist and to facilitate listening among the potential collaborators (Gray, 1989). In multistakeholder partnerships parties often hold different forms of power stemming from the societal sector to which each partner belongs. For example, government agencies may hold decision authority, private-sector organizations may have financial resources, and nonprofit organizations may have representational or grass roots power. Recognizing these different forms of power as valid and significant can assist in *leveling power differences*. Partners may tend to emphasize the power of decision authority, or of having significant human, informational, or economic resources, but the relational and perceptual aspects of power are also important in social partnership contexts (Purdy, 2012). For example, power can exist in the ability to catalyze constituents or in the ability to speak on behalf of societally important ideals such as human rights (Purdy, 2012). While government agencies may be reluctant to partner with social movement activists because they consider them as uninformed fanatics (Hanke et al., 2003), the presence of third parties can ensure these agencies that the dialogue will remain civil while ensuring access to the decision-making forum for the activists. Acknowledging different types of power is a means of balancing power among participants; doing so can increase the effectiveness of the partnership by reducing the need for displays of and contests over power. Attending to power differences among partners allows adjustments to be made to the process design, the participants, and the approach to substantive issues, creating a more level playing field on which parties can participate fully and genuinely (Purdy, 2012).

Another useful tactic for conflict-initiated partnerships is *synchronized de-escalation* (Osgood, 1962). This tactic helps parties to "step back from the ledge" while saving face and maintaining the integrity of their identity. In synchronized de-escalation, one party offers a small concession to signal good faith and an intention to improve the relationship. Other parties are invited to reciprocate with their own concessions to reciprocate the extension of good faith. Since none of the partners knows whether the others will follow through, offering concessions signals trust and provides a means for the partners to move into a problem-solving mode.

Once parties have agreed to participate and have begun to share information, *exploring each other's frames* is a particularly vital tactic for partnerships rooted in conflict. Participants in multistakeholder partnerships frame conflicts through their taken-for-granted institutional logics. For reframing to occur, the parties must reassess the stance they are taking in light of the frames proffered by others (Schon & Rein, 1994). Differences in frames may not be immediately evident, but may be exposed by role reversal and imaging processes in which parties share views of themselves and how they appear to others (Alderfer, 1977). For example, in a workshop among irrigators and government regulators in Queensland, Australia, a key feature of the partners' interaction was described as follows:

> The small group discussion...transformed the process of understanding value, into collaboratively linking issues and concerns to potential strategies. The positive discourse enabled "reframing" to identify shared interests and find common ground about equity and triple-bottom-line sustainability...that resulted in irrigators agreeing on words about fairness and environment for the first time...They realized they could talk about sustainability in a way that was nonthreatening to their members and still seen as legitimate by government
>
> (Baldwin & Ross, 2012: 225 and 227).

In a similar conflict in Southern Ecuador between government engineers and indigenous peoples to improve irrigation systems, reframing was also critical (Dewulf & Bouwen, 2012). The engineers conceptualized irrigation using a theoretical flow rate model while the local farmers based their arguments on a practical frame stemming from years of experience. To bridge these differences, several conversational techniques for reframing were useful, including incorporating each other's frames, accommodation, and reconnection (Dewulf & Bouwen, 2012). By exposing different frames, participants have the opportunity to construct a hybrid shared frame that recombines the extant logics (Djelic & Quack, 2008) and reshapes expectations about outcomes of the partnership (Gray, 2007).

Shuttle diplomacy is another tactic that may be needed in conflict-initiated partnerships. Shuttle diplomacy involves the mediator meeting individually with each partner to learn their concerns in order to convey them to the other partner(s) in a subsequent private meeting. This tactic can prove beneficial when the dynamics among the potential partners are deemed to be initially explosive and face-to-face meetings would likely to escalate the conflict. Through shuttle diplomacy a mediator may be able to diffuse or dampen escalatory tendencies.

Although the above tactics have been suggested explicitly for conflict-initiated partnerships, even partnerships that start from opportunities, rather than conflict, may face conflict as they develop. As partnerships move toward creating solutions and making deals, conflicts may emerge that ignite or reignite tensions and move the partnership closer to impasse. In such cases, many of the tactics described here may prove useful for keeping the partnership on track. Some partners have even acknowledged that conflict was beneficial to the partnership.

Even if partners do not see eye to eye, conflict can stimulate deeper investigation of the issues and generate new understanding and novel solutions.

For example, in the partnership between INEOS Chlorovinyl and World Wildlife Fund for Nature, an initial campaign against PVC (polyvinyl chloride) by Greenpeace was pivotal in getting the company to the table with WWF, although Greenpeace eventually elected not to pursue the partnership. Nonetheless, according to Jason Leidbetter, formerly of INEOS, "Greenpeace was nipping at our heels. We were forced into partnership kicking and screaming, but Greenpeace has done us a lot of good." He believes there is a role for NGOs who will raise tough issues for business.

Conclusion

Multistakeholder partnerships draw together stakeholders with varying institutional logics whose interests have either clashed or converged around a problem or opportunity. Whether initially rooted in conflict or opportunity, such partnerships are likely to generate conflicts at some point as participants work through the processes needed to try to achieve resolution. Various structural and relational challenges can generate conflict, such as differential power or a mandate to participate. More deeply rooted institutional logics can also drive conflict, such as when participants hail from diverse societal sectors or when the core logic of an organizational field is being negotiated. In this chapter we have offered means by which to understand conflict in multistakeholder partnerships and have reviewed several techniques that can be used to support progress toward resolution, unleashing the full potential of such partnerships to create a collective impact (Kania & Kramer, 2011) on society's most daunting challenges and inspiring opportunities.

7

Power and Collaboration

An Institutional Perspective on Power and Partnerships

Multistakeholder partnerships are governed by power dynamics that affect and are affected by the structure, processes, and relationships of the partnership. We draw on multiple meanings of power here. The first is the idea that the exercise of power is actor-based activity intended to influence; the second is the Foucauldian notion that power is a force embedded in discourse and elements of everyday life (Purdy, 2012). When considered through the lens of institutional theory, the exercise of power involves bestowing legitimacy upon actors and the ability to define the boundaries of what is acceptable and possible according to norms, practices, and beliefs that are negotiated by participants in a field. Present in every social interaction, power incorporates both repressive and productive elements, and operates on multiple levels of social organization simultaneously. As a result, we will treat power in this chapter as having social and relational aspects that incorporate both capacity and action, such that "power is the medium in social relations to structure fields of action" (Göhler, 2009: 36).

As noted in Chapters 2 and 5, legitimacy is an important aspect of partnerships. Legitimacy refers to "a generalized perception or assumption that the actions of an entity are desirable, proper, or appropriate within some socially constructed system of norms, values, beliefs, and definitions" (Suchman, 1995: 574). Within partnerships it pertains to who is viewed as a legitimate partner, whether partners gain legitimacy from joining a partnership, and whether the partnership has legitimacy to act within a field. According to Stinchcombe "a power is legitimate to the degree that, by virtue of the doctrines and norms by which it is justified, the power-holder can call upon sufficient other centers of power, as reserves in case of need, to make his power effective" (1968: 162).

A thorough analysis of power must consider two modes of power that span from everyday interactions to broader social structures, norms, and sanctions

(Clegg, 1989). The first mode, episodic power, describes how power is used during interactions among parties to create or reduce dependence through communications and actions such as influence and force (Lawrence, 2008). This approach to power draws attention to relatively discrete acts of strategic mobilization initiated by self-interested actors (Clegg, 1989). On the other hand, systemic power is linked to ongoing, taken-for-granted practices that advantage some groups even when those groups do not participate in creating or propagating them (Clegg, 1989). The institutional fields we discussed in Chapter 3 are a basis for systemic power that comes in two forms: disciplinary power, where the institution shapes meaning and action by specifying rules and rewards that provide a sense of identity and motivation (Lawrence, 2008), and domination, where the institution restricts the range of actions that are available (Lawrence et al., 2001). From a systemic perspective, power is deter-mined not by individual actions and dependencies but by legitimacy within the social order, yielding differential levels of voice, access, and acknowledg-ment among field level actors. Systemic power often operates behind the scenes and goes unchallenged, hampering partners' ability to reach broadly acceptable and sustainable agreements. The systemic approach to power also recognizes that, once formed, collaborative partnerships may also have difficulty achieving legitimacy within the broader social field (Provan et al., 2008).

Episodic Aspects of Power

Scholars of collaborative governance have offered several insights about the nature of power exercised when parties to a governance process interact.[1] Reed (2013: 197) describes one of the enduring debates in sociological theories of power as argumentation over the "long-standing distinction between power to (capacity) and power over (domination)." "Power to" is a capability or precondition (Göhler, 2009) that represents a disposition toward how power is used (Clegg, 1989), while "power over" is exercised power that represents episodic agency (Clegg, 1989). Huxham & Vangen (2005) note that "power to" imbalances among partners are a potential threat to collaboration because they may generate distrust among participants when one believes the other has more power to influence the partnership process. For example, Gray (1989) identified the power to mobilize and the power to organize or convene a collaborative process as examples of "power to" behavior. Concerns about "power over" come into play when participants have difficulty agreeing on a shared purpose and some have the ability to steer outcomes in their own favor. Under these conditions, governance of the partnership becomes more difficult because of the threat that some actors may attempt to impose their will on others. Research on collaborative interorganizational processes suggests that a third orientation toward power, "power for," is possible. "Power for" emphasizes the sharing or expansion of power to reduce power imbalances or advance a position that is not solely self-interested (Huxham & Vangen, 2005).

To fully understand episodic aspects of power, we must consider why actors are perceived to possess the capacity to take action or the ability to coerce others to accept their will. The framework we adopt here to understand forms of power proposes that organizational power in collaborative contexts is generated primarily through the authority, resources, and discursive power held by organizational actors (Hardy & Phillips, 1998). Each of these three forms of episodic power is discussed in greater detail below.

Authority refers to the socially validated right to make a decision or take action on behalf of others. While it may be derived from coercion, authority is more commonly understood as a delegation of power by those who are governed, through social and political structures that are sanctioned and legitimate. For example, government agencies have the authority to establish and enforce rules because citizens share a belief in the "rationalization and the regulation of human activity by legal and bureaucratic hierarchies" (Friedland & Alford, 1991: 248). Private organizations and nongovernmental organizations rely on corporate governance structures and the strength of institutional structures such as the law to vest authority in designated actors.

Resources serve as a form of episodic power because they can be used to influence dependency relations among organizations. Whether resources are human, technical, financial, informational, or cultural, they represent the ability of actors to grant or withhold something that other actors desire. The value of resources as a form of power is not absolute; it is specific to the episodic domain in which actors have an interest and the needs of those actors in relation to each other. For example, scientific knowledge might prove to be a more valuable resource in solving an environmental challenge than having access to money. However, perceptions of resources as well as actual resources are relevant to how actors perceive power. Kanter notes that "people who are thought to have power already...who look like they can command more of the organization's resources...may also be more influential and more effective in getting the people around them to do things and feel satisfied about it" (1977: 168–9). This insight reminds us that people may act in ways that reflect their perceptions of power rather than reflecting the objective dependency relationships that might otherwise determine power.

Discursive legitimacy is a form of power that recognizes the ability of an organization to exercise voice on behalf of an issue in the public sphere (Hardy & Phillips, 1998). The ability to manage meaning by influencing how information is presented is particularly important in collaborative partnerships because the process involves complex negotiations designed to develop

119

shared frames about the problem or issue (Huxham & Vangen, 2005; Elliott et al., 2003). Expertise in shaping meanings yields discursive power; Hallett (2003) describes this as "the power to define the situation" (p. 133). Furthermore, discursive power represents access to a means of catalyzing social groups to take action. Grassroots organizations that generate social movements such as "Occupy Wall Street" provide a familiar example of discursive power in action (Reineke & Ansari, 2015); however, other organizations have access to this form of power as well if they can organize themselves and others to act on the values or principles they hold. Government agencies typically represent the principle of democracy or the rule of law, corporations may represent the desire for prosperity and economic well-being, and nonprofit organizations may represent values such as equality, sustainability, or freedom from want. Like other forms of power, discursive power exists in the eye of the beholder but can be restricted by systemic power. For example, an organization that presumes to have discursive power linked to the value of equality is unlikely to be powerful in a social context where significant social inequities are accepted as the norm. Conversely, an organization that serves or is comprised of individuals with low power (such as children, the poor, or immigrants) can have considerable discursive power by speaking on behalf of a value such as compassion if other actors also see this value as important.

When evaluating power dynamics in collaborative partnerships, these three forms of power can be juxtaposed with the three power orientations described earlier to create a framework for assessing possible power responses of actors based on their perceived characteristics (see Table 7.1). Placing an actor within the framework requires careful assessment because forms of power and power orientations are subjective characteristics that involve an element of judgment. As noted above, forms of power are not absolute and depend in part on perceptions or attributions within contexts; thus actors and observers make judgments about which forms of power are present and to what degree various actors have them. Power orientations are largely a matter of judgments by actors about others, although social and cultural influences as well as past experience can also significantly influence the orientation an actor brings to a partnership.

Table 7.1 provides examples of potential power moves that arise from the various combinations of power forms and power orientations. It identifies the capacity for action that is generated by power when taken at its most extreme. The framework is not predictive of the actions that actors will take; rather it illustrates the range of possibilities that are available to them. The actions taken by actors are dependent on their assessments of the power of other actors as well as the costs and benefits of taking action. For example, the first row of Table 1 indicates that actors who are perceived to have authority may

Table 7.1 Actor capacities based on forms of power and power orientations

		Power orientations		
		Power over	Power to	Power for
	Authority	Impose unilateral decision	Decide how to decide	Endorse collaborative efforts
Forms of power	Resources	Take action independently	Participate in decision making	Provide means for broad participation
	Discursive power	Create social pressure for a given action	Manage meaning or sanction a decision	Represent those who cannot participate

have the capacity to impose a unilateral decision, as in the case of a regulatory agency that has the ability to promulgate regulations in a particular domain. However, they may not choose to exercise that capacity and may instead elect a collaborative approach (such as regulatory negotiation) rather than a rational-legal one. As described in Chapter 4, such a choice was made by the Federal Energy Regulatory Commission (FERC), the US federal agency responsible for governing the electric power system, when it was rewriting the laws for hydroelectric power project relicensing in the United States. Rather than drafting regulations and limiting stakeholder involvement to a public comment period, FERC engaged in collaborative governance through a series of meetings across the country that culminated in stakeholders joining with FERC to draft the new regulations (Purdy, 2012).

As the second row of Table 7.1 shows, actors with access to resources have the ability to select the degree to which they wish to influence the dependencies among stakeholders in a partnership context. Depending on their assessments of the power of others and their own preferences, these actors may act unilaterally or may level the playing field to support broad participation in collaborative governance. In the hydroelectric relicensing example, FERC expended its own resources to travel to thirteen locations throughout the country near hydroelectric facilities to facilitate the participation of Native American tribes in the licensing process, and designated 50 percent of all meetings specifically for tribal participation (Purdy, 2012). In contrast, Yanococha Mine in Peru did nothing to respond to indigenous people's concerns when they complained about the mine's impact on their communities. Consequently, some of these groups refused to participate in the Mesá de Diálogo y Consenso process, believing that the table was tipped in favor of the mine. Finally, the third row of Table 7.1 illustrates ways in which actors with discursive power are able to influence public opinion and change the nature of the discourse around an issue. For example, nongovernmental organizations such as Greenpeace walked out of United Nations climate change talks in

Warsaw, Poland in 2013 to indicate growing global frustration with slow progress on an agreement (Twidale & Chestney, 2013). Some attribute agreement on greenhouse gas emissions at the 2014 talks in Lima to "peer pressure" that resulted from this action (Davenport, 2014).

Episodic aspects of power are concerned with elements of influence that are specific to the actors, contexts, and relationships associated with a particular issue the partners intend to tackle. These perceptions and calculations of power occur through interactions that are relatively immediate to the situation and to the interests and actions of those involved in it. However, the situation itself is infused with power dynamics that emerge from the taken-for-granted practices and processes that are fundamental aspects of social organization. These forms of power may be invisible even to the actors themselves. Power in the forms of discipline and domination (Lawrence, 2008) is hidden in the technologies, physical settings, and practices that we use to interact in the world. "Lawrence and Suddaby (2006: 230) argued that maintaining practices involves developing and policing the normative, cognitive and regulative structures that underpin them" (Zietsma & Lawrence, 2010: 195). Only when we consider the role that these kinds of institutional elements play in organizations and society can we begin to see some of the less visible aspects of power that position actors in the social order and limit or control what they are able to accomplish. These systemic aspects of power will be considered next.

Systemic Aspects of Power

Power dynamics emerge from a complex web of varied understandings about the interdependencies between participants' interests, resources, and influence.[2] One of the challenges of thinking of power in relation to partnerships is to recognize that power is an attribution rather than solely an objective quality. Further, the attribution of power is influenced by institutional forces. Beliefs about the power held by any party are formed in relation to the observer's beliefs about the institutional fields in which the party operates: is the entity central or on the periphery of its field? Does it influence the standards of the field or struggle to adapt to them? Does the entity have a stream of resources that allows it be idiosyncratic with respect to institutional norms and practices? Does it bridge multiple fields in a way that marginalizes or extends its power?

A systemic view of power recognizes that communication and action are sources of domination that are imbedded in the very structures of social interaction. The role of systemic power in partnerships is most easily seen as top–down, where "the way things are" determines the possible avenues of influence and alternatives available to participants. However, the systemic form of power exerted by institutions does not exist a priori in a society or field; it is created through bottom–up activity that involves "doing legitimacy" (Barley, 2008: 506) and enacting power. For example, the power of organizational elites within organizations is maintained by collective "class work" that includes creating firewalls to separate groups, developing nets of accountability, constructing legitimating myths about meritocracy, and establishing differential levels of autonomy (Gray & Kish-Gephart, 2013). The behavior of partners is influenced by their ability to influence legitimacy norms within the field. Changing these norms depends on a number of factors including: (1) the state of the boundaries between groups, (2) the level of acceptance of the practices, and (3) the capacity to undertake the boundary and practice work needed to introduce a different set of institutional norms (Zeitsma & Lawrence, 2010:189). Variations in these conditions can move stabilized fields to conflict, move conflicted fields to become innovative collaborative ones, and ultimately prompt reinstitutionalization of the field with new norms and practices (Zietsma & Lawrence, 2010). Additionally, in some cases, collaborative partners begin to operate in the interstitial spaces between fields or transcend their respective fields to engage in new field creation (Purdy & Gray, 2009). Thus, a systemic view of power must view the institutional context as socially constructed, meaning that it provides structures of discipline and domination, but these are also malleable and able to be changed or recreated in certain contexts.

As partnership participants consider the array of options available to them based on existing field conditions, they also may consider whether they want to maintain or change the legitimacy standards in a field to support the goals of their partnership. Challenging existing legitimation norms requires the introduction of new bases for evaluating the legitimacy of actions (Suddaby & Greenwood, 2005). It also involves judgments about the types of power within a field that might facilitate or impede the change. These judgments acknowledge that interactants and actions "are embedded in situationalized arrangements of power and resources" (Clemens, 1996: 226) that influence interactants' perceptions of which situations appear possible and impossible to change. Systemic power differences that are largely invisible, and exercised through ongoing rules and sanctions that privilege certain groups while concealing their role as beneficiaries, are difficult to dismantle and often require the strong mobilization and confrontation tactics of social movement groups (Gamson, 1992; Strang & Soule, 1998) to force change. On the other hand, episodic power is less entrenched and stratified and affords interactants more room to maneuver. When interactants perceive a field as characterized by episodic power, they feel less constrained by rules and taken-for granted assumptions, which allows them to imagine and enact alternatives with less fear of reprisal and greater ease in finding agreement among partners.

Table 7.2 Orientation toward field creation or restructuring in collaboration

		Domination: Perception of power relations	
		SYSTEMIC	EPISODIC
Legitimation: Stance toward field norms	CHANGE	**REVOLUTION** **Externally induced reframing** *Focal interactant promotes new frame imposed on issue field* **Internal reframing** *Focal interactant promotes revising frame of issue field* **Importing a master frame** *Focal interactant promotes higher order frame in issue field*	**EVOLUTION** **Merging frames** *Focal interactant participates in constructing a new frame in the issue field from existing ones* **Situated improvising** *Focal interactant gradually creates new frame in the issue field*
	MAINTAIN	**STATUS QUO** **Maintaining frame dominance** *Focal interactant reinforces existing frame of issue field* **Institutional distancing** *Focal interactant insulates itself from existing frame of issue field*	**POWER SHARING** **Maintaining frame plurality** *Focal interactant supports coexistence of multiple frames in the issue field*

Source: Adapted from Gray, Purdy & Ansari 2015.

In Chapter 3 we described the importance of partners finding agreement on a shared frame to guide their partnership efforts. As studies on power and institutional work (Martí & Fernández, 2013; Rojas, 2010) and discursive institutional entrepreneurship (Rojas, 2010) have emphasized, framings are always embedded in power relations that authorize certain actors and perspectives and neglect or exclude others (Meyer & Höllerer, 2010). We build on this work by showing how different perceptions of power relations and varying stances toward the legitimacy of field norms may impede or facilitate partners to challenge, initiate, and/or enforce institutional change.

In Table 7.2, we present a matrix that illustrates four patterns linked to partners' perceptions of power as either systemic or episodic and whether they seek to maintain or change legitimation norms within the field their partnership is addressing. Each pattern represents a different orientation toward constructing or restructuring the field from the perspective of a focal interactant: revolution, evolution, status quo, or power sharing. In describing framing processes associated with these orientations we note that the term "partner" can refer to individuals, groups, organizations, or even nation states.

A *revolutionary* pattern occurs when the focal interactant perceives systemic power but seeks to change legitimation norms. In this case, other interactants' power and their stances toward legitimation in the field will shape the action the focal partner is able to take. For example, if another partner is relatively more powerful than the focal partner, the latter may be limited to leveraging normative and rhetorical power from outside the field in order to build their own power to change the legitimation norms within the field. This was the situation in the Rabobank case when a coalition of environmental groups led by FOE challenged several Dutch banks' commitments to sustainability. Although the banks had entrenched power, the FOE coalition pressed for change in defining what was considered a "legitimate" lending portfolio with respect to sustainability. Consequently, in order to protect its reputation, Rabobank was forced to revise its own norms about what constituted an acceptable sustainability portfolio. Where one partner enjoys strongly entrenched systemic power, less powerful partners must muster sufficient countervailing power to force field level change. This could occur in the form of social movement pressure from outside the field, internal pressure for change, or by leveraging master frames that apply broadly across multiple fields (such as civil rights frames). Which mechanisms are likely to be invoked will depend on the relative power among interactants.

A *status quo* pattern occurs when the focal partner perceives a systemic power configuration and prefers no changes to existing legitimation norms. If other partners are more powerful, the focal interactant may invoke *institutional distancing* to preserve the framing and legitimacy norms already in place within the field and resist the framing advanced by another partner. This mechanism may also be activated when the focal interactant anticipates that revolutionary mechanisms might yield even less advantageous institutional arrangements. Conversely, if other partners are less powerful, the focal partner may be able to *maintain the dominant frame* without the need to distance or resist. In both these cases, little variation in interpretations occurs, the extant frames in the field persist and no change in legitimation norms occurs.

An *evolutionary* orientation occurs when the focal interactant perceives episodic power within the field and seeks to change legitimation norms. Systemic power differences do not dominate in such situations, thus if the focal partner offers a revised framing of the problem, other partners may have sufficient power to resist the new framing, but may not be able to prevail with their own framings either. Since power is more evenly distributed, the field is fluid enough to entertain variations in framing but change in the legitimation norms depends on both interactants. This creates the possibility of negotiations resulting in a *merged frame* that combines the differing frames of the partners into an overarching new frame. However, if one or both interactants are unwilling to shift their frames (e.g., they resist new framings), change can only happen incrementally through *situated improvising* as interactants gradually revise their frames through trial and error over time. They may "build a variety of ambiguous frames, investing little in any of them, since it is not yet clear which coalition or set of rules will organize the arena" (Armstrong, 2005: 167). This pattern best characterizes the Mesá process because although the Yanococha mine owners resisted the consensus process and the proposed changes in mine operations emerging from it, the Mesá did make inroads in improving the water quality delivered to residents of the communities surrounding the mine by agreeing to water quality and quantity standards and by engaging in inspections of water quality and quantity in many communities. The evolutionary orientation is more likely to occur when partners perceive a context to be institutionally complex, that is, characterized by multiple frames, structural fragmentation, and moderate centralization (Greenwood et al., 2011) and consequently, difficult to change. Whether true field level change occurs in this context largely depends on whether the partners both seek to change the field's legitimation norms.

The final pattern represents an orientation of power sharing, where the focal interactant perceives episodic power and desires to maintain the extant legitimation norms. Although other partners may also want to maintain the extant norms, interpretations of them or what they are intended to accomplish is different, leading to ongoing tensions. Since power is dispersed, no dominant interactant is able to force a settlement (Fligstein & McAdam, 2012; Rao & Kenney, 2008) around a single set of legitimating norms and no interactant wants to give up its preferred framing of legitimation norms within the field. With power perceived to be relatively equal, each party seeks to preserve its own autonomy and distinctive frame but also needs to accept others' distinctive frames as legitimate. This tension may be handled by agreeing to disagree and mutually coexist with differing interpretations regarding the best approach (Murray, 2010). This pattern *maintains frame plurality*, which is likely to occur in contexts that permit a heterodoxy of interpretations, identities, and practices (Durand et al., 2010; Kraatz & Block, 2008), but may not work in partnerships where partners need to agree on fundamental framings and goals in order to take joint action. Or it may lead some partners to resort to decoupling (Meyer & Rowan, 1977; Oliver, 1997) in which they separate their actual activities from their espoused identity in the face of conflicting frames. In forming partnerships, indigenous peoples may decouple by having their interests represented by agents whose appearance, modes of expression and cultural behaviors are aligned with more dominant institutional orders. In some cases, the tension may be buried and simmer below the surface of interactions as suppressed contradictions

(Seo & Creed, 2002) or the inability to reconcile conflicting frames may generate intractable conflict foreclosing the possibility of partnership (Gray, 2004).

Dealing with Legitimacy Threats

If pressures to remain legitimate within one's own institutional order are
significant, one may ask how any partnership process could succeed since
no participant would tolerate legitimacy threats in order to reach an agreement.[3] However, some organizations reduce legitimacy pressures in other
ways. Elite actors may have sufficient resource streams and power sources
that are not controlled by external observers that allow them to set aside
concerns about legitimacy (Greenwood & Suddaby, 2006). Other organizations may operate in contexts where the legitimacy of certain practices is
ambiguous (Goodrick & Salancik, 1996) or the institutional context is complex or changing (Greenwood et al., 2011), which creates greater organizational discretion to act because the parameters of legitimacy are unclear or in
transition. This is often true for sustainability partnerships where the frontier
of what is considered sustainable practice is fluid and evolving. Still, these
problems may be thorny and difficult to resolve simply because of the sheer
number of issues in play (scope) and/or the geographic breadth (scale) of the
issues. For example, stakeholders grappling with issues such as whaling must
contend with different and incommensurable frames related to species sustainability, cultural heritage, subsistence and economic power, animal rights,
and the sovereignty of indigenous peoples. Finding common ground in this
morass of issues will always be challenging even when partners exhibit relatively equal power at the negotiating table.

Although the frequency of cross-sectoral partnerships has increased in
recent years, problems with power in partnerships persist. Existing power
dynamics between parties can heavily influence the interactions of parties
(Helms & Oliver, 2015) or amplify power struggles (Walker & Hurley, 2004).
Some parties may withhold information or effort to gain or retain power
in partnership processes intended to be collaborative (Gray & Schruijer,
2010). Power issues also can be more subtle, such as when representatives of
some communities are not organized in a way that allows them to fully
participate, or when the interests of some stakeholders are not noticed or
not acknowledged. Scholars have identified practices that can improve positive outcomes for collaboration, including having a powerful and credible
actor convene the partners (Wood & Gray, 1991), supporting voluntary
participation (Genskow, 2009), and using procedures that treat stakeholders
equally (McKinney & Field, 2008); however these are focused primarily on
influencing episodic aspects of power rather than systemic ones. Such

127

solutions do not address challenges that are embedded in the structure of the social system, such as the established models for how problems are recognized and framed that are typically derived from the dominant cultures and institutional orders, reducing or eliminating from consideration the concerns of lower power participants. These concerns are often exacerbated in developing countries where governments are either fragile or autocratic. Partnerships in these contexts run the risk of low levels of inclusiveness and legitimacy because low power stakeholders are, at best, often included in name only (Bäckstrand, 2006; Brown, 2008; Schäferhoff et al., 2009). The Mesá case is illustrative in that the federal government (through the Ministry of Mines) exerted no enforcement pressure on Yanococha to reform its unsustainable mining practices.

This chapter's examination of both episodic and systemic power suggests that successful collaboration within a partnership is unlikely to succeed unless two conditions are met. First, collaboration requires a context for interaction that allows participants to sustain sufficient power to (1) satisfy their existing expectations regarding their own institutional legitimacy or (2) to modify legitimacy standards in a way that ensures their legitimacy going forward. A collaboration partner that does not have sufficient power to garner legitimacy is unlikely to continue participating, as we saw in the Mesá case when some indigenous groups dropped out of the process. However, the relative power of the actors does not determine whether a relationship is collaborative (Gray, 1989). Instead collaboration is dependent on settings where roles and practices are not predetermined by markets or hierarchies (Phillips et al., 2000b). To successfully construct a shared context for partnering, actors need to "build upon, work around, recombine, reinvent and reinterpret logics and institutional arrangements" (Djelic & Quack 2008: 308). Actors must remain open to suspending and even revising the assumptions embedded in their sectors and fields about how problems should be framed, how information should be interpreted, and how they should relate to each other when working together. Thus it is necessary to construct a collaborative partnership that is mutually valued by all participants.

A second important condition for successful collaborative partnerships that stems from this analysis of how power influences partnership dynamics is the acceptability of the collaborative effort itself. For common pool resource issues, collaborative governance networks are one option for partnering among several alternatives that can be used (Hanemann & Dyckman, 2009), but rational-legal approaches may be preferred because they are more deeply institutionalized or they offer paths that are perceived to be less risky for obtaining one's preferred outcomes (Layzer, 2008). Partnerships on environmental issues in particular face a difficult task in changing understandings of how people should behave and how resources should be managed because they are complex, multi-jurisdictional and often poorly suited to compromise solutions that would be acceptable to all participants. For example, the distributive, zero-sum nature of some problems, such as whaling, makes a compromise solution impossible because some parties are unwilling to accept a complete ban on whaling while other parties are unwilling to accept the killing of a single whale. Such problem structures are not uncommon in environmental contexts where naturally occurring critical values (such as extinction thresholds) impose absolute limits on solutions and serve as barriers to compromise and creative, win–win partnership solutions.

Progress on problems such as climate change is difficult to achieve through collaborative approaches, not only because power dynamics and institutional expectations make finding solutions difficult, but because partnerships may identify solutions that challenge the basis of the dominant institutions of society. Helms and Oliver note that "when institutional constituents resolve conflict in ways that radically alter how they relate to one another, fields change. Radical settlements can also lead to major redistributions of power among field members" (2015: 473). Changes in the institutional order occur more commonly and easily through "institutional shocks" such as natural disasters and similar catastrophic events than through deliberate incremental change via sustained collective action (Wijen & Ansari, 2007). Nevertheless, gradual change is occurring in many democracies where it is no longer assumed that the nation-state should dominate governance or that relations between society and government should be uniform and at arms-length (Paquet, 2007). Accountabilities in environmental governance are not unidirectional; instead they are multidirectional among all the relevant stakeholders, leading to effective and creative social learning (Paquet, 2007). Collaborative partnerships that recognize and embrace this intelligent accountability take a step toward overcoming the hierarchical dominance structure of institutional orders. For example, partnerships that bridge across the domains of law, social services, business, healthcare, and transportation have made some progress in disrupting the oppressive institution of human trafficking, which spans the globe (Foot, 2016).

Conclusion

Multistakeholder partnerships are not merely vessels in which power dynamics play out. They are arenas for the social construction of power, and they influence participants' subsequent forms of power and orientations toward power within a field. MSIs have the potential to yield new and changed relationships that affect access to information, levels of trust, and participants' placement within a field. The outcomes of collaborative partnerships may expand or diminish a partner's access to authority, resources, or discursive power, or precedents may be set that reposition partners relative to the issues and the future sources of power related to them. Despite the difficulty of studying a dynamic, relational, multilevel concept such as power, further research is needed to understand the episodic and particularly the systemic aspects of power that affect and are affected by multistakeholder partnerships. We begin this exploration in the final chapter of this book.

Notes

1. We draw selectively from Purdy (2016: 249–53) in this section.
2. We draw selectively from Gray et al., 2015: 131–3 in this section.
3. We draw selectively from Purdy (2016: 258–61, including Table 11.1) in this section.

8

Partnerships for Sustainability

In the last fifteen years, there has been an exponential rise in the use of multistakeholder partnerships to address sustainability around the globe. In this chapter we build on a systematic review of two related but distinct literatures that address the evolution of MSPs for sustainability: the management and the public policy literatures (Gray & Stites, 2013). The overall question we address is: *What are best practices for firms to collaborate with other organizations to advance sustainable business?*

The management and public policy literatures reflect the increase in the use of partnerships to address sustainability concerns, often, but not exclusively, revealing partnerships between businesses and NGOs. Figure 8.1 shows the increases in partnership articles published per year in these two literatures between 2000 and 2012. These partnerships actually come in many forms, ranging from alliances between businesses and NGOs, to networks of small rural farmers working with micro-financiers, to government-led efforts to manage natural resources or design transportation infrastructure, to industry-level, norm-setting bodies designed as substitutes for government intervention.

The chapter is organized as follows. First, we provide brief definitions of sustainability and corporate social responsibility to set the stage for what sustainability partnerships are designed to achieve. Next, we describe the different forms that partnerships for sustainability may take, from those that just involve one firm and one NGO to much broader partnerships that bring together many businesses, NGOs, and even government(s) to tackle larger-scale issues and problems for which individual organizational efforts would be insufficient. Next, we discuss factors that partners should consider in selecting an appropriate partner. Finally, we review criteria that each type of partner needs to satisfy to consider a sustainability partnership a success.

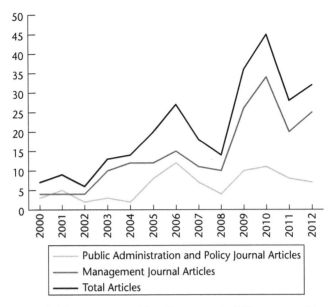

Figure 8.1 Increase in articles about sustainability partnerships

Defining Sustainability and Corporate Social Responsibility

Countless definitions of sustainability are available. One general definition stresses the importance of bringing industrial systems into harmony with nature by balancing use and regeneration of resources and striving to preserve the lives of humans, other species, and future generations (Senge et al., 2007). However, because sustainability is "a broad and evolving construct that defies a universally agreed definition" (Haugh & Talwar, 2010: 385), understanding this variety is important for potential partners. Their definitions of sustainability will influence how they define their orientation to problems and their motivations for engaging in partnerships in the first place. Thus, how partners define sustainability will affect the ease or difficulty with which they find common ground.

Explicit links have also between made between sustainability and corporate social responsibility (CSR). CSR traditionally has been defined as encompassing "the economic, legal, ethical, and discretionary expectations that society has of organizations at a given point in time" (Carroll, 1979: 500). Additionally, so-called Base-of-the-Pyramid advocates argue that improvements to the livelihoods and well-being of the world's poor are also critical to sustainability (Hart, 2005; Prahalad, 2004).

Synthesizing these various approaches, we define sustainability as improvements to the total quality of life, both now and in the future, in a way that maintains the ecological processes on which life depends while satisfying the basic needs of all stakeholders (Gray & Stites, 2013: i). Additionally, the Natural Step has identified four basic conditions that help to operationalize our definition of sustainability. These are depicted in Figure 8.2.

Organizations have many motivations for linking with others to address sustainability challenges. For businesses, the desire to enhance their reputations as socially responsible is critical, along with finding leaner ways to produce and reducing their environmental footprint. For governments, partnerships are becoming the governance structure of the future (Ansell & Torfing, 2014). For NGOs, the challenge involves taking up the role that, in many cases, governments are no longer able to fulfill because of shrinking resources or weakened social mandates. For communities, their paramount desires are to escape poverty, eliminate human rights abuses, ensure sustained supplies of natural resources, and enhance their overall health and well-being. Combining resources, skills, and knowledge from a wide range of stakeholders to address the challenges of creating a sustainable planet, these multisector partnerships draw on diverse competencies of partners from many sectors to tackle problems that individual organizations (or even whole sectors) cannot solve or cannot solve as well, working independently (Bryson et al., 2006; Gray, 1989; McGuire, 2006).

In a sustainable society, nature is not subject to systematically increasing...

...concentrations of substances extracted from the Earth's crust,

...concentrations of substances produced by society,

...degradation by physical means,

and, in their society...

...people are not subject to conditions that systematically undermine their capacity to meet their needs.

Graphics based on The Natural Step's Sustainability Criteria

Figure 8.2 The Natural Step's Sustainability Criteria

133

Types of Sustainability Partnerships

As we discussed in Chapter 1, multistakeholder partnerships may involve members from two or more sectors: business, nongovernmental organizations, governments, and civic society or community. Sustainability partnerships are no different. A strong business case has been made for business involvement in partnerships for sustainability. A global survey of 766 CEOs in 100 countries revealed that "seventy-eight percent believe that companies should engage in industry collaborations and multi-stakeholder partnerships to address development goals" (Lacy et al., 2010: 11). So, for many scholars and sustainability experts, the question of whether business should be (or needs to be) involved in partnerships is moot (Zammit, 2003). The more important questions are "how and to what effect?" (Zadek, 2008: 379). While many business–NGO partnerships involve only one business and one NGO (dyadic), many others join more than one business and/or multiple NGOs. The Rabobank case (in Chapter 4) exemplifies a sustainability partnership between a single business and two NGOs.

As we diagrammed in Figure 1.1, when three or more sectors participate in a partnership, this constitutes a multisector partnership. Multisector partnerships for sustainability range in scale from the local to the global. At the local level, climate action partnerships have been created to implement Agenda 21. At the transnational level, many multisector partnerships for sustainability have been set up as policy dialogues or roundtables (such as the Soya Roundtable, the Marine Stewardship Council, and the Better Cotton Initiative) in which multiple businesses, NGOs, and civic society members explore the development of sustainable standards for producing a commodity and certifying its production.

An increasingly common type of multisector partnership is called *collaborative governance*, a term describing partnerships that involve the governmental sector and seek to address public policy issues. Government actors are encountering more challenging public issues and have limited resources with which to create innovative solutions. Further, policy implementation increasingly involves an array of stakeholders. Consequently, a new form of governance, which is generally referred to as "collaborative governance" or "network governance" (Provan & Kenis, 2008) has emerged. Public policy scholars describe governance as "a set of legitimate and authoritative relationships and processes that define public goals and stimulate collective action to achieve them" (Waddell & Khagram, 2007: 262). Put more simply, governance involves the processes of managing the delivery of public good (Gray & Stites, 2013). A useful way to map types of collaborative governance is to think of them as falling on a continuum of government involvement.

At one end, governments "play a minimal role in directing the economy, stepping in only when markets fail," while at the other end, decisions and their implementation are handled within a governmental bureaucracy (Regéczi, 2005: 208). Collaborative governance would fall in the middle, between these two extremes. We expand on the notion of collaborative governance in Chapter 9.

Types of Business–NGO Partnerships for Sustainability

Within the broader constellation of partnerships, those involving businesses and NGOs can take many forms because they reflect a heterogeneous set of activities, "with some initiatives resembling conventional forms of philanthropy while others are characterized by more substantive forms of multistakeholder engagement" (Utting & Zammit, 2009: 43). Now we will drill down to consider a number of different forms that these types of partnerships can assume. Figure 8.3, arrays several of these types along two axes. The X axis displays the scope of the partnership, which increases with the number of players and sectors involved and the size of the problem arena (e.g. local, regional, national, global). The Y axis displays the degree of shared ownership and responsibility for the partnership exhibited by the partners. Each partnership type is described in detail below.

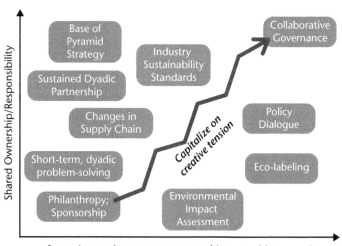

Figure 8.3 Types of business–NGO partnerships

Philanthropy or Sponsorship

This is the simplest form of partnership, in which "businesses approach partnerships as philanthropic initiatives consisting of uncoordinated and piecemeal donations to worthy causes" (Jamali et al., 2011: 376). Typically, this form of partnership involves donations from a single business to a single NGO. A move toward social alliances, which are business–NGO partnerships linked to corporate social responsibility, has shifted some philanthropic partnerships upward toward sustained engagement and outward toward including multiple partners. For example, a longstanding partnership exists between Toyota Motor Sales USA and the National Environmental Education Foundation (NEEF), a nonprofit extension to the Environmental Protection Agency which is a US government regulatory agency. Toyota and NEEF support National Public Lands Day which engages Toyota employees and thousands citizens in projects such as refurbishing the Kentucky Department of Fish and Wildlife's Salato Wildlife Education Center (http://corporatenews.pressroom. toyota.com/releases/toyota+kentucky+npld+2014.htm). The collaboration around environmental stewardship has grown such that Toyota and NEEF now jointly offer capacity-building grants, professional development, and educational resources to local nonprofits that support individual public lands sites (www.neefusa.org/resource/our-commitment-public-lands-every-day).

Environmental Impact Assessment

When a business considers other stakeholders' input on its plans for a new facility or site it conducts an environmental impact assessment. The degree of stakeholder involvement varies, from offering one-time input to providing substantial input as the plans unfold. Business might also consult NGOs for *short-term problem-solving* on a single sustainability issue or might develop a more *sustained dyadic partnership* with one NGO. For instance, Dupont and the Environmental Defense Fund (EDF) teamed up to work together on nanoproduct development. Either short-term problem solving or a sustained dyadic partnership might generate changes in the firm's supply chain as were evident when Loblaw (a Canadian grocery chain) teamed up with World Wildlife Fund to develop a line of sustainable seafood. *Eco-labeling* is an industry-level effort that generates standards for certifying which products are sustainable.

Policy Dialogues

Policy dialogues (e.g. Canada's Royal Commissions and US regulatory negotiations) involve stakeholders in discussions with government to recommend legislation or regulations. Similar discussions among industries and NGOs are convened to develop voluntary *industry sustainability standards,* such as the chemical industry's Responsible Care Initiative, which focuses on health, safety, and environmental performance, or the Canadian Precast/Prestressed Concrete Institute's (CPCI's) new Sustainable Plant Program, which sets sustainability standards for manufacturing facilities in the concrete industry.

Base-of-the-Pyramid Strategies

As we discussed in Chapter 2, these are partnerships in which businesses work closely with income-poor communities around the globe to develop new sustainable business opportunities that are locally embedded and generate value for all the partners.

Collaborative Governance

As noted earlier, collaborative governance involves businesses and other stakeholders in the design and implementation of governmental activities. We devote the whole of Chapter 9 to this topic.

Mapping Sustainability Partnerships on a Continuum

Many researchers have proposed typologies or continua to capture differing levels of commitment by businesses and/or partnerships to corporate social responsibility. Most continua have four levels, although some only have three, and a few have five. Almost all the continua seek to reflect increasing levels of business involvement in partnering with their stakeholders, and many build on each other. Austin and Seitanidi (2012) offer a synthesis of the four-part models that includes a progression ranging from philanthropic to transactional to integrative to transformational. In Figure 8.4 we overlay these gradations on the types of partnerships we presented in Figure 8.3 to reflect the increasing levels of responsibility and complexity that partners face as they move from partnerships in the lower left to the upper right of the figure. Achieving successful partnerships at the upper right of the continuum requires that partners learn to capitalize on the creative tensions inherent in the partnership. The different levels also help to distinguish partnership outcomes, with those focused on reputation and image in the bottom left and those with wider societal impact in the top right.

Partnerships in the lower left corner (the hashed area) largely represent threat-induced, compliance or charity-driven responses. In this level of response, sustainability activities involve providing welfare to society by

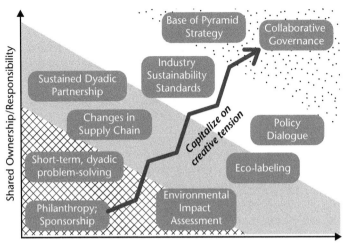

Figure 8.4 CSR sustainability continuum

responding to government regulations or by providing charitable giving to sustainability-related causes. The second level from the left in the continuum (the shaded area) represents largely transactional sustainability partnerships, where the primary motive for business is improving profitability or market share. The third level in white captures integrative/sustainability partnerships, in which businesses move beyond bottom-line considerations to consider how to balance those considerations with social and ecological concerns. Finally, partnerships in the upper-right area of the figure (the dotted area) represent a final type in which other key stakeholders are involved in sustained interactions designed to agree on and enact sustainability objectives that are equally responsive to all partners' needs (Van Marrewijk & Werre, 2003). This approach most likely refers to what others have called transformational (Bowen et al., 2010) or transformative (Austin & Seitanidi, 2012) engagement. Businesses that respond at this level not only embed CSR/sustainability in every aspect of their operations and tie it into their strategic objectives (Valente, 2012) but are also interested in managing and integrating stakeholder expectations (Bhattacharya et al., 2009), and their partnership efforts empower and give equal voice to stakeholders and communities with whom they partner. Vurro and her colleagues (2010: 48) explain that a firm operating at an empowerment-driven level might "act as brokers between governments and communities, through participative leadership styles and governance models aimed at mobilizing local capacity around a social mission, that is, the improvement of local conditions."

The stages of the continuum appear to be in a chronological order, implying that they represent chronological steps. While firms that are new to sustainability partnerships may likely begin with transactional types of partnerships and may progress along the continuum as they gain experience and enjoy success in their partnership efforts, a firm doesn't have to start on the left and move through the levels stepwise. A firm could enter into partnerships anywhere along the continuum and skip levels as it becomes more involved in sustainability activities. Partnerships often evolve by means of a "'reactive-turned-proactive' strategy, where pressures from NGO activists lead the company to go from resistance and mere compliance to strategic actions" (Perez-Alemen & Sandilands, 2008: 30). However, as Van Marrewijk and Werre (2003: 97) wisely observe, the partnership types toward the upper right of the Figure 8.4 generally appear later in a firm's development "because they have to wait for the emergence of the parts that they will then integrate." In other words, considerable previous learning and investment is necessary to reach the final stage of the continuum.

Partner Selection

As we discussed in Chapter 2 on motivations for partnering, each partner evaluates the utility of partnering on the basis of the outcomes they expect to achieve from the partnership. Their motivations may stem from the desire for greater legitimacy or to acquire new competencies, to gain access to resources or to transform society in some way. Matching these motivations with key partner and partnership characteristics enables each partner to make a business case for partnering.

Once the decision about whether to partner is made, an equally important question is "with whom" to partner. Selecting an appropriate partner, however, is not necessarily an easy task. Eight key partner or partnership characteristics should be weighed in making such a selection decision including:

(1) the potential partner's resource profile,
(2) their previous partnership experience,
(3) their reputation,
(4) the type of NGO (relational or confrontational),
(5) the representational status of participating stakeholders,
(6) power dynamics among the partners,
(7) cultural fit, and
(8) the time horizons for the desired activities.

These decisions should not be made lightly, because, as we explained in Chapters 6 and 7, partner selection can impact how the partnership process unfolds and can have a direct impact on partnership outcomes.

Resource Profile

Perhaps one of the most important bases for partner selection is each partner's resource profile. Typically, for-profit organizations have deep financial pockets and business-oriented expertise. Non-profit organizations often lack financial means, but do have other important assets, such as expertise regarding the generation and distribution of public goods, negotiation and facilitation skills and are not compelled by stockholder demands for short-term results. Partners in any collaborative relationship should know how each partner's capabilities complement others' and select partners with the resource profile necessary to meet the objective (Dahan et al., 2010). Thus, the current financial standing of each partner is another important characteristic, as the presence or lack of funds are likely to influence the process and outcomes of the collaboration. In particular, "if corporate finances take a nosedive, compassion is likely to be jettisoned in favor of survival" (Van Sandt & Sud, 2012: 323).

Previous Partnership Experience

Each partner has its own experiences of partnering (or not partnering) with other organizations, or perhaps with the same organization but in a different context. Such experience, positive or negative, will likely have a significant impact on collaborative processes and outcomes. Positive experiences will likely pave the way for trust, which is another important partner characteristic. Although trust is often developed in the process of collaborating, it is also inherent in relationships that have continued over time, as trust begets trust (Gulati & Nickerson, 2008). Similarly, previous grievances are likely to have detrimental effects on subsequent partnerships. Hence, partner experiences are an important component to consider during partner selection.

Partner's Reputation

Whether corporate, nonprofit, community, or government, a potential partner's reputation and therefore legitimacy is important to the subsequent processes and outcomes of the partnership. Partners that have positive reputations are likely to complement one another, whereas partners that team up with others that have a poor reputation run the risk of delegitimation. This effect is particularly true for NGOs that are perceived as having been co-opted, or "in bed with the enemy," when they join forces with stigmatized firms (Baur & Schmitz, 2012). On the flip side, firms looking to improve their image via partnerships should investigate their partner's ability to draw positive attention. Additionally, a partner's degree of network centrality, or influence in the community, is an important characteristic to consider in advance (Rowley, 1997). "As high centrality combines with increasing inter-connectedness of the actors within a supply chain network, instrumental approaches are progressively replaced by more relational attitudes aimed at joint value creation among partners" (Vurro et al., 2009: 607). The level of support and energy for sustainability within one's potential partner is another important consideration. One way to assess this is to ask about the level of commitment to sustainability by a potential partner's top leaders.

NGO Type

For businesses working with NGOs, it is crucial to understand the implications that NGO type may have for partnership processes and outcomes. Whereas some NGOs follow a partnership strategy to achieve their goals, others prefer to act independently (Ählström & Sjöström, 2005). Although an independent NGO may engage in dialogue with other organizations, it is much less likely to want to engage in an ongoing collaborative relationship. A common distinction between NGOs that do engage with business labels the first as reformative and the second as radical. While "reformative NGOs prefer using symbolic gain strategies (e.g. positive publicity) and material gain strategies (e.g. 'boycott' — mobilizing consumers to buy a certain product) to induce reinstitutionaliza-tion, radical NGOs will use symbolic damage strategies (e.g. negative publicity) and material damage strategies (e.g. boycott) to effect deinstitutionalization" (Van Huijstee & Glasbergen, 2010a: 595). In addition, NGOs too have different competencies. Operational NGOs are likely to have expertise with regard to providing social services, whereas advocacy NGOs are likely to have greater expertise in lobbying governments but are unlikely to be able to provide the same support processes for sustainable development as operational NGOs.

Representational Status

For a collaborative partnership to have the best results, partners should know the representational status of all stakeholders implicated in the partnership. That is, to what extent are various players included in partnership decisions. Particularly when the issues impact many different stakeholders, partners should "consider carefully their entire stakeholder network, not only who directly affects, or is affected by, organizational outcomes but those who are directly or indirectly affected by these outcomes" (Gray, 1989; Polonsky, 2001: 44) and whether they have a voice in the proceedings. In particular,

> the broad participation of multistakeholder partnerships across sectors forms the basis of inclusiveness and thus the possibility of overcoming a participation gap, meaning that all parties relevant to a specific issue have a say in matters and also

> ensures that "dissident," more critical voices about different approaches, are being heard and can be taken into account, which increases credibility and quality
>
> (Pinkse & Kolk, 2012: 184).

This approach often results in a situation where affected stakeholders are represented by another party. However, when stakeholder groups are represented by only one or a few participants, the "two-table problem" may emerge in which "these stakeholders must seek consensus within their organization as well as at the stakeholder table" (Margerum, 2007; Putnam, 1988). It is thus important that the stakeholder representatives have the authority to make decisions on behalf of the group they represent (Cheng & Sturtevant, 2012; Gray, 1989).

Cultural Fit

Organizational, national, and ethnic cultural considerations are important characteristics of partners that almost inevitably affect partnership dynamics. Differences in organizational cultures between business and NGOs stem largely from their differing missions and accountability systems. Each organization has its own culture and goals, and the degree of fit or alignment between partners' cultures and goals may influence processes and outcomes. Differences between business and governmental cultures also stem from the stakeholders to whom they are accountable, with businesses often being quicker to make decisions than the more stodgy decision making processes of bureaucracies (Gray, 1995). For example, one case recounted a practitioner saying "I don't know if you've heard this about collaborating, but everyone thinks it's a wonderful idea. They don't account for how much time it takes to have organizations trying to do projects together, and when two organizational cultures deal with turf issues, all that takes a lot of time" (Suarez, 2011: 320). Cultures don't have to be similar for partnerships to work; however, partners need to be aware of cultural issues and their possible impacts. Partners also need to have similar or at least complementary goals. For example, the CEO of Timberland claims "if you can find at least one common goal ... you've also found at least one reason for working with each other, not against" (Austin & Seitanidi, 2012: 734).

Partnership success may also be influenced by differences in national and ethnic cultures. Generally, national culture has a greater impact than organizational cultures on views regarding sustainability and cooperation. For example, a study on the differences between France and Brazil showed that the weak monitoring processes in Brazil and strong government intervention in France pose differing constraints for organizations (Sobczak & Martins, 2010). Further, "the successful implementation of ... partnerships, is based on the assumption of a strong state that is capable of providing an enabling institutional environment for partnerships to evolve in; yet, these conditions are largely absent in most developing countries" (Bitzer & Glasbergen, 2010: 223). As a result, less-developed countries, where many social partnerships occur, may pose additional complications for partnership organizations. Finally, in some settings, the context is rife with conflict: for example, in the Democratic Republic of Congo. In such conflict-ridden areas, partnerships must put extra effort into trust and capacity building and explicitly consider the local cultural context (Kolk & Lenfant, 2012).

The role of indigenous peoples in partnerships deserves special mention because of the "'distinctiveness' of their culture and economy and their special attachment to and historical continuity with the lands they have traditionally used or occupied" (Sawyer & Gomez, 2008:12). Although they have often been marginalized in the past, indigenous people's involvement as equals in partnerships is not only necessary but also offers the potential for shared benefits, including new business ideas, improvements in handling disruptive change and techniques for sustainable ecosystem management (Murphy & Arenas, 2010). Because of the scars left by past colonial relationships, designing partnerships to ensure voice for indigenous peoples is especially critical and is consistent with the broad definition of sustainability as ensuring the well-being of all people. An example from Canada illustrates how a partnership between a government and a First Nation evolved. In 2011, the Government of Canada and the Assembly of First Nations began a partnership, acknowledging the importance of communication and coordination to achieve positive change in their relationship. The agreement is governed by several guiding principles that include:

1. improving relationships and strong partnerships between Canada and First Nations respectful of Aboriginal and Treaty rights as recognized and affirmed in the *Constitution Act, 1982*;
2. building effective, appropriate, transparent and fully accountable governance structures;
3. empowering success of individuals through access to education and opportunity;
4. enabling strong, sustainable, and self-sufficient communities;
5. creating conditions to accelerate economic development opportunities and maximize benefits for all Canadians; and
6. respecting the role of First Nations' culture and language in our history and culture.

The challenges inherent in implementing the agreement are apparent from a recent example in which a memorandum of understanding (MOU) was

143

signed by Canada's Minister of Fisheries and Oceans and the First Nations in British Columbia (BC) to create a joint dialogue process regarding issues related to fisheries and aquatic resources in BC (UNFAO, http://www.fao.org/fishery/legalframework/nalo_canada/en. Accessed March 8, 2017). However, only a few weeks later, concerns surfaced over the degree of voice that First Nations have in drafting education legislation. These events point to the difficulties inherent in trying to design partnerships across these historically problematic boundaries (Globe & Mail, 2013).

Power Dynamics

Similar to issues regarding representation, power dynamics and imbalances or dependencies are also very important to partnerships and collaborative processes and outcomes, as we discussed extensively in Chapter 7. Asymmetric dependence occurs when there is an imbalance of power in a partnership. In these cases, "a stronger partner will tend to influence or manipulate a weaker one" and "in response, the weaker partner may pretend to be cooperative while actually trying to avoid its partner's requests so as to protect its own interests" (Liu & Ngo, 2005: 1131). Businesses often have more power because of financial considerations; however, NGOs potentially have a great deal of power as they can mobilize social movements and campaigns against partnering organizations (Reed & Reed, 2009). In general, "large power imbalances are viewed as problematic because they may lead partners into political or opportunistic behavior that can serve one or both partners' interests at the expense of partnership performance" (Selsky & Parker, 2005: 858).

Time Horizons

Another important partner consideration is a potential partner's time horizon for realizing results. One source of difficulty can arise when funders expect a turnaround and impact in a time period that is not realistic (London & Rondinelli, 2003: 34). Sharing time frame expectations should be done during the exploratory phase of a partnership to ensure that partners have compatible expectations. Additionally, as noted above, partners' time horizons may shift because of contextual factors, such as economic downturns or political contingencies, or because of changes within the partnership itself that may require the partners to renegotiate their relationship as the partnership evolves.

Selecting the right partner and partnership design does not, however, guarantee a successful outcome from partnering. As we discussed in the Chapter 5, several process issues are critical to achieving optimal partnership outcomes.

In addition to thoroughly vetting potential partners, how these process issues will be addressed if the partnership goes forward should be an important part of pre-partnership discussions.

Outcomes of Sustainability Partnerships

A key benefit of partnerships is that outcomes occur that the partners could not accomplish on their own. This follows the reasoning that "two heads are better than one," and many are better than two! In many cases, without the knowledge and resources of all relevant stakeholders, problems simply cannot be addressed. Like the motivations described earlier, some outcomes of cross-sector partnerships are sector-specific, while others benefit all partners and even the planet, in terms of improvements in sustainable practices. Clarke and Fuller (2010: 19) refer to these kinds of outcomes as "environmental-centric" which they define as "unexpected outcomes related to the ecological, economic, governmental, legal, political, regulatory, social, and/or technological environments beyond the context of those involving the focal issue(s) of the collaboration." There are also individual outcomes that accrue to those who serve as partnership representatives such as learning, enhanced organizational status, and networking (Harrison & Easton, 2002: Kolk et al., 2010). In addition to the short-term outcomes that specific partners seek (e.g., governance vs. corporate innovation), there may also be longer term results that spill over into other sectors. For example, Loblaw's Sustainable Seafood Initiative with WWF has led the firm to make short-term decisions about which fish to sell in its stores at any given time. Loblaw elected to carry sustainable cod, which has become virtually unavailable. However, this shortage prompted a longer-term partnership between WWF, the Canadian government and representatives from fish processors and fishing unions to participate in fisheries' improvement plans in Eastern Canada—a co-management process that will eventually have payoffs for Loblaw and many other stakeholders. Table 8.1, Partnership Outcomes, summarizes the collective outcomes of partnering and the outcomes that accrue to stakeholders in each sector. We now examine possible outcomes sector by sector.

Outcomes for Business

As we noted in the discussion of motivations to partner in Chapter 2, the early outcomes that many businesses seek from partnering are improvements in their reputations that would assure them a license to operate. Plentiful evidence shows that partnerships have in many cases generated such improvements (Austin & Seitanidi, 2012; Kolk et al., 2010; Yarnold, 2007).

Table 8.1 Positive and negative partnership outcomes by sector

			OUTCOMES		
	Business	NGOs	Government	Community	Environment
POSITIVE	Improve CSR reputation; ensure license to operate Supply chain improvements Innovative products New markets Attractiveness to employees Gain critical competencies Integrate sustainability in core business practices De facto rules for regulating industries	More focus on efficiency and accountability Enhanced reputation Garner needed funding Entice action by business on sustainability projects	Improved project designs Greater transparency and acceptance of plans More efficient resource usage Strengthen data management Meet sustainability targets Garner greater public accountability Insight into economic and demographic trends Improve interagency coordination	Greater voice in policymaking Improved quality of life Models for other projects Integrated service delivery Retain control of lives Gain culturally-suited products and outputs Build networks for self-reliance	Environmental advocacy Deal with complexity Institutionalized attention to problem Environmental conditions improved
NEGATIVE	Perceptions of greenwashing	Suffer tainted reputation Cooptation	Need to deal with conflict Less thorough study of research Funds shrinking	Inequitable outcomes Need to balance subgroup vs. greater public interest	Continued degradation Replacement of nature with human-produced products

The Rabobank case presented in Chapter 4 is a good example. Reputational gains are especially likely when partnership efforts simultaneously produce other outcomes, such as invention of new products or changes in corporate supply chains. Additionally, businesses that pursue partnerships for sustainability can gain critical competencies, gain new knowledge about existing problems, identify new problems and opportunities (e.g. for products or markets), increase networking and social capital, and enhance their attractiveness to existing and potential employees (Austin, 2000; Kolk et al., 2010; Selsky & Parker, 2005). Positive outcomes for businesses increase when the partnership is widely publicized within the firm and both top management and employees are engaged. "Only then will they yield desired company benefits, such as an enhanced corporate image, reputation, higher product sales, and increased attractiveness to (potential) employees, and also be effective in reaching non-profits' and societal goals" (Kolk et al., 2010: 127).

Some scholars writing about evaluating partnerships make an important distinction among outputs, outcomes, and impacts (Brown, 2008; Kolk, 2014). Outputs refer to distribution of goods or services (e.g. repair of roads or distribution of books), whereas outcomes encompass new practices and behaviors (e.g. new procedures for recycling waste). Impacts, which are the most difficult of the three to measure, capture actual improvements in sustainability (e.g. reduced air pollution) or in material well-being (e.g. reduction in infant mortality rates). These longer-term outcomes are also illustrated in voluntary environmental programs (VEPs) that "foster collaborative relationships between government and the regulated community while promoting environmental learning and capacity-building. In the short-term these activities may not lead to pollution reduction, but they may create a foundation for long-term environmental management improvements" (Darnall & Carmin, 2005: 86). For example, in some programs, the "declared intention of the partnership was to create rules for a well-defined domain of activities intended for application to those involved in such activities, whether private commercial actors or public governmental or intergovernmental bodies" (Zadek, 2008: 375). Examples of such partnerships that adopted this approach include the Extractive Industry Transparency Initiative (EITI), the Forest and Marine Stewardship Councils (FSC and MSC), the Equator Principles, the International Council on Mining and Metals (ICMM), the Global Reporting Initiative (GRI), and the World Commission on Dams (WCD). Many VEPs do not set out to establish new forms of governance for a sector. Nonetheless, both the UK-based Ethical Trading Initiative (ETI) and the US-based Fair Labor Association (FLA) have created de facto rules of the game for how many retailers and their suppliers approach labor standards. Both the ETI and FLA have, with other initiatives, created a new governance environment for labor standards linked to, but operating independently from, existing bodies of agreed international labor standards, or indeed national labor law and the statutory means by which these standards are, or should be, enforced. Both have, in practice, mutated into "governance micro-climates" (Zadek, 2008: 375). With respect to legitimacy, these non-statutory collaborative governance approaches have also created some public good because they have "overcome the historically confrontational, inflexible, and self-limiting basis on which the social contract between business and society has been defined and outcomes created" in the past (Zadek, 2008: 378).

Outcomes for NGOs

A key outcome of sustainability partnerships that is of importance to NGOs who partner with business is the acquisition of resources (including investments, goods, services, a greater base of volunteers, and technical and managerial expertise) to ensure their continued operation (Austin, 2000; Kolk et al., 2010). According to Suárez (2011), NGOs have increasingly become focused on greater efficiency and effectiveness, both in their operations and in developing accountability standards to assure their supporters that they are meeting their strategic objectives. Partnerships can provide them with business strategies and models for rationalizing their operations. And, in many developing countries, larger NGOs often provide the glue that holds partners together. "They bridge the skills, knowledge, relationship, and resource gaps between multinational companies and local governments" (Worthington, 2014).

NGOs also stand to improve their reputations through partnerships if they are able to bring additional resources to bear on the causes they champion. Environmental Defense, for example, has seen an exponential growth in its operating funds and reputation as a result of its many partnering efforts. The biggest risk noted for NGOs in partnerships, however, is a tarnished reputation should they align with a corporate partner who fails to deliver the level of commitment needed to effect real change (Argenti, 2004; Millar et al., 2004; Yaziji & Doh, 2009). For example, Friends of the Earth does not partner with business because it is "wary of the risk of 'green wash' that could stem from business collaboration" (Ählström & Sjöström, 2005: 233). In general, research finds the risks of partnering to be higher for NGOs than for businesses (Austin & Seitanidi, 2012). The ultimate risk to NGOs is cooptation: being used by the business for its reputational gain without any realization of the NGOs' goals.

Outcomes for Government

A desirable outcome of partnering for governments is finding ways to ensure that they meet their sustainability targets. This means that various constituents need to agree on action plans for protecting resources in the future. Often this also means finding ways to reconcile various stakeholders' competing interests (Bingham & O'Leary, 2006; Brown, 2008). The good news for governments is that "participatory approaches have demonstrated their value and viability" (Castro & Nielsen, 2001: 231). For example, a report by a World Conservation Union Working Group to the Intergovernmental Panel on Forests observed: "In many countries, community involvement is proving to be a cost-effective, socially just, and environmentally sound approach to stabilizing natural forests" (Poffenberger, 1996: 2). In addition to achieving greater sustainability, governments can benefit from being able to depend on the "certainty of the process, knowing when the review process has ended, improved project design through meaningful public participation in the design stages, and greater project acceptance in affected communities" (Doelle & Sinclair, 2006: 204) will ensue. These outcomes, of course, depend on the use of collaborative governance processes characterized by high levels of participation and constructive resolution of conflicts. Processes that were deemed unsuccessful often could not find common ground among long-standing adversaries or simply engaged in contractual exchanges without real citizen input (Andrews & Entwistle, 2010).

Through partnering, governments can also gain greater insight into economic and demographic trends, improve their public accountability and improve coordination with other agencies (Provan et al., 2009; Smith & Roberts, 2003). On the technical side, they can strengthen their data management processes and information infrastructure (Smith & Roberts, 2003). According to Margerum (2007: 127), "the nested collaboration approach also has the advantage of encouraging innovation and allowing flexibility by providing clearer direction from the policy level." In the face of shrinking budgets and broad trends in governance toward decentralization and economic liberalization (Castro & Nielsen, 2001), collaborative governance approaches seem both necessary and inevitable for government agencies. Such efforts may also be aided by government sponsorship of university research on key issues. The implications of collaborating for governments are discussed in detail in Chapter 9.

Outcomes for Civic Society

Wheeler and colleagues (2005) reported fifty examples of local networks that have been developed to provide increased income to local people in poverty through partnerships with entrepreneurs, NGOs, and governments. While other partners view communities as outlets for products or suppliers for their own economic endeavors, communities view partnerships as avenues to self-reliance for individuals and themselves. Commercial investors, financial institutions, and businesses:

> saw the payoffs of partnerships primarily in terms of profits and returns on investment but often also in terms of fulfilling a social mission or sustainable development mandate. Development agencies and donors saw the potential for enhanced quality of life through human development and ecological enhancement (Wheeler et al., 2005: 37).

Collaborative processes have the potential to give local community members an increased sense of control over their lives, as in the decisions about the

Lockyer catchment area in Queensland, Australia, which met both irrigators' concerns for equity and the government's sustainability commitments. This successful outcome was accomplished by allowing irrigators to participate in detailed negotiations about water allocations that directly affected their livelihoods (Baldwin & Ross, 2012). Ensuring a participatory rather than a service focus is critical if partnerships are to significantly enhance the voice of less powerful communities (Andrews & Entwistle, 2010). The expectations of the poor regarding business were expressed in the World Bank's Voices of the Poor survey. Low-income people were reported to express clear hopes that business enterprises would generate sustainable livelihoods for them and their families (Narayan et al., 2000). However, care must also be taken not to advance the interests of one particular subgroup over another, since such action can conflict with the broader public interest (Brecher & Wise, 2008).

In developing countries accomplishing this kind of power-sharing is more difficult, however. Understanding the local culture and social expectations is critical to success in partnering in poverty-ridden economies. London and Rondinelli (2003) detail a variety of characteristics that distinguish successful from unsuccessful business initiatives in such settings. Ventures fail because they misjudge the market environment and do not consider the interests of local partners. Successful firms, on the other hand, develop pricing structures appropriate for the market (2003) and devise and distribute enabling artifacts, such as solar-powered stoves, and quality-of-life enhancing social structures (e.g. teaching communities how to set up a daycare facility) (Pearce et al., 2012).

Some business-NGO partnerships allow corporations to gain access to new markets while enabling them to try out new models for sustainable business. In one example, Heifer International partnered with the Bill and Melinda Gates Foundation to create the East African Dairy Development (EADD) program; an innovative farm-to-market initiative that boosted milk production and incomes of small-scale farmers. The partnership intends to connect over 200,000 farmers to dairy markets and thereby promote their financial independence and boost social equality in these farming communities (Worthington, 2014). In another example, Plan International USA (a US-based NGO) forged a partnership with Microsoft to extend digital access to classrooms in African countries (Worthington, 2014). When NGOs team up with businesses that "are not solely focused on short-term growth," they can play a vital role in linking "marginalized populations to markets" (Doelle & Sinclair, 2006: 188).

For local communities to benefit from partnership efforts, governments too must play a role. The 2004 report of the UN Commission on the Private Sector and Development argued that "the public sector must foster property rights, simplify regulatory and fiscal systems, apply the rule of law and ensure transparency and good governance in developing countries in order to 'level the playing field' and enable entrepreneurship to flourish" (Wheeler et al., 2005: 38). The report's authors also stressed the necessity for financial services reform to improve access to capital and the need to develop human skills and knowledge in the developing world. The report proved to be "an excellent starting point for more specific recommendations about opportunities for meaningful, high-leverage investments in human, social, financial and ecological capital at both the global and local levels" (Wheeler et al., 2005: 38). In 2012, the World Bank also revised its sustainability criteria for judging its internal investments, noting the enormous investment needed by low-income countries to achieve sustainable growth.

Considering the impacts of partnerships on indigenous communities is also critically important for several reasons. Historically, these communities have borne the brunt of oppression and colonization while clinging unwaveringly to their communal and spiritual traditions, which are rooted in strong attachment to their land and the natural environment (Burton, 2002). As recent economic development has often challenged not only their lifestyle but their well-being (by destroying sacred sights, polluting rivers and streams, and disturbing natural habitat) (Murphy & Arenas, 2010), their voices in these changes and the consequences they produce are often nil or minimal. In the eyes of multinational corporations undertaking development projects, indigenous populations have often been regarded as "fringe" stakeholders because they are "typically disconnected from or invisible to the firm because they are remote, weak, poor, disinterested, isolated, non-legitimate, or non-human" (Hart & Sharma, 2004: 10). While the advent of indigenous people's movements has generated protests to call attention to their plight and has gradually enabled some of these groups to gain seats at collaborative tables, even when they are seated, these groups are often mistrustful of collaborative processes (for good reason) because their voices (and the issues of importance to their communities) have for decades been dismissed or overshadowed by more powerful stakeholders' interests in these settings. They come to the negotiations with the viewpoint that development projects are "fundamentally unjust, despite the proliferation of corporate codes on social responsibility, and detailed programs for stakeholder relations and community consultation" (Whiteman, 2009). Overcoming this fundamental mistrust is often a slow process that may require extraordinary measures to ensure that the table is level and open enough to hear and address their dissident voices, as we have explored in both the Mesá and the hydroelectric relicensing cases (in Chapters 4 and 7). In many cases, indigenous groups who partner with corporations have received investments in infrastructure, social services, and/or employment in exchange for granting a license for firms to operate in their communities, but "rather than providing compelling examples of collaboration, these efforts have often been considered as serving primarily to neutralize and depoliticize indigenous resistance to business activity" (Murphy & Arenas, 2010: 105–6) rather than as serious efforts to hear and incorporate their views into a joint agreement.

When care is taken to respect indigenous people's rights to express their own visions of development (UNDRIP (UN Declaration on the Rights of Indigenous Peoples), 2006; OAS Declaration on the Rights of Indigenous Peoples, 2016), steps are enacted to ensure balance at the negotiating table, and final agreements reflect the concerns and interests of indigenous groups, then such partnerships may represent true-power sharing and reflect procedural and possibly distributive justice for indigenous communities (Whiteman & Mamen, 2002). Using mutual learning approaches is also a valuable method for approaching conflicts between indigenous communities and natural resource extraction firms (Bouwen & Tallieu, 2004; Whiteman & Mamen, 2002). When these factors are utilized in the design and execution of partnerships, some of them have been able to forge fair and just agreements in which indigenous views are well-represented and the outcomes agreed to appear to benefit those partners as well (Andersen, 2000; Gaworecki, 2016; Murphy & Arenas, 2010). Such projects require grappling with how to integrate differences in methods of knowing (DeWulf & Bouwen, 2012) as well as finding solutions for the more potentially distributive issues that can arise in natural resource conflicts.

Outcomes for the Environment

While no final evaluation of the long-term impacts of multisector partnerships on the environment is possible, the resounding conclusion from scholars studying sustainability is that partnerships provide the best chance of bringing the necessary resources, technology, and commitment to ensuring a sustainable future for the planet. Evidence of multisector partnerships' effectiveness, however, is largely anecdotal and prescriptive. In the wide array of sustainability partnerships reviewed by Gray and Stites (2013), at least small environmental improvements have been documented. These included reducing carbon footprints, using less energy, reducing waste, and carefully managing natural resources. As David Yarnold of Environmental Defense concluded: "The environment is not a special interest, it's a public interest" (Yarnold, 2007: 24). Sustainability partnerships are milestones on the road to a new brand of environmental advocacy. Such phrases as "sound outcomes" and "substantial reductions" appear repeatedly, and the fact that these efforts garner widespread, multisectoral commitment from their participants is also a testimony to their success. Doelle and Sinclair (2006: 188) sum up the criteria likely to guarantee success of sustainability partnerships by concluding that if the process considers "all interests affected by it equally and fairly" it "is much more likely to produce a contribution to sustainability." They go on to conclude that "NGO and private sector partnerships are here to stay and are rapidly evolving as both parties find ways to further align their objectives in areas of sustainability, access to markets and job creation" (Doelle & Sinclair, 2006: 188).

Despite this enthusiasm for the partnership model, several critiques of partnerships as a vehicle for achieving sustainability have also been levied. Some critics point out trade-offs inherent in the very definition of sustainability. For example, Page et al. (2016:1) conclude that sustainability partnerships may face inevitable trade-offs between innovation and agreement,

> Because some of the factors that enable innovation and agreement among collaboration partners differ and may undermine one another, producing both innovation and agreement is even more challenging than producing either one in the absence of the other.

Such trade-offs may compromise the degree to which such partnerships can be truly transformative. Similarly, others have pointed to tensions and trade-offs faced by transnational standard-setting partnerships. For example, Riisgaard et al. (2017) point to three fundamental tensions faced by stakeholders in the Better Cotton Initiative (BCI) that may prevent them from achieving their goal of making 30 percent of world cotton production sustainable. As the partnership scaled up, they found it necessary to balance stakeholder inclusion with process control and efficiency. A second trade-off between "upscaling the BCI standard system and the relative stringency of the system in relation to other similar standards systems became an issue" (p. 15). A third tradeoff involved capacity building for local farmers versus monitoring their progress in meeting the standards—a process that was counterproductive.

Others have raised issues of a more critical nature about potential co-optation when powerful MNCs and NGOs launch partnerships. For example, Laasonen et al. (2012: 521) criticize the dialogic processes that most partnerships are reported to adopt, claiming that "they privilege collaborative and deliberative ways of engaging and marginalize more adversarial subject positions." They go on to suggest a potential bias in the business and society literature on partnerships, arguing that "an articulation of adversarial relationships as potentially good for society—and for instance democracy—may be suppressed as a result of the more instrumental nature of most article aims" (p. 528). Finally they suggest the importance of acknowledging "the potentially constructive role that can be played by conflict" (p. 528). Others have raised similar concerns to those we addressed in Chapter 7 about power imbalances within partnerships. "Alliances and cooperation may also imply the 'co-optation' of critics into the decision making of business if stakeholders participate only symbolically in decision making without exerting any actual power" (Holzer, 2008: 50–1). A study of the outcomes of the Forest Steward-ship Council (FTC), for example, found that one unintended consequence of this transnational regime was that the increased costs of the system were borne by the small-scale farming operations at the bottom of the value chain (Bass et al., 2001).

Finally, the importance of the context in which the partnership activities are being conducted is also critical to evaluating their success. Those address-ing problems in the developing world face special challenges (Batliwala & Brown, 2006; Kolk & Lenfant, 2012). A study of 59 NGO-business partnerships in the Democratic Republic of Congo (DRC) found that little data was avail-able for assessing their success except output measures, which did little to indicate whether transformational outcomes were actually achieved by these partnerships (Kolk & Lenfant, 2012). Trying to move beyond output measures, Kolk and Lenfant (2015) focused their assessment in coffee-supply chain partnerships among businesses, NGOs, and cooperatives in the Congo at the organizational and individual levels as well as on the dynamic interactions among partners. The assessment focused primarily on outcome measures such as improved managerial capacities, skill transfer; and improved functioning of cooperatives, economic gains for the farmers, decreased tension in the com-munity, and creation of new governance infrastructures (Kolk & Lenfant, 2015), but the long-term, truly transformative impacts of these partnerships on society and the environment remain unclear. Accordingly, they note that partnerships that are truly transformative in developing contexts need to also play a peacekeeping role.

> In complex settings such as those in the DRC, transformative partnerships are best equipped to tackle root causes of conflict and bring about positive and sustainable change, thus ultimately serving the cause of peace. In the Central African context, collaboration agreements that do not take into account the conflict context or address conflict-related issues such as ethnicity, identity, land, power, and natural resources are less likely to be relevant or sustainable (Kolk & Lenfant, 2012: 506).

Conclusion

To sum up, those partnerships for sustainability that seek to establish broad goals and plans for the future will be easier to enact than those that seek to change the institutional norms of the field and attendant practices within partnering organ-izations (Page, 2003). The more they seek to be transformational, the greater the challenges they will face in the process of working together. Yet, these trans-formational partnerships are likely to accomplish more substantial changes and make greater inroads to improving sustainability on the ground than the former

(Page, 2003). Evaluating the success of partnerships for sustainability (and other collaborative partnerships in general) necessitates taking into account the historical, social, and political dynamics of the context in which they are being conducted and looking beyond the transactional exchange process to assess whether the partnership advances broader development goals such as enhancing the well-being and empowerment and peace of civic society.

In the next chapter we consider the role of government in promoting and convening cross-sector partnerships. We also offer additional information on how collaborative partnerships that adopt a collaborative governance model can be assessed for their effectiveness and transformational capacity.

Acknowledgment

Dr. Jenna Stites contributed substantially to the material in this chapter.

9

Collaborative Governance

In this chapter we consider the role of government and how collaborative partnerships have generated changes in governance processes. Governance involves the processes of managing the delivery of public goods (Gray & Stites, 2013). Historically, approaches to governance have emphasized a command-and-control, regulatory approach; however, as problems increase in complexity, adversarial and managerial modes of policy making and implementation are no longer sufficient for governance (Ansell & Gash, 2008). As we discussed in Chapter 2, in order to implement public policy, governments need capabilities that lie beyond the scope of their agencies. Many problems have become so complex they exceed the level of governmental resources available. Governments need both the expertise and the financial resources of partners from other sectors to address these problems. They are increasingly turning to collaboration with citizens and communities as well as private and non-profit organizations to help them make improvements or solve problems (Sorensen & Torfing, 2011; Walker & Senecah, 2011), placing public managers in roles where they have sustained involvement in facilitating and operating in multi-organizational arrangements (O'Leary et al., 2009). This has transformed the way public business gets done (Emerson & Nabatchi, 2015) and has given rise to a new form of governance which is alternately referred to as participatory management, inter-active policy making, stakeholder governance, co-governance, collaborative management, or our preferred term, collaborative governance (Ansell & Gash, 2008; Bingham et al., 2005).

Several definitions of collaborative governance have been offered in the literature; all emphasize nongovernmental stakeholders participating in the work of government and using deliberative processes designed to strive for consensus. For example, Ansell and Gash (2008: 544) describe collaborative governance as "a governing arrangement where one or more public agencies directly engage non-state stakeholders in a collective decision-making process that is formal, consensus-oriented and deliberative and that aims to make or implement public policy or manage public programs or assets." This definition emphasizes formal partnerships that are initiated by government parties. An alternate definition refers to "joint efforts by public and private actors, each wielding a degree of discretion, to advance a goal that is conventionally considered governmental" (Donahue, 2010: S151). This characterization broadens the scope of what is considered collaborative governance by including informal participatory processes and removing the requirement of government initiation, recognizing that government guidance of collaborative governance processes falls along a continuum. Other definitions include the idea that collaborative governance should "carry out a public purpose that could not otherwise be accomplished" (Emerson et al., 2012: 2), acknowledging that a primary goal of collaborative governance is to develop a more comprehensive approach to planning, policy, and implementation than government could achieve on its own (Gray, 1989; McGuire, 2006; Wondolleck & Yaffee, 2000).

A special case of collaborative governance is the collaborative governance regime (CGR), a term used to describe "a type of public governance system in which cross-boundary collaboration represents the predominant mode for conduct, decision making, and activity between autonomous participants who have come together to achieve some collective purpose defined by one or more target goals" (Emerson & Nabatchi, 2015: 18). Collaborative governance regimes include organizational systems of state and non-state actors with institutionalized norms that persist over a long period; the term "regime" emphasizes the stability of conventions that are in place for a particular issue or a particular group of actors. Examples include the United Nations and the Kyoto Protocol, which are organized at the transnational level and function in place of or as a form of government (Rosenau, 1992) since no single country's government can preside over every other country. For example, ICANN (Internet Corporation for Assigned Names and Numbers) is a public–private partnership with members from around the world that provides governance of the Internet worldwide. ICANN's mission is to keep the Internet secure, stable, and interoperable. It develops policy on the Internet's unique identifiers. Through its coordination role of the Internet's naming system, it promotes competition and has an important impact on the expansion and evolution of the Internet (https://www.icann.org).

Collaborative governance regimes may also be organized at the regional level to manage public issues that span jurisdictions, such as the Everglades Restoration Task Force (Heikkila & Gerlak, 2015) or the Newtok Planning Group, which is working to relocate a native community in Alaska threatened by rising sea levels (Bronen, 2015). Collaborative governance regimes describe those collaborative governance processes that involve state and nonstate actors in sustained engagement around a public policy issue in which procedures and norms of engagement become institutionalized.

Uses of Collaborative Governance

Collaborative governance can be used to address many different substantive aspects of public life, from education to transportation to water management and beyond. Torfing (2016) emphasizes the value of collaborative governance as a source of innovation that has the capacity to address complex problems and challenges. Participants in collaborative governance collectively must develop strategic, governance, operational, and practice capacities among others (Sullivan et al., 2007) that allow them to manage group dynamics and make progress on the issues at hand. Collaborations also "need sufficient capacity to enable them to exercise appropriate control" to prevent domination by powerful actors or pursuit of unproductive activities (Sullivan, et al., 2007: 73).

One area particularly suited to collaborative governance is the management of natural resources. The collaborative management of shared resources has been studied extensively, yielding the institutional analysis and development (IAD) framework developed by Elinor Ostrom (2015). Derived from decades of studying cooperative arrangements for managing shared and limited natural resources, the IAD framework explains co-management by emphasizing the importance of (1) the rules that people use to order their relationships, (2) the attributes of the physical environment, and (3) the structure of the community. A chief benefit of this framework is that it incorporates law, politics, and management (Amsler, 2016) as well as recognizing the immutability of the natural world.

In the context of natural resource management, a term used synonymously with collaborative governance is *co-management*, which refers to "a situation in which two or more social actors negotiate, define, and guarantee amongst themselves a fair sharing of the management functions, entitlements, and responsibilities for a given territory or set of natural resources" (Borrini-Feyerabend et al., 2000: 1). The suitability of collaborative processes for managing this type of public good stems from the highly interconnected relationships among stakeholders concerned about natural resources—from those who live on the land (e.g. indigenous and First Nations' peoples), to those who extract the resources for a livelihood (e.g. loggers, farmers, and irrigators), to those who enjoy natural resources for recreation (e.g. hikers and anglers), to those who advocate for their preservation (e.g. conservation groups). Often, these co-management partners find themselves at odds with one another, so collaborative governance can also serve as a dispute resolution process (Borrini-Feyerabend et al., 2000; Lewicki et al., 2003; Wondolleck & Yaffee, 2000).

Other co-management efforts may be more agency-centered regulatory negotiations such as those at the national level in the United States; notable examples include efforts by the US Environmental Protection Agency, Department of Energy and other US federal agencies to involve stakeholders in rule-making decisions (Fiorino, 1999; Department of Energy, 2015). The hydroelectric relicensing case in Chapter 4 is an example of a regulatory negotiation. At the transnational level, collaborations may address truly global issues such as climate change or plastic pollution of the oceans. At this level, the boundaries between business–NGO partnerships and collaborative governance initiatives may begin to blur, since collaborative forums such as the Soya Roundtable or the Sustainable Forestry Initiative attempt to develop voluntary norms and standards to "govern" the behavior of all businesses, governments, and members of civil society; hence, the norms are global in nature. A key expectation associated with collaborative governance is that compliance with the agreed-upon policies and practices will be substantial, since participants were given a voice in their creation (Van de Kerkhof, 2006). McGuire (2006) reported that considerable new legislation in the United States requires that collaborative processes be used for policy implementation.

One interesting example of a failed attempt at co-management occurred in Australia (Brown, 2002). In an effort to forge regional forest agreements (RFAs), bioregional assessments of the country's forests were conducted between 1995 and 2000. These brought timber companies and environmental NGOs together who typically were at odds on how to make harvesting of timber more sustainable. The NGOs specifically sought to prevent long-term damage to old growth forests, while the logging firms wanted to ensure enough lumber for profitable future harvests. As we explained in Chapter 6, resolution of this presumed impasse was made possible when the stakeholders re-examined the government's starting assumption that a compromise solution was the only one possible. Instead, an integrative agreement emerged because the negotiating group realized that a switch away from old-growth forests was consistent with the industry's projected future needs for the softer wood offered by purpose-planted trees. This realization enabled a collaborative outcome to be achieved and agreed to by the government of South Queensland. Unfortunately, however, the Federal Government was unwilling to accept the agreement because it contravened a principle set forth in the overarching framework established for the regional assessments. In this case, conflicting decisions by different levels of government (provincial vs. federal) derailed a creative agreement among traditional adversarial parties. This foreshadows the potential problems cross-sector governance partnerships may have in moving across jurisdictional levels—a topic we address in detail in Chapter 10.

Forms of Collaborative Governance

Collaborative governance efforts include several different kinds of structures that have been described as integrated cooperation structures (Emerson

& Gerlak, 2014) and complex adaptive networks (Booher & Innes, 2010). The key structural features of collaborative governance can be evaluated on whether they: (1) engage partner organizations, (2) have an oversight entity, (3) enable partners to implement the strategy in their own organizations, (4) have a communication system, and (5) have a monitoring system (Clarke, 2011).

Government Led

The most common form of collaborative governance structure is one that is led predominantly by a government agency. This includes deliberative forums that are designed to increase citizen participation in governing (Newman et al., 2004), rulemaking processes, regulatory negotiations, government advisory committees, and policy dialogues (Amsler, 2016). The US hydroelectric licensing case described in Chapter 4 was a government-led collaboration, dominated by the agency that held the regulatory power to make the rules for how hydroelectric dams received authorization to operate.

One of the key challenges in government-led collaborations is managing the power dynamics among participants. A government agency with authority to act that also leads the collaboration runs the risk of dominating the process. The logic guiding some agencies is an oppositional "promulgate and enforce" approach while others utilize a procedural "consult and coopt" approach. In either case, the agency retains the responsibility for drafting any new plans or regulations. The logic of the process of collaborative governance, on the other hand, is grounded in consensus decision making, which has well-established meanings, norms, and practices: "In consensus decision making, all group members express their opinions, discuss the issue, and then choose an alternative they all can agree to, at least in part" (Tjosvold & Field, 1983: 500–1). Opposing opinions are addressed directly and this open controversy results in a thorough exploration of the problem with greater understanding among group members (Hall, 1971; Cronin et al., 2011).

Careful process design plays a role in mitigating concerns about power imbalances at the table. The hydroelectric relicensing case presented in Chapter 4 in which the Federal Energy Regulatory Commission (FERC) gave equal status to a coalition of participants in presenting their ideas for revising hydroelectric licensing standards illustrates how a balance of power could be designed into the process. FERC also elevated the status of Native American tribes by designating half of its nationwide forums to prioritize tribal input. An additional challenge is that governments may convene partners and frame the collaborative agenda according to their own perspectives and authority. An advantage of government-led collaborations is that they eliminate the need for additional coordination to manage governmental requirements and deadlines and thus are less likely to be considered illegitimate. Further, governments typically have sufficient resources to initiate and manage a collaborative process, and their engagement in a leadership role may help influence the allocation of government resources toward implementing the partnership's work.

Shared Leadership

Rather than government assuming full responsibility for leading a collaborative governance effort, another model is to use a steering committee, usually comprised of a select group of primary stakeholders to an issue. For example, a steering committee of 16 members was created to manage a 130-organization collaborative process to guide the City of Montreal's regional sustainable development strategy (Clarke & Fuller, 2010). Similarly, the Construction Sector Transparency Initiative (CoST) grew from a seven-country pilot project in 2008 into a fifteen-country initiative to increase knowledge and assessment of public infrastructure efforts by 2016. Participants organized a multistakeholder steering committee to oversee production of the group's report and to arrange ongoing review and information assurance in member nations (Brockmyer, 2016). Virtually all global multistakeholder initiatives operate with a steering committee. If designed carefully, steering committees can reinforce the team mentality and ensure that multiple perspectives are represented in agenda-setting and process design. To maintain their influence, the steering committee must be closely associated with the power of government, either through membership or endorsement (Painter, 2001), but this could run the risk of marginalizing lower power stakeholders if they are not adequately organized and represented in this decision-making body.

New Entity

Collaborative governance may also involve organizing an entirely new entity. Because creating a new organization is relatively costly, this approach is most often used to manage a complex situation where ongoing dialogue is needed over a long period of time involving a substantial number of parties. An example of this is the Pacific Forest and Watershed Lands Stewardship Council which was formed in 2004 in California (Middleton, 2013). This group, composed of a private power company, state and federal agencies, tribes, and citizens, is charged with managing complex issues of land ownership, water rights, habitat preservation, recreation, sustainable forestry, historic preservation, and hydroelectric power production (Middleton, 2013). The Council has negotiated settlement agreements for the California Public Utilities Commission and advises various agencies on policy and practice.

Public–Private Partnerships

Public–private partnerships (PPPs) have become popular globally as a means of linking the capital and entrepreneurialism of private sector businesses with the authority and public benefit focus of government. For projects such as building bridges or housing, PPPs are sometimes arranged as purely contractual relationships, which places them outside the scope of this book (Hodge & Greve, 2007). However, PPPs may also be constituted as collaborative partnerships, for example in managing the provision of healthcare or social services over a long period.

Efforts to improve food security and nutrition in Bogotá, Colombia were initiated after the passage of a new law on national health in 1993. A program called The Food and Nutrition Plan of Bogotá was developed in 1999 that brought together participants from a dozen different government agencies as well as hospitals, nutritionists, and educational institutions. By 2003 this had developed into a permanent organization called the Bogotá Nutrition System. Commissions comprised of public officials were created to work across different sectors and institutional boundaries to implement changes through public agencies. Challenges in governing the complex partnership emerged when officers in charge of coordination felt decreasing commitment from agencies at the central and local levels. New stability emerged in 2009 with the introduction of a shared information system. For a PPP to move beyond a program-based network to a true collaboration, high-level government sponsorship is needed as well as clarity of roles, consistency of staff, and incentives to sustain engagement (Montoya et al., 2015).

PPPs can generate significant public benefit and economic impact beyond the immediate focus of their work. Through investments in public–private partnerships for genomics research, among medical, research, pharmaceutical, and other commercial entities as well as NGOs advocating for specific medical conditions, the US has generated an economic output of nearly a trillion dollars (Battelle Technology Partnership Practice, 2013). These partnerships are designed to generate and compile large databases of sequenced genomic data ostensibly for future medical research but also for commercial applications such as targeting electronic advertisements to consumers based on their health and behavior patterns. A 2013 research study concluded "the growth of genetics and genomics science and applications in the U.S. has been a true public-private partnership, with private sector entities supporting and benefiting from federal research and generating significant tax revenues," which included 3.9 billion in federal tax dollars (Battelle Technology Partnership Practice, 2013: 3).

Mandatory Collaboration

In India, collaborative governance was used to monitor and evaluate the implementation of a 2006 government policy related to poverty alleviation, the Mahatma Gandhi National Rural Employment Guarantee Act (MGNREGA) (Vij, 2011). The law guarantees wage employment, providing over 50 million households with income, and provides for social audits of every project at least every six months. Recognizing that discrimination, social exclusion, and structural inequality still exist within communities, beginning in 2011 the federal government required state governments to partner with local civil society organizations to improve the quality of social audits (Vij, 2011). This example is interesting because it includes mandatory collaborative governance, where state government was required to partner with NGOs and community members to conduct audits of the MGNREGA. Mandated collaboration has not received as much research attention as it merits (Gray & Wondolleck, 2013). Some scholars have been skeptical about the level of collaboration that is achievable when partnering is mandated (Rodriguez et al., 2007; Genskow, 2009). When partnerships are generated by a legal mandate or regulatory requirement, at least four possible problems may occur: (1) the parties are collaborating perfunctorily or "in name only" just to appear to meet the regulatory requirement; (2) local relevance/ownership is lacking (Taylor & Schweitzer, 2005); (3) the requirements for how to structure the partners' interactions constrain the flexibility with which they can interact; or (4) one partner is able to exert greater leverage over the others. In the latter situation, Hardy and Phillips (1998) argue that this is no longer collaboration but rather may be compliance, contention, or contestation instead. Another consequence of differential power among potentially collaborative partners is collusion in which some partners conspire to keep secrets in order to keep an upper hand and avoid exposing their weaknesses or vulnerabilities (Gray & Schruijer, 2010).

While mandated collaboration may have the liabilities noted above, in some circumstances it may be necessary and even prove beneficial as it gives regulatory agencies the opportunity to garner input from a wide array of stakeholders as in regulatory negotiations (Gray & Wondolleck, 2013). Mandated collaborations can force potential partners to get on with addressing problems that need attention. Partnerships for managing natural resource issues at the ecosystem level often warrant mandated approaches to ensure that coordination across the ecosystem occurs (Agranoff, 2007; Wondolleck & Yaffee, 2000), but as we saw in the Queensland Forestry Agreement, this requirement led the Australian government to foreclose on a creative agreement negotiated between loggers and environmental NGOs because it fell outside the initial guidelines set out by the government for such agreements.

Recent research suggests the relationship between mandatory participation and partnership effectiveness is not a simple one. A study of mandated collaborations between a wildfire management agency and citizens revealed that the degree of social learning that occurred varied depending on other factors such as number of partners, duration of planning, and quality of the facilitation (Brummel et al., 2010). Often, learning consisted of enhanced coordination, but not innovation. Additionally, the nature of the mandatory requirements (e.g., annual review by an outside party and use of a standard template) produced different degrees of learning. Finally, these authors raised questions about the longevity of the learning and suggested the need for evaluation beyond the end of the mandated relationship.

We will now consider barriers to collaborative governance that stem from the issues, the context, and the likely participants in such processes.

Barriers to Collaborative Governance

While many examples of successful collaborative governance exist globally, significant barriers remain. Decisions made in the earliest stages of partnership formation, often unilaterally by government entities who have the authority to convene partners, determine how issues are framed and who is eligible to participate in the process (see Chapter 5). Such choices about the scale and scope of the issue also play a significant role in determining which barriers to effective partnership may impede a collaborative governance attempt.

Nature of the Issue

Although collaborative governance can be used for issues with many different kinds of content, some substantive issues that are overseen by governments may not be seen as fitting for collaborative partnerships. For example, governments may not elect to use this approach in situations of policy making around highly technical and complex issues such as nuclear energy, in situations involving public security and military operations (Torfing & Ansell, 2017), or in zero-sum situations such as formulating economic development policy (Feiock et al., 2012). Particularly when the stakes are high, governments may be unwilling to share sensitive information or cede decision-making power to non-expert participants.

Competitive or Cooperative Context

The content of substantive issues is not the only potential barrier to collaborative governance; context also influences its availability for use and its feasibility. One influencing factor is partners' perceptions about whether participants are working together for mutual benefit (cooperation) or whether participants are seeking to win (competition). Tjosvold and Fields (1983) found that people making consensus-based decisions were affected by whether the context was initially perceived as cooperative or competitive. In cooperative contexts, people making consensus decisions viewed their group as more effective and desirable, and they were more committed to their team's decisions than when consensus was used in a context initially viewed as competitive. Similarly, actors in contexts with a history of centralized government decision making or winner-take-all political contexts may find collaborative governance more difficult or less desirable than those in contexts where power is more widely distributed or stakeholder consultation is common (Torfing & Ansell, 2017).

The competitive or collaborative dynamic extends to dyadic relationships within a collaborative partnership. Participants may variously have cooperative, competitive, neutral, or no relationships with other participants, and as the number of participants grows, the complexity of managing the number and variety of relationships increases. Some partners may be in competition with each other for resources or legitimacy which incentivizes them to differentiate themselves from other organizations (Brandsen & van Hout, 2006), particularly if they have previously operated successfully in a context governed by noncollaborative arrangements that are hierarchical, contractual, and/or competitive. In contrast, collaborative governance requires organizational participants to integrate with other organizations by sharing their interests as they work together to try to develop shared views/frames of the issue, identify solutions, and determine implementation plans. For example, a regional collaborative partnership to address homelessness would generate different perceptions than partnerships within individual jurisdictions enacting policies that shift the homeless population and their need for services to an adjacent jurisdiction. A context characterized by such competition limits the capacity of local units to solve problems and makes collaboration riskier although perhaps even more important (Feiock et al., 2012).

Identifying Participants

Where issues are broad in geographic scope (e.g. national, transnational, or global), one key barrier to collaborative governance is identifying sufficiently representative nongovernmental actors who have the time and resources to fully engage in the work (Torfing & Ansell, 2017). Such contexts require careful attention to how participants, process design, and content framing interact with collaborative partners' authority, resources, and legitimacy (Purdy, 2012). As Torfing (2016: 131) notes, mobilizing relevant and affected actors helps "enhance the collective capacity to design innovative responses to the problems, challenge and opportunities at hand. The ultimate goal is to include all affected actors in order to provide a pluralistic and comprehensive understanding of the problem at hand and to fully grasp the stakes involved in constructing an innovative solution. However...involving all the affected actors might prove impossible." Identifying relevant actors who have the appropriate knowledge, competencies, and capacity to engage in collaboration is especially challenging in addressing transnational challenges such as climate change. For example, the Asia-Pacific Partnership on Clean Development and Climate includes numerous governments of industrialized and developing countries with some private sector involvement and limited participation by NGOS and intergovernmental organizations (Bäckstrand, 2008). However, restricting size for efficiency of operation can leave key stakeholders' without a voice in decisions that may impact them directly.

Jurisdictional Authority

Another potential barrier to collaborative governance at larger scales is that decisions made at the transnational level or across multiple jurisdictions may lack the force of law or executive authority to back them up. Although most instances of collaborative governance involve governmental authority, our earlier definition of collaborative governance noted that it can describe partnerships that advance goals which are traditionally considered governmental. An example of this is global governance partnerships that address complex challenges with implications for stakeholders worldwide that transcend the jurisdiction of any one government. At least 45 such global partnerships have emerged since 1992 to develop transnational business and human rights standards for industries such as fishing, mining, and technology (MSI Database, 2017). An example is the Extractive Industries Transparency Initiative, which is organized in multistakeholder groups in each participating nation. An assessment of these global governance efforts indicated that participating groups often needed to improve their governance practices; one common concern is that the national secretariats are often not accountable to the multistakeholder groups (MSI Database, 2017). This suggests that global governance efforts must build strong linkages to governments in specific contexts to ensure legitimacy and accountability during local implementations.

Individual Participation

The participation of individual citizens in collaborative governance is often seen as desirable and representative of a modern approach to representative democracy where citizens are engaged and empowered (Newman et al., 2004) rather than "passive individual bearers of legal rights" (Torfing, 2016). Further, individual participants simplify collaboration in that individual actors need not attend to the shadow negotiation that organizational agents must engage with to ensure that the communications, decisions, and actions undertaken in the collaborative partnerships are acceptable to other organizational members back home (see Chapter 5 for more on back-home buy-in). However, the contexts in which collaborative governance occurs can discourage individual participation because government processes may be seen as too "hierarchical, bureaucratic and party bound to be able to deal effectively with questions of identity in a multi-cultural and global/local world" (Newman et al., 2004: 204). Deliberative processes, especially those addressing the local impact of issues, must enable citizens to voice their interests, experiences, and identities, but individual participants are likely to be perceived as naïve and lacking in skills, or to be categorized into either the "general public" or "special groups" based on ethnicity, ability, or socioeconomic status (Newman et al., 2004). Collaborative governance requires real involvement in decision making, and this may be hard to achieve without intermediary structures such as organizations representing key stakeholder groups' interests (Pestoff, 2006). Often these need to be organized first before effective representation of these voices can occur.

Tensions of Collaborative Governance

Provan and Kenis (2008) identify three tensions that exist in collaborative governance processes: efficiency vs. inclusiveness, internal vs. external legitimacy, and flexibility vs. stability. Efficiency versus inclusiveness recognizes that effective collaboration requires time and effort to build trust, share information, and engage in dialogue that yields consensus on problem definitions and appropriate actions. Increasing efficiency (reducing inputs relative to outputs) decreases the inclusiveness of collaborative governance through fewer participants, a narrower scope, or less time to engage, which in turn may yield less information sharing, less engagement with the issues, and lower commitment to proposed actions and policies by non-governmental participants (Provan & Kenis, 2008). Ultimately, this can influence the quality and durability of the decisions taken as well. The tension related to internal versus external legitimacy is linked to societal expectations about who is responsible for managing the public good and how that work should be carried out. Internal legitimacy considers how participants view the process of collaborative governance and whether interactions and efforts within it are seen as credible, while external legitimacy refers to whether nonparticipants see the collaborative governance process as legitimate and sufficiently representative (Human & Provan, 2000). Finally the tension of flexibility versus stability recognizes the dual challenge of creating nimble and adaptable partnerships while ensuring their stability and sustainability (Provan & Kenis, 2008).

Tensions may also emerge within stakeholder organizations as a result of their participation in collaborative governance. Such tensions arise when stakeholders are potentially competitors for customers, donors, employees, contracts, legitimacy, or attention. These partners "find that they must both compete and cooperate, trust and distrust" (Brandsen & van Hout, 2006: 548). For example, the provision of care for elderly citizens in the Netherlands links state agencies with hospitals, nursing homes, insurance companies, housing associations, etc. While elder care is guaranteed and ongoing collaboration is needed to meet this public standard, stakeholders must work with direct competitors, vendors, and suppliers whose individual interests oppose their own interests.

Page et al. (2016) note that "a number of the tactics that help to produce agreement among divided parties run directly counter to the conditions and characteristics of collaboration that favor innovation" (2016: 6). These include reducing diversity by restricting participation to a small, stable group; focusing on shared interests and common ground instead of exploring differences; and structured processes focused on consensus decisions that limit creativity and collective learning. For collaborative governance processes seeking innovative solutions to challenging issues, the tensions among these tactics must be managed to support achieving agreement that does not resort to agreeing on a minimally adequate solution that all parties find acceptable just to get some agreement.

The final tension we'll highlight in this chapter is the tension between traditional and collaborative approaches to governance. Traditional governance involves "a top-down hierarchy under central control, with a closed boundary and a single authority" while collaborative governance "is characterized by interdependent network clusters under distributed control, with an open boundary and shared authority" (Booher & Innes, 2010: 35). The goals, planning, management, and leadership functions for government agencies differ radically between these two approaches, as do the perceptions and activities of stakeholders. Collaborative governance processes unfold in contexts with different shared expectations about whether the traditional collaborative approach should be more dominant. Furthermore, the stance of a single collaborative governance process may shift over time as participants, political dynamics, and external conditions change. Tensions are experienced as the capabilities and responses of participants adapt to the dynamics of governance as it emerges and unfolds over time.

Evaluating Collaborative Governance

Evaluation of collaborative partnerships is important to allow us to understand and assess governance outcomes as well as to improve collaborative process design and implementation. In Chapter 2 we identified some outcomes of partnerships that pertain to specific partners, which could be used to assess the value of the partnership for individual participants. Here we consider evaluation schemes that consider outcomes at the collective level.

Clarke and Fuller (2010) suggest an outcomes-based framework that identifies categories of assessment for collaborative governance of environmental issues:

1. plan-centric outcomes related to the underlying issues;
2. process-centric outcomes related to collaboration;
3. partner-centric outcomes related to learning and changes among partners;
4. outside stakeholder-centric outcomes related to nonparticipating partners;
5. person-centric outcomes related to one or more individuals;
6. environmental-centric outcomes beyond the context of the focal issue.

This scheme emphasizes separating the elements of the partnership into distinct components, and accentuates the importance of interactants in the form of partners, stakeholders, and individuals. Page, Thomas, and Kern suggest two dimensions on which outcomes of collaborative governance can be evaluated (2016): innovation and implementation. Collaborative innovations can be classified as synergistic, independent, or borrowed, while the implementation continuum includes no agreement, agreement in principle, implementation agreement, and implementation fidelity which involves good faith efforts to fulfill the agreement.

A different approach is offered by Gray (2000), who identified five bases on which collaborative partnerships could be assessed using different perspectives. Each perspective suggests a fairly specific mechanism for measuring partnership outcomes. The first perspective focuses on the degree to which the problem for which the partnership was organized has been ameliorated. The second approach is based on social capital formation, specifically, "the aggregate of actual or potential resources" that were mobilized among partnership members (Gray, 2000: 245–6). This could include, for example, the extent of capacity building directed at lower power stakeholders or reduction of mistrust among partners. The third perspective focuses on the level of shared meaning the partners construct about the issue(s). Shared meaning will evolve as partners understand and integrate each other's frames about the issue and can agree on norms for governing the field. These have been referred to variously as shared frames (Lewicki et al., 2003), or joint sensemaking (Maitlis, 2005, Maitlis & Sonenshein, 2010). The fourth perspective is structural and involves whether changes in network relations among stake-holders have occurred such as increased density of connections within the network or restructuring of initial relationships. The fifth perspective concerns distribution of power within the field, specifically whether a more equitable power distribution emerges. This may involve increased voice with regard to the issue for some stakeholders and sharing of governance responsibilities by those who began from a privileged position.

Another approach to considering outcomes focuses on capacity building, specifically the development of five governance capacities that are necessary for coping with wicked problems: reflexivity, resilience, responsiveness, revitalization, and rescaling (Termeer et al., 2015). Rather than focusing on outward impacts, these capacities emphasize the internal capabilities to govern that are required and potentially are enhanced by the process of collaborative governance. A given partnership could be assessed according to these governance capacities over time to evaluate changes in its ability to address challenging problems. Reflexivity refers to cultivating the capacity to sift through the tangle of interwoven factors inherent in a wicked prob-lem. Resilience "ensures that the social-ecological system is able to adapt to unpredictable, changing circumstances without losing identity and reli-ability" (Termeer et al., 2015: 684). A responsive governance system devel-ops the capacity to take wise decisions in the face of continually changing conditions. In governance systems with the capacity to revitalize, actors are able to recognize and side-step counterproductive interactions before they derail progress. Finally, rescaling includes the capacity to understand cross-level dynamics and address them. We discuss cross-level issues in more detail in Chapter 10.

Emerson and Nabatchi (2015) recommend using multiple units of analysis to assess collaborative governance regimes, including the participant organ-ization, the partnership, and the target goals. For each unit of analysis, one can assess levels of performance including actions, outcomes, and adaptation. This results in a three-by-three matrix of assessment in which (for example) the actions of an organization can be assessed in terms of efficiency, the outcomes of a collaborative governance regime as a whole can be assessed in terms of external legitimacy, and the adaptation of target goals can be assessed in terms of sustainability. This complex approach to analysis creates a rich picture of the productivity and effectiveness of collaborative partnerships, while revealing areas of robustness and vulnerability.

Evaluation frameworks should also take the specific objectives of the col-laborative governance partnership into account. If its purpose is largely explorative and informational, then an evaluative focus that stresses partners' learning may be more appropriate than assessing progress on milestone achievements. The approach to evaluation would also differ for governance processes focusing on technical versus adaptive change. For the former, outcome measures would likely be in order whereas, for the latter, the extent of capacity building and learning might be more appropriate measures. For standard-setting governance processes, the tripartite factors of output, outcome, and impact should probably be assessed. We examine these factors and their applicability to all types of partnerships in more depth in Chapter 11.

10

Cross-Level Dynamics

In this chapter we continue our theoretical discussion of partnerships by focusing on how potential partners may frame issues at different levels and the difficulties that can ensue for partnership formation as a result. These differences in interpretations among stakeholders can lead to a clash of frames because partners are viewing the focal problem or issue through different lenses—often originating from two or more different institutional fields. For example, an issue like fishing rights may be framed as jurisdictional by government, economic by business, or ecological by NGOs. To be sustained, multistakeholder partnerships require participants to establish a shared frame that situates the issue within a field or recasts the issue as a newly emerging field. The difficulty of creating shared frames depends not only upon how the issue is bounded and who participates in a given setting, but also on how the issue is unfolding outside the immediate setting of the partnership. "What precedes all the formal steps of decision-making is the generation of narratives in the informal public sphere, narratives about experiences of conflict over collective resources, the impacts of public decision, normative claims about what should be done to whom, and so on" (Parkinson, 2012: 29). The problem is compounded when the partnership is cross-level (i.e., involves partners from different geographical or jurisdictional levels) because agreements that make sense at one level do not necessarily translate to levels above or below the original one. Nonetheless, developing a robust understanding of the problem at the outset and ensuring successful implementation of partnership agreements often requires cross-level analysis and actions. Thus, the level at which partnerships are formed can have implications for other potential and existing partnerships in other locations and at other levels of action. Consequently, to adequately characterize partnerships, we need to view them as cross-level phenomena.

Scale of Organizing

The most important consideration in understanding the cross-level dynamics of multistakeholder partnerships is the scale of organizing. The scale of organizing refers to the space or place in which partnerships are operating. Space in this context refers to the physical setting, while place indicates those setting filled with meaning, symbols, memories, narratives, norms, and power relations (Gieryn, 2000; Parkinson, 2012). The boundaries of space may be seen easily in the substantive focus of multisector sustainability partnerships that consider the future of organisms, resources, and physical features in a particular setting. The scale of physical space may be less easy to define but it plays an equally important role in partnerships that address social issues such as health, human rights, and governance. When we refer to place, we acknowledge the overlay of human agency, conflict, and power onto physical space:

> claims to control not territory for its own sake but the resources that come with a given territory: food, commodities, climate, and even the myths and narratives that are told about those territories, along with the access routes to those things. This means that they can be used to rule out claims to common resources by some disadvantaged people against wealthier others by ruling that the other is not part of "us", and so has no claim on "our" collective resources; or, on the contrary, by swamping and assimilating invaded or colonized groups, to deny public claims on the grounds that the larger "we" does not agree   (Parkinson, 2012: 30).

When we consider how collaborative partnerships are organized around space and place, we may describe them according to community boundaries, market reach, or governmental jurisdictions. All three of these organizing schemes allow for differences in scale. By scale, we mean "the spacial or temporal dimension of an object or process" (Turner et al., 1989: 246). For example, community boundaries could include town, tribe, race, class, or nation state. Government jurisdictions may be organized at the local, tribal, regional, national, or international level. The reach of markets, as arenas of exchange, can vary from local to global. To illustrate different scales of organizing, consider that partnerships to mitigate environmental damage could be organized at the level of a single estuary, a watershed level, or a global level, while partnerships to address refugee migration could be organized within nation-states or regions as well as trans-nationally all at the same time. Scale plays an important role in shaping how issue fields are defined. For example, a healthcare partnership that operates locally to address the needs of a single urban area will differ from one that seeks to address population health issues for a whole continent in terms of issue-framing, participants, resources, legitimacy, authority, process, and implementation, and the efforts of one partnership will likely have implications for others organized at other levels.

To illustrate the importance of scale in cross-level analysis, we share two examples related to ecosystem management. Both examples are set in Canada and involve some of the same partners. First, we consider the Canadian Boreal Forest Agreement (CBFA) partnership, which created the world's largest conservation initiative, covering 76 million hectares, with its May 2010 agreement (http://cbfa-efbc.ca/agreement). This partnership, initially between the forestry industry and environmental NGOs (ENGOs), was spurred by aggressive "do not buy" campaigns by Greenpeace and ForestEthics against Kimberly Clark Company and Victoria's Secret because of their use of Canadian Boreal old growth pulp in their products and advertising respectively (Riddell, 2014). Another impetus for the agreement was a Canadian federal law that took effect in 2005 requiring creation of caribou recovery plans in each Canadian province. Because the Boreal Forest spreads across all of Northern Canada spanning seven provinces, the logging industry faced a potential patchwork of different regulations. Facing pressure from ENGOs, the Forest Products Association of Canada (FPAC) saw an opportunity to "gain competitive advantage by branding Canadian wood as ecologically sound" by partnering with the ENGOs (Riddell, 2014: 145). According to the agreement (http://cbfa-efbc.ca/agreement), the key goals of the partnership were to:

1. implement world-leading sustainable forest management practices;
2. accelerate the completion of the protected spaces network for the boreal forest;
3. fast-track plans to protect boreal forest species at risk, particularly woodland caribou;
4. take action on climate change as it relates to forest conservation;
5. improve the prosperity of the Canadian forest sector and communities that rely on it;
6. promote and publicize the environmental performance of the participating companies.

Signatories to the agreement included the FPAC, 21 forest products companies, 7 ENGOs and 2 funders (Riddell, 2014). Given these broad goals, the huge geographic scale, and the dozens of forestry companies and ENGO organizations involved, the partners planned "to forge the CBFA first bilaterally, and then based on this common agenda to seek collaboration and new legislation with both provincial and First Nations governments across Canada" (Riddell, 2014: 147). Another outcome of the agreement was that the ENGOs involved agreed to stop boycotting the forest products companies that are signatories to the agreement in exchange for a suspension of logging operations on almost 29 million hectares of the forest—the area inhabited by boreal caribou. During the suspension, the signatories agreed to develop action plans for caribou recovery in certain places and to generate guidelines for improving ecosystem management and forestry practices. Such action would require the involvement of communities, provincial and local governments, local civic organizations, and tribes across multiple forest ecosystems. However, moving from broad national principles to formal local agreements proved challenging. For example, over 100 First Nations indigenous tribes with distinct legal jurisdictions had been left out of the initial overarching agreement in spite of their requests to participate, generating mistrust and reluctance to partner on implementation. Furthermore, an independent progress evaluation in May 2012 noted that the CBFA had begun work on five of the six goals it had targeted for its first year, but that progress on completing its milestones was lagging (http://cbfa-efbc.ca/independent-progress-report). In December 2012, two ENGOs withdrew from the agreement, citing lack of sufficient progress toward objectives, failure to legally designate protected areas (Riddell, 2014), and violation of the agreement by one partner (Myles, 2012). By February 2017, the CBFA secretariat had been shut down with no immediate word on the future of the agreement (Foster, 2017).

The CBFA faced significant challenges because of cross-level issues. Not only were multiple committees involved in implementing the agreement, but new partners were being added as CBFA engaged Canadian provincial and First Nations' governments in an effort to influence ongoing planning initiatives—thereby magnifying the potential for additional process conflicts and erosion of trust among participants.

In contrast, an example of a smaller scale forest partnership on Canada's west coast has similar beginnings but a very different outcome. Environmentalists seeking to protect the temperate rain forest bordering the Pacific Ocean created the name "Great Bear Rainforest" in the late 1990s to launch a media campaign against the commercial logging of old-growth trees. After waves of local and international protests, a multistakeholder dialogue was held among representative of the provincial government of British Columbia, indigenous First Nations groups, environmental organizations and the forest industry, leading to conservation agreements in 2006 and 2009 that improved forest protection and recognized the rights of First Nations (Saarikoski et al., 2013). A final agreement was reached in February 2016 between the stakeholders to protect 85 percent of the 6.4 million hectare Great Bear Rainforest from industrial logging, with the remaining 15 percent subject to strict rules for logging (Hunter, 2016). The rights of indigenous people are recognized in the agreement, which includes assurance of shared decision making, a greater share of timber rights and $15 million in funding for 26 First Nations (https://www.for.gov.bc.ca/tasb/slrp/srmp/plan17.html). This partnership agreement has been lauded as an effective model of multistakeholder collaboration that generated not only improved relations among the key stakeholders but sustainable outcomes for forests as well (Riddell, 2014).

The Canadian Boreal Forest Agreement, on the other hand, was perhaps doomed by its complex multilevel dynamics. It was characterized by a broad scope with respect to physical geography, the range of interdependent issues (e.g. trees, caribou, watersheds, etc.) and the number of parties, creating dissatisfaction around who was invited to participate. Significantly, the CBFA could not be implemented without a cascading series of local agreements that would provide management and oversight of a multitude of issues, and these proved to be longer and more difficult to negotiate than anticipated. The Great Bear Rainforest partnerships found success with a more focused geographic domain and early inclusion of a wide range of stakeholders who had direct links to the means of implementation. The differences in scope between the cases signal the importance of considering cross-level issues in addressing process design, conflict, and power in partnerships.

The US hydroelectric licensing case presented in Chapter 4 provides an example of a different approach to cross-level dynamics, where the partnership was designed with cross-level issues in mind. Although hydroelectric licensing conditions are primarily determined by national laws and overseen by the Federal Energy Regulatory Commission (FERC), the consultation process designed by FERC explicitly included regional actors and authorities who would have a stake in hydroelectric licensing agreements. While the physical geography associated with hydroelectric projects is varied and dispersed, the narrow focus on the issue of licensing within a unified national legal framework made cross-level inclusion easier, especially when coupled with FERC's "roadshow" approach where partnership meetings were repeated in multiple locations to support the participation of many stakeholders. Such cross-level inclusion would be notably more difficult for an issue of transnational scope where the level of implementation involves different political-legal jurisdictions.

As we suggested in Chapters 6 and 8, scale differences can arise in evaluating partnerships' outcomes and impacts as well, just as they can when considering the impacts of social movements on their targets (King, 2008a; De Bakker et al., 2013; Kolk, 2014). Partnerships can be assessed in terms of whether they succeed in getting issues onto the agenda for public deliberation (Schumaker, 1975) and whether they gain compliance from those for whom standards are set (Bartley & Child, 2011). They may also be evaluated as to whether conditions on the ground—such as improvement of working conditions in sweatshops, health protocols followed in local villages, or the adoption of more sustainable farming methods by smallholders—are achieved (Arbruster-Sandoval, 2004; Riisgaard et al., 2017), and whether partners' reputations are enhanced by partnering. Partnerships may succeed at one level (such as crafting an overarching agreement in principle or fostering good public relations) but fail miserably in delivering on real change where it counts the most, for example, among those who have the least capacity to effect it by themselves.

Levels of Analysis

In addition to scale, we consider a second dimension that is important to cross-level understanding of partnerships: level of analysis. Levels of analysis can be viewed as lenses that are used to analyze problems rather than to describe locations where a specific nexus of activity is occurring. They are artificially imposed perspectives that are used by researchers to focus attention on specific interactions or phenomena. The labels micro, meso, and macro are used by social scientists to distinguish small-, medium-, and large-sized social phenomenon (Gibson et al., 2000). For example, one way to understand a partnership is to focus at a micro level on the language used by partners as they negotiate, whereas another understanding would be gained by considering the political dynamics among nation states at the macro level.

Considering a partnership through different levels of analysis can reveal hidden conflicts, underlying commonalities, or aspects outside the partnership's focal field that influence its substance and/or process (Pattberg, 2007) or reveal differential impacts on different stakeholders (Bass et al., 2001). This is illustrated by the Great Bear rainforest example, where at the macro level, the partnership is considered to be highly effective (Riddell, 2014), but a micro level analysis of the language used in the partnership reveals some unresolved conflicts. The name "Great Bear Rainforest" was originated by environmentalist Ian McAllister of Pacific Wild in 1997 (Hopper, 2016), for the purpose of galvanizing an international campaign for its protection. This name was chosen without consulting First Nations, who have various traditional names for the areas including Txalgiu, Tsee-Motsa, Waglisla, Klemdulxk, and Aweenak'ola (McSheffrey, 2016). When the "Great Bear Rainforest" name became widely used in the early 2000s, First Nations accepted it as a means of protecting the land, but "the emotive significance of such a name cannot be underestimated" (Reed, 2004: 33). The language suppresses the fact that indigenous peoples had stewarded the land "for thousands of years before environmentalists ever painted 'Great Bear Rainforest' on a banner" (McSheffrey, 2016). Further, some ENGOs involved in the partnership take issue with statements that the agreement creates "protection" when some aspects are not formalized in legislation, for example with respect to the availability of commercial licenses for trophy bear hunting (McAllister, 2016). This micro level of analysis calls our attention to the back home negotiations that occur among coalitions and within organizations who participate in partnerships and reveals new insights about a partnership that is seemingly very successful when viewed at the macro level.

Cross-Level Analysis and Fields

Scott (1995: 56) defines a field as "a community of organizations that partake of a common meaning system and whose participants interact more frequently and fatefully with one another than with actors outside the field." The concept of a field is particularly useful in studying multistakeholder partnerships because it is not limited to a single level of analysis. Individual organizations are clearly evident in fields, as are collections of organizations, and the behavior of field members is "guided by institutions ... that provide stability and collective meaning to social interactions" (Wooten & Hoffman, 2008: 131). However, the degree of institutionalization within a field can vary over time depending on the degree of shared interpretations and routinized behavior that evolve, and the extent to which these become taken-for-granted among the field's members. We develop these ideas further in Chapter 11.

We assert that the relationship between field dynamics and multistakeholder partnerships is multifaceted and reciprocal; that is, partnerships can emerge from field dynamics, field dynamics can influence partnerships, and fields can change as a result of partnerships. Fields may be contested spaces in which actors compete for legitimacy and power to shape the field's norms (Bartley, 2007; Wooten & Hoffman, 2008; Purdy & Gray, 2009). An example of this occurred when US states created offices to support dispute resolution both within and outside the boundaries of the legal system. These offices worked on a variety of complex problems in partnership with public agencies, civic organizations, businesses, and the courts depending on local needs, and sought to influence each other about which goals and model should become the "ideal." The contest over norms persisted for nearly two decades, shaping the activities of the offices and the partnership opportunities they pursued (Purdy & Gray, 2009). This case illustrates the potential for fields to remain in conflict about norms and practices for extended periods of time (Gray, 2004; Levy & Scully, 2007; Van Gestel & Hillebrand, 2011) while others forge agreements and move toward settlement (Fligstein & McAdam, 2012).

New fields may also be created when engagement around an issue becomes energized. Fields come into being as relational spaces when partners "begin to take note of one another ... through this process of referencing one another, actors bring a field into existence" (Wooten & Hoffman, 2008: 138). For example, Barley (2010) describes a partnership of large corporations, law firms, foundations, and trade associations that was expressly created to help corporations shape US government policy. In the Rabobank case introduced in Chapter 4, the emergent field can be thought of as sustainable banking. When the NGO Friends of the Earth Netherlands challenged Dutch banks whose sustainability portfolios they deemed problematic, they were helping to define this emerging field as were World Wildlife Fund Netherlands and Rabobank when they embarked on creating a green credit card. In Chapter 4's US hydroelectric licensing case, the field was national (US-based) in scale, and new rules for how some decisions within the field would be made were being negotiated among the agency and key stakeholders. Defining the field in the Mesá case is a bit more difficult. The scale of the dialogue was regional although some national level actors, such as the Ministry of Mines, were also implicated as stakeholders. However, the scope of the Mesá's discussions was more problematic to define. Clearly, the dialogue sought to alleviate neighboring communities' concerns about pollution and scarcity of water in the Cajamarcha region. Toward those ends, some concrete actions to evaluate the quality and quantity of drinking water in the communities surrounding the mine were taken, but the dialogue was also circumscribed to avoid discussing at least one key issue, namely Yanococha's culpability for environmental damage to the water. Because the issue was never resolved either within or outside the Mesá's purview, this restricted the Mesá's ability to address the issue and hence to establish new standards for the field that were more responsive to the concerns of the broader community within which the mine operated.

Cross-Level Dynamics

To fully understand how collaboration emerges and changes fields, it is necessary to shift levels of analysis when examining collaborative partnerships. That is, a framing that starts at the organizational level can amplify to higher levels where, through collaborative negotiations, it is revised, merged, or amplified further to become institutionalized among a group of organizations or even adopted more broadly as a norm, law, or practice at the societal or transnational level.

Scale Frames

Another consideration related to scale concerns how stakeholders' framing of the problem may change at different scales. Stakeholders who join a partnership will likely bring these differences in scale framing with them into the deliberations (van Lieshout et al., 2011). We illustrate this with data about a conflict over implementation of national law in the Netherlands that requires municipalities to designate new agricultural development areas (ADAs) and to specify the rules with which farms in ADAs have to comply. The designation of an ADA in a municipality led stakeholders to clash over the scale at which the problem should be defined. An alderman in the local community framed the issue in terms of finding a balance between agricultural and other types of activities in the community and used a high-level sustainability frame to argue against the development of a "new mixed company" (NMC) at the local level. In contrast, the founder of a local action group used a local, place-based frame to evaluate the impact of all the multiple developments around one village, claiming that the cumulative impact of these developments would have negative consequences for the village. In contrast to both of these, an entrepreneur interested in building a new NMC framed the problem at the regional level and pushed for the approval of the NMC concept broadly, saying he could locate his company anywhere in the Netherlands, but would move to India if the NMC idea was not adopted (van Lieshout et al., 2011). He was adopting a space-based frame that discounted the local, place-based perspective of the citizen's group. This example reveals differences both in the focal problem (ADA vs. NMC) and in the scale at which each stakeholder is framing their views. This difference in scale framing led the action group to form in the first place because they believed their concerns were not being addressed in the public deliberations resulting in gridlock in the municipal deliberations. Each actor's scale frames were based on different scale dimensions (e.g., spatial, agricultural, administrative, and time scales) that highlighted different aspects of the issue (van Lieshout et al., 2011) and were positioned on different levels of analysis of the problem. Failure to recognize these differences in scale framing made it impossible to craft a common definition of the problem.

Representation and Scale

One clear implication of addressing problems that cut across multiple scale levels is that partners from different levels of scale will need to be included even though their framing of the issues may complicate deliberations. In the case above, for example, some stakeholders represented the local level (alderman and citizen's group), while the entrepreneur was a national (or even global level) player. When partnerships bridge levels, determining how to represent stakeholders from different levels in the deliberations poses a design challenge and possibly a logistical nightmare. For global agricultural partnerships (like the one in Chapter 2 to which Oxfam raised considerable objection), major partners were multinational corporations and global level NGOs and governments of African countries, but the decisions by these parties would have major implications for local farmers. How to integrate them into the global discussions raises interesting challenges for partnership design,

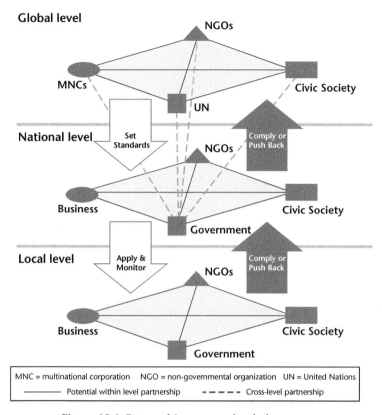

Figure 10.1 Partnerships as cross-level phenomena

including the need to work across many legal jurisdictions and cultures. Figure 10.1 depicts partnerships as cross-level phenomena to convey the complexities that are introduced when partners from different jurisdictional levels are included. This is particularly true in standard-setting partnerships such as the Better Cotton Initiative (BCI) because decisions are made by global level partners that impact the practices of stakeholders at lower levels.

Spanning Levels of Scale

As partnerships span levels of scale, tensions can emerge that would not be present at a single scale level. This problem is well illustrated by deliberations to establish the BCI between 2003 and 2009 (Riisgaard et al., 2017). This initiative grew out of efforts by the WWF (an NGO) and the International Finance Corporation (IFC) to identify commodities that generated substantial negative impacts on sustainability. The WWF and IFC believed that by developing sector-wide multistakeholder initiatives, improvements in the sustainability performance of these commodities could be realized (Riisgaard et al., 2017). Cotton was one of these commodities, along with soy, sugar cane, and palm oil. With respect to cotton, the WWF and IFM thought that a multistakeholder partnership could identify and develop a performance-based approach to reduce up to ten of the "most significant environmental impacts of cotton production" including reductions in the use of water, pesticides, fungicides, (and) fertilizers while also increasing agricultural productivity and producers' incomes (Riisgaard et al., 2017: 5).

However, the BCI faced three major trade-offs in meeting its intended outcomes. First, it found it was necessary to balance stakeholder inclusion with process control and efficiency. Second, as the scale of production on farms increased, the stringency with which standards could be applied decreased. Third, although capacity building was an intended outcome for farmers, the need for auditing of farm practices discouraged learning on the part of farmers, causing them to push back against these higher level imperatives (see Figure 10.1). Additionally, the trade-offs among these imperatives were exacerbated as the project tried to scale up its efforts (Riisgaard et al., 2017). Consequently, although donors and end-users may exert pressure for increased production, it may not be logistically feasible for MSIs to maintain sufficient quality, ensure capacity building among smallholders, and satisfy donors' needs for auditing of on-farm activities. "In short, the more MSIs attempt to ensure the quality of standard implementation, the more difficult it becomes to rapidly scale-up the implementation of a given MSI" (Riisgaard et al., 2017: 10). Thus, ensuring governance that is both flexible and can manage complex interactions across different levels (Termeer et al., 2010) poses a hurdle that many multistakeholder partnerships have yet to clear.

Shared Ownership/Splitting

As we have stated, enduring multistakeholder partnerships require participants to establish a shared frame that situates the issue within a field or recasts the issue as a newly emerging field. Shared ownership of problems is an important pre-condition for creating shared frames. In environmental problems, shared ownership is "the collective recognition that this natural heritage contains value, that a larger problem or crisis exists, and the acceptance of at least part of the responsibility not only for creating the problem but also for correcting it" (Bryan, 2004: 882). For example, achieving the requisite level of shared responsibility has been one of the major stumbling blocks to reaching a robust global climate change agreement (Ansari et al., 2013).

Collaborative partnerships are more likely to create shared ownership than traditional approaches to governance that emphasize compliance and enforcement (Bryan, 2004). The presence of shared ownership in collaboration helps motivate information sharing, the expression of interests, and the search for solutions that are widely acceptable, and a commitment to enacting solutions. Further, collaboration allows the paradoxes that are inherent in conflicts to be addressed (Bryan, 2004). We have shown how paradoxes are inherent in public problems because of different frames and different levels of analysis from which stakeholders approach them. For example, local conventions may be in conflict with national laws or global principles such as human rights. Typically such paradoxes provoke "splitting" (Smith & Berg, 1997) in which part of a paradox is compartmentalized and becomes a stakeholder's sole focus. Within a field, for example, stakeholder groups organize around split-off elements of a paradox and assume roles that position them against each other. For example, "when a timber industry executive... remarks that he is responsible only to the company's shareholders, he is arguably severing the paradox—the contradiction—of balancing economic gain with social and environmental responsibility" (Bryan, 2004: 888). As we observed just above in the BCI case, splitting generates problems with scale and jurisdiction because it implies that responsibility for the paradox resides elsewhere. When NGOs focus exclusively on capacity building and end-users insist on rigorous auditing at the expense of the former, partnerships can encounter splitting. Parties are unable to focus on the larger problem because they wish to avoid the paradoxical tension:

> Because of our tendency to own parts of the paradox, while disowning other parts, it makes sense to bring people together who individually carry the various parts. Only then, it appears, do we stand a chance of making paradoxes salient to participants and working through the arduous process of addressing the contradictions... Collaboration enables the inherent paradox to be restored and managed (Smith & Berg, 1997: 889).

However, if relevant stakeholders do not have the opportunity to participate in deciding the standards that will ultimately prevail in the field or to push back when they are counterproductive, collaborative outcomes can be skewed to satisfy the interests of some groups over others thereby shifting power, or perhaps maintaining an already unequal distribution of power among field level actors. In drafting guidelines for preventing human rights violations by contractors in the private security industry, for example, corporations were permitted to meet recommended standards (ANSI/ASIS PSC.1 and ISO 18788) by considering human rights risks as part of their normal risk assessment processes (DeWinter-Schmitt, 2017). This reduces transparency and makes certification more difficult as it obscures the actual practices of the companies with respect to specific human rights "as a normative good codified in international law and essential to the realization of human dignity" (DeWinter-Schmitt, 2017: 13).

11

How Partnerships Can Transform Institutional Fields

In this chapter we return to our premise that multistakeholder partnerships have the potential to transform institutional fields. Investigating this possibility requires broadening one's view of partnerships to a higher order level that aligns with evaluating the *impact* of partnerships rather than measuring their immediate *outputs* or general *outcomes*. As we presented in Chapter 8, outputs refer to the immediate result of partnership activities; outcomes capture changes in behavior of partners and others targeted by partnership decisions or in the application and implementation of services, knowledge, or standards; and impacts, "the most far-reaching of the three," refer to reductions or improvements in the problem the partnership set out to address as well as any negative side effects that were generated (Kolk, 2014: 27–8). Because of the difficulties of measuring the impact of multistakeholder partnerships, many studies only measure output by assessing the match between programs, reports, activities, and the functions originally planned (Kolk, 2014: 28). For example, these kinds of measures were utilized for evaluating partnerships spawned by the UN's millennium development goals, revealing that only partnerships focusing on energy, water and health satisfied functional output measures (Pattberg et al., 2012; Schäferhoff, et al., 2009; Szulecki, et al., 2011). Output assessment was also described in Chapter 4 in the US hydroelectric case, where a collaborative governance process yielded new licensing rules that decreased the time and cost of licensing. Subsequent assessments of outcomes associated with this multistakeholder partnership indicate that the revised licensing rules support better mitigation of environmental impacts (McCann, 2006) and favor the development of smaller, more sustainable hydroelectric projects over big dams (Tarlock, 2012), but that the government agency FERC still wields significant regulatory authority on an ad hoc basis when licensing particular projects (Viers, 2011).

To build toward assessing the broad and far-reaching impact of multistakeholder partnerships, so far we have offered several ways to understand the results of multistakeholder partnerships. Chapter 8 describes a range of possible outcomes for the sectors of business, NGOs, governments, and civic society with a lens that is focused both on results for individual stakeholders and for the environment writ large. In Chapter 9 we reviewed a variety of evaluation frameworks that widen the lens and consider partnerships more holistically by considering whether a partnership has built the necessary capacity for managing a particular issue. Chapter 10 considers how the scale of a partnership influences effectiveness at implementation. In this chapter, we expand the lens even further to consider how partnerships impact the institutional fields in which they are constructed. We build on the institutional theory framing we offered in Chapter 3, which provides a useful lens for evaluating this wider impact of multistakeholder partnerships.

The Reciprocal Influence of Fields and Partnerships

Institutional fields have been defined as "relational spaces where disparate organizations involve themselves with one another in an effort to develop collective understandings regarding matters that are consequential for organizational and field-level activities" (Wooten & Hoffman, 2008: 138). Fields are "the basic building blocks of political/organization life in the economy, civil society and state" and a fundamental unit of meso-level social order (Fligstein & McAdam, 2012: xiii). The level of institutionalization of a field refers to the extent that there are "rules, norms and beliefs that describe reality … explaining what is and is not, what can be acted upon and what cannot" (Hoffman, 1999: 351). In nascent fields, members have less solidarity of purpose, fewer agreed upon practices and field boundaries are likely to be ambiguous or contested (Brown, 1980; Wooten & Hoffman, 2008; Purdy & Gray, 2009; Zietsma & Lawrence, 2010), and introducing new logics can evoke controversy, debate, and conflict within fields (Schneiberg & Lounsbury, 2008). At the other extreme, when field-level institutionalization is low, shared meanings and agreed upon rules are absent and stakeholders have fewer or more conflicted interactions. In these fields, conformity around rules, norms, or practice is lacking (Vurro & Dacin, 2014). In fields with high degrees of institutionalization, frames are widely shared among the field's participants and norms and rules are well-established, agreed to and adhered to—a condition some refer to as settled fields (Armstrong, 2005; Fligstein & McAdam, 2012: xiii) or "settlements" (Rao & Kenney, 2008: 353). In highly institutionalized fields, members also share a collective identity (Hardy et al., 2005) that yields stability, regularity, and control to field members (e.g. Strang & Soule, 1998).

The Embeddedness of Partnerships within Fields

When multistakeholder partnerships form, they do not do so in a vacuum. Instead, they are embedded within one or more fields, and the contexts in which they are embedded shape how the partnerships unfold (Sharfman et al., 1991; Bartley, 2007; de Bakker et al., 2013; Vurro & Dacin, 2014). For example, Bartley (2007: 299) argues that the host of transnational certification schemes created by multistakeholder partnerships emerged from "political conflicts about the regulation of global capitalism and the embeddedness of these conflicts in neo-liberal rules and scripts." This is consistent with our argument in Chapter 2 that globalization has contributed to the formation of partnerships. However, rather than adopting a strictly political lens (as Bartley does), we take an issue field perspective, arguing that partnerships typically arise in unstable or contested fields where potential partners' actions interfere with each other, creating hyper-turbulent conditions within the field (Emery & Trist, 1965; McCann & Selsky, 2014) from which no stakeholder is exempt. We believe this adaptation allows us to account for a broader range of partnerships than just those at the transnational level. These disparate actions have destabilizing effects on each other creating both conflicts and interdependencies among field members that impede their efforts to diffuse their preferred frames for how the field should be organized.[1] In the face of these destabilizing influences, field members either envision them as opportunities for initiating needed change within the field or as sources of conflict about the fundamental premises on which the field is organized. Either can serve as a launching pad for multistakeholder partnerships which can be seen as attempts to restore informal or even formal field level governance and stability to these turbulent fields. The latter is especially true at the global level where no overarching government exists to legislate rules for the field. Relatively speaking, the impact of a single bilateral partnership, such as that of Rabobank and Friends of the Earth Netherlands, is unlikely to transform the entire field of sustainable banking, but can serve as a proto-institution (Lawrence et al., 2002) that has the potential to be emulated and diffused through the field of banking. When stakeholders elect to jointly tackle the problems created by their interdependent actions through partnering, they increase the possibility that they can directively correlate their actions (Trist, 1983) and establish stable governance arrangements within the field while also meeting their own needs for approval and legitimacy (Dacin, 1997; DiMaggio & Powell, 1983; Suchman, 1995).

Impact as a Change in Structures of Signification,
Legitimation and Domination

One way to assess the impacts of partnerships, then, is to examine the degree to which they have added to or changed the level of institutionalization within the field (Phillips et al., 2000b). When they successfully collaborate, partners build a joint interpretation of the problem and forge agreements about collective steps to remedy it. Evidence of such change would be manifest in the instantiation of new, more widely shared meanings as well as new rules and routines within the field. These respectively correspond to what Giddens (1984) refers to as changes in signification and legitimation within the field—the outcomes of structuration processes within fields in which social actions are tried and eventually become routinely reproduced (Barley & Tolbert, 1997; Giddens, 1984).

Changes in Signification and Legitimation Structures. Signification refers to the development of interpretive frames that guide behavior in a social context, while legitimation describes the construction of norms that guide interactions as well as establish rights, obligations, and sanctions to enforce conformity (Gray et al., 2015: 119). Changes in signification occur when partners construct joint interpretations and align their frames with each other, as eventually occurred among environmentalists and waste handlers when the field of recycling was born (Lounsbury et al., 2003). In the partnership between the Brazilian government, the Nature Conservancy and IBM to prevent further deforestation of the Brazilian Amazon (described in Chapter 1), old frames about the ranchers' role and privileges (e.g., the forests were there for the taking) were gradually replaced with new frames favoring sustainable grazing practices and alternative ways for the ranchers to generate gainful livelihood. At the same time, changes in legitimation structures were underway. New routines and concomitant training to support them were adopted, and new laws were passed that made these changes legitimate and previously unsustainable practices illegitimate.

Similar observations have been offered by Pattberg (2007: 183) about how transnational multistakeholder partnerships such as the Forest Stewardship Council (FSC) influence fields. He identified three types of influences including (1) cognitive and discursive influences that comprise "the framing of issues and key concepts of the decision-making process" and "other forms of social learning"; (2) regulatory influences that pertain to "the establishment of new norms, rules and standards at various levels"; and (3) "more direct material and structural influences 'on the ground'." Negotiations within multistakeholder partnerships designed for standard-setting, such as the FSC or the Soya Roundtable, are cross-level in nature, usually occur in highly uncertain fields and require expertise from many issue areas to craft agreements. "Brokering knowledge and organizing effective learning processes among different stakeholders is therefore key to influencing the behavior of relevant actors" (Pattberg, 2007: 184) including states who decide to adopt the transnational standards. Ultimately, multistakeholder partnerships may shift the discourse about an issue area (Hardy & Maguire, 2010) by successfully defining the content of key normative concepts such as "sustainable forest management" (Pattberg, 2007: 184), establish new norms, practices, and responsibilities for actors within the field, and foster collective learning and action about the issue or problem.

In summary, one way to assess impact of a partnership on the issue field is to compare to what degree and how it is institutionalized before and after the partnership became operational. Table 11.1 maps how the potential impact of partnering on field level institutionalization varies as the scope of the problem and the partners' shared level of responsibility for it increases. In the bottom left corner of Table 11.1, for example, the scope of the problem is limited and partners' shared levels of responsibility are low, thus the potential for field-level change is small. Partners are unlikely to develop a broad and/or deep understanding of the problem and are unlikely to learn much from each other. If the scope of the problem is much larger but the partners' shared level of responsibility remains low, there may be increased potential for learning (because more facets of the problem will be explored), but conflict may remain unresolved and the potential for lasting institutional change seems unlikely without higher levels of partner responsibility. This seems particular likely for commons problems, such as climate change, because partners may be unwilling to accept responsibility for their complicity in the problem (Ansari et al., 2013). Moving toward the top and middle of Table 11.1, the potential for partners to develop a shared framing of the problem and to agree on limited new norms increases, but, because the scope is limited, the potential for wholesale reinstitutionalization is still restricted. We would expect that the greatest likelihood of field transformation in partnerships would fall in the top left of Table 11.1 where agreement is reached on new shared frames and widely shared norms are negotiated.

Changes in Structures of Domination. So far we have examined changes in signification and legitimation structures within fields that can occur when partnerships are formed. We now look further at the dynamic contexts in which institutionalization processes are unfolding and aspects of domination within them. Domination refers to power interactions that create, affirm, or enforce patterns of autonomy and dependence among a collective (Giddens, 1984). We subscribe to the premise that, regardless of their age, fields are not static entities; instead, they are characterized by "constant jockeying going on . . . as a result of their contentious nature" (Fligstein, 2013: 43). Their actors differ in their ability to exercise power and often engage in conflicts about how and for what purposes the field should be governed (Purdy & Gray, 2009; Fligstein, 2013). "Power is the medium in social relations to structure fields of action" (Göhler, 2009: 36). Therefore, how fields evolve depends on who has

Table 11.1 How collaborative partnerships impact field structure

	SCOPE OF COLLABORATION		
LEVEL OF SHARED RESPONSIBILITY	**Narrow**	**Moderate**	**Broad**
High	Greater regularity and frequency of interaction Greater emotional intensity Greater likelihood of working through conflicts More likely that parties become aware of their own taken-for-granted institutional expectations and their impact on others	Greater understanding of complexity of problem and interdependencies Increased willingness to examine impact of one's own practices on field Greatest chance for replication in other contexts	Agreed-upon institutional meanings and practices more likely to be transmitted across field Potential for field-level change in signification and legitimation structures Alternative meanings and practices more likely to move up and down levels More likely to engage in new field creation and enforcement
Medium	Some potential for learning Increased possibility of changes in practices	Moderate potential for frame change	Substantial potential for one or both partners to change frames Substantial potential for agreements, but durability may suffer
Low	Least likelihood that learning occurs Less likelihood of seeing past positions Less trust in partners Unwillingness to examine impact of own practices on field Extant structures of domination will prevail	Limited exposure to alternative frames and practices Some learning may occur Reaching agreement is unlikely	Exposure to alternative frames and practices from a greater number of other sectors and fields Possibility of importing practices from another field into an existing field Fragile compromise agreement may be reached, but low durability Potential to become overwhelmed and quit the process

INCREASING POTENTIAL FOR FIELD CHANGE

and wields power within the field and whether this shifts during field level contests. Many institutional changes within fields occur without shifts in power relationships because "actors empowered by existing institutions use their advantages to elaborate institutions in ways that preserve their power and preclude alternatives" (Schneiberg & Lounsbury, 2008: 651).

When shifts occur in the distribution of power among field members, Giddens refers to these as changes in the structures of domination within the field. As we discussed in Chapter 7, substantial differences in power can prevent field members from forging collaborative agreements. To remain legitimate, existing power configurations must be enacted and re-enacted by field members in the form of societal rules and practices (Phillips et al., 2000b). In order to understand how power dynamics can transform fields, we first introduce four different field configurations and then describe possible pathways of change from one configuration to another.

Field Level Configurations: Starting Points for Change

Figure 11.1 presents a model of four states in which fields can exist. The model is built on the premises that stakeholders within a field may not only differ with respect to power, but also in terms of the purposes, aims, and directions they prefer that field members undertake (Galvin, 2002; Huxham & Vangen, 2005)—a fact that cannot be more evident than in the recent US debate over legislation for healthcare. Figure 11.1 shows four prototypic institutional fields distinguished by differing power dynamics and purposes that may

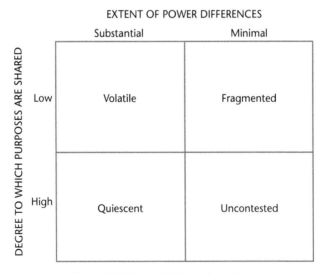

Figure 11.1 Issue field configurations

characterize fields at any given moment. The horizontal dimension in Figure 11.1 indicates differences in actors' power, which varies from substantial to minimal. The vertical dimension captures the degree to which the field's actors enact shared purposes. Juxtaposing these two dimensions generates a model of four generic field level configurations. These serve as starting conditions from which field level institutional change can emerge, induced either by shifts in the configuration of power among the field's actors or in the level of shared purposes enacted by the field's members.

Those fields in which actors share a common purpose and have minimal power differences are labeled *uncontested* fields. In fields that comprise this category, contests among stakeholders are, at least temporarily, resolved yielding what others have called settlement conditions (Armstrong, 2005; Fligstein & McAdam, 2012; Rao & Kenney, 2008). In contrast, in *fragmented* fields, power differences are minimal, but actors enact very disparate purposes. Such fields have variously been called "fragmented" (Nathan & Mitroff, 1991), under-organized (Brown, 1980) or contested (Lounsbury et al., 2003; Purdy & Gray, 2009; Wooten & Hoffman, 2008), and have been linked to widely differing frames and logics among field members (Fan & Zietsma, in press; Gray, 2004; Purdy & Gray, 2009). In *volatile* fields large power differences and disparate purposes privilege some voices over others, and more powerful parties shape the rules and rituals for how the domain will be organized, enabling weaker parties to be coopted by more powerful ones (Baur & Schmitz, 2012; Selznick, 1957). Those with power have the ability to "rule in" certain issues and "rule out" others from consideration (Fairclough, 1992), enabling them to privilege interests that benefit themselves while ignoring or subrogating other actors' interests yielding differential levels of voice, access, and acknowledgement among field level actors (Foucault, 1979). This kind of power operates behind the scenes, often unchallenged, and can hamper actors from forging broadly acceptable collaborative agreements. Failed states fall into this category as do fields with a lot of social upheaval and social movement activism. In *quiescent* fields low-power actors enact the powerful's purposes, but only because power differences are severe and repressive. In these fields, some actors with high levels of systemic power wield so much power over others that the latter may even be unaware that they are oppressed (Freire, 1971; Gaventa, 1980). This can lead to a highly stable field with little turbulence because contention and protest are quashed.

Our view is that all of these characterizations of fields are possible at different times in the field's evolution as the degree of institutionalization within the field shifts. Shifts in either the relative power dynamics among actors or in the actors' perceptions about the purpose of the field can produce institutional changes that cause fields to shift from one configuration to another. Such shifts begin from changes in an existing institutional relationship among field members within one of the four cells. Pressure from certain stakeholders can generate differentiation and ambiguity within a field (Podolny, 2001), leaving it vulnerable to both exogenous and endogenous sources of change and creating enabling conditions for new institutionalization initiatives to emerge. In the next section we consider several pathways by which institutional changes within fields may occur, shifting the field from one configuration to another.

Pathways of Change within Field Configurations

We begin by considering the possibility of change in uncontested fields where purposes are widely shared and power differences are minimal. Changes in the norms and meanings of a field can be generated from outside a field, for example through broader technological or social change, or from inside a field through the individual or joint efforts of field members such as in standards-setting partnerships. If changes start in an uncontested field and power differences are unaltered, the meanings that undergird institutional norms may shift (Lounsbury et al., 2003; Hardy & Maguire, 2010; Gray et al., 2015), but institutionalization may simply reproduce or reconstitute the existing pattern of power relations among actors (Phillips et al., 2000b). If some actors question a field's shared purposes and raise new conflicts, the field may shift from uncontested to fragmented and then back again to uncontested if new settlements are reached and are deemed legitimate (Green, 2004; Suddaby & Greenwood, 2005). For example, changes in the fields of accounting (Greenwood et al., 2002) and publishing (Thornton, 2004) introduced new guiding logics but did little to change the fundamental power differences among field members. On the other hand, Maguire and his colleagues (2004) reported how AIDS activists gained ground in advancing their agenda in the public sphere and thereby gained influence and agenda-setting power for their cause. To construct a framework for understanding the impact of partnerships on institutional fields, we identified patterns of activity that created shifts from one issue field configuration to another. Figure 11.2 illustrates four pathways of change driven by shifts in power among field actors as well as by changes in the degree to which shared purposes in the field are enacted.

Pathway #1 (from quiescent to volatile fields) is labeled *consciousness raising* after the term "conscienticization" introduced by Paolo Freire (1971) in the *Pedagogy of the Oppressed*. Consciousness raising is a signification process that enables oppressed peoples to come to understand their oppression and take steps to reframe their own identities. This pathway may involve the most difficult shift because it necessitates that the oppressed members of a field overcome the culture of silence and muster enough power to change the

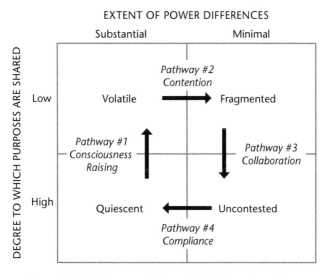

Figure 11.2 Pathways of change in field configurations

structures of domination within the field. This means that low-power stakeholders need to develop "self-awareness or critical understanding of the existing social conditions in which their needs and interests are unmet" (Seo & Creed, 2002). Freire (1971) labels this process conscienticization because it involves developing a critical consciousness about one's oppression as well as acknowledging one's complicity in perpetuating the current power relations. Social movement theorists refer to such efforts as diagnostic framing (Benford & Snow, 2000) when they highlight the experience of these stakeholders as victims of injustices perpetrated by more powerful actors. Consciousness raising does not change the power dynamics of the field, but occurs when low power actors in a field challenge the idea that field purposes are shared and express different frames about themselves and their relationship to other actors that were previously unspoken.

To illustrate how the degree of shared purposes enacted in a field can arise, we examine the case of CONAIE, a confederation of indigenous people's groups in Ecuador that emerged in the 1980s. Indigenous peoples in Ecuador, like many places in Latin America, have historically remained repressed and been denied access to political voice and participation. Despite neoliberal state reforms during the 1980s that generally created a more open society, indigenous peoples were left "politically marginalized as individual citizens" and "disempowered as corporatist peasant actors" (Yashar, 1998: 31). However, during the 1980s steps were taken by indigenous leaders to mobilize these groups on the basis of their indigenous identity as citizens, rather than organizing them around their ethnic or regional identities. This involved "challenging the historical image of Indians as a submissive, backward, and anachronistic group" (Yashar, 1998: 23). This consciousness raising was led by two separate indigenous people's groups which eventually merged to become CONAIE (Confederation of Indigenous Nationalities of Ecuador). "The CONAIE not only supported the transformation of indigenous consciousness but also provided a mechanism for the movement to project itself into economic policy debates" (Jameson, 2011: 65). Along with the demand to recognize their collective indigenous rights as citizens, CONAIE championed "territorial autonomy, respect for customary law, new forms of political representation, and bicultural education" (Yashar, 1998: 23). In effect, CONAIE discursively contested the very meaning of citizenship in Ecuador, and, in so doing, has challenged the meaning of politics and how it has been conducted in that country.

CONAIE's efforts at consciousness raising are akin to those advocated by Paolo Freire (1971) in Brazil, that he labeled "conscientização" or "conscienti-cization" (95). This term conveys a fundamental signification or sensemaking process (Giddens, 1984) in which oppressed people come to understand their oppression in a new way—not governed by a fatalistic attitude—but instead as something they can resist—over which they can exert leverage. It involves a fundamental reframing such that, in the Ecuadorian case, the opportunity to see oneself as a citizen precisely because of one's indigenous roots became a reality for them, and they were able to assert their own frames that didn't conform to those prescribed by the state.

Pathway #2 in Figure 11.2 is called *contention,* which involves moving from volatile to fragmented fields. Volatile fields are characterized by large power differences and histories of conflict in the absence of a common field-level purpose. Although power differences are substantial in volatile fields, they are not viewed as immutable, and radical change is possible (Greenwood & Hinings, 1996; Seo and Creed, 2002) if low power stakeholders can engage in power-building tactics to challenge elites. A strategy of contention (McAdam et al., 2001) enables suppressed resentments to emerge (Brown, 1980; Seo & Creed, 2002), but not without potentially explosive conflict because this pathway threatens existing structures of signification, legitim-ation and domination that serve elite interests. "In contention, new entrants (to a field) struggle to overturn existing domain parameters in order to make space for themselves and, in so doing, challenge dominant stakeholders" (Hardy & Phillips, 1998: 226). Contention introduces conflict into a volatile field, in this case through mobilizing human resources to engage in protest and exert coercive pressure on elites. For example, when social movements arise, they challenge the systemic power structure of the field (Benford & Snow, 2000; Davis et al., 2005) through protests or inciting boycotts, they can reshape institutional relationships (Bartley & Child, 2014; den Hond & de

Bakker, 2007; King, 2008b; McCarthy & Zald, 1977; Schneiberg & Lounsbury, 2008), resulting in a change in the domination structure of a field. The connection between social movement activities and partnership formation, however, has been underdeveloped in institutional theorizing (for exceptions, see Gricar & Brown, 1981; Zietsma & Lawrence, 2010) although there are many examples of how NGO campaigns against businesses created the impetus for partnerships to form as we have seen in the Rabobank case (Chapter 4) and the Canadian Boreal Forest Agreement (CBFA) discussed in Chapter 10. Similarly, "NGOs used the strategy of consumer boycotts to force companies to rethink their timber procurement policies" (Pattberg, 2007: 182), thereby increasing the demand for sustainable timber—to which the formation of the Forest Stewardship Council (FSC) was a direct response. Bartley & Child (2014) found similar dynamics in the formation of other standard-setting partnerships.

As social movements engage in contestation, they attempt to build discursive legitimacy (Hardy & Phillips, 1998) both for the issue and for themselves as legitimate stakeholders whose concerns need to be taken seriously by elite actors (Gray, 1989). By building discursive legitimacy, movement organizers may be able to "compensate for a lack of traditional power sources" and exert sufficient influence to modify the dominant institutional frames of the field (Hardy & Phillips, 1998: 182). In these cases, the exercise of contention can move a field from a volatile to a fragmented configuration by adjusting the power relationship among the actors. Contention enables a less powerful contender to disturb the entrenched stranglehold the powerful have in the field and successfully establish their own legitimate voice as a stakeholder and reshape the issues on the public agenda.

We return to the CONAIE example to illustrate how changes in the extent of power differences can occur, in this case through contention, to address agrarian land reform in Ecuador. In 1990 CONAIE brought indigenous groups from across the country to stage a protest in the middle of the Panamerican Highway, effectively blocking transport of goods through the country for several days. Because of this leverage, the group was able to gain access to high-level government negotiations that focused on sixteen of their demands (Jameson, 2011). Among them was the demand to dismantle new laws that would have effectively stripped them of rights to own their own land. While such mobilization tactics are essential for moving from volatile domains to fragmented fields, lower power actors may also need to leverage other sources of power such as bridging social capital with well-placed elites who care about their cause to effect such field-level transformation. In this case, contention, coupled with intercession by the Catholic Church, enabled CONAIE to regain legal control of territorial lands for indigenous people in Ecuador. As a powerful player in their own right, the Church's involvement helped to level the playing field and overcome the systemic power differences between CONAIE and the Ecuadorian government.

The CONAIE's experience illustrates to what lengths low-power groups may need to go to get access to power and change the domination structure within the field. Their protests blocking the Pan American highway enabled them not only to mobilize as a social movement and mount an effective protest but to gain access to collaborative negotiations with the country's most powerful actors—negotiations that led to further power-balancing within the field by restoring to them control over their lands. Thus, the CONAIE's experience demonstrates an extreme case of challenging the systemic power structure within a field and effectuating changes in domination as well as signification and legitimation structures. Through CONAIE's efforts, indigenous peoples in Ecuador now have an ongoing, established voice in Ecuador's political process.

The third pathway of field-level change we label *collaboration*, which enables stakeholders to transform a fragmented field to an uncontested one. This pathway is depicted by arrow #3 in Figure 11.2. Collaboration is a "mechanism by which a negotiated order emerges among a set of stakeholders" within an institutional field or from diverse fields that come together to deal with a joint problem (Gray, 1989: 228). It affords field members a chance to search for and enact a common purpose. When fields are fragmented, they experience extreme turbulence (i.e., a rapid increase in the number of uncontrollable environmental jolts to organizations within a field). Collaboration has been suggested as a mechanism of institutionalization in such contexts (Gray, 1989; O'Mahoney & Bechky, 2008) building on the partners underlying interdependence.

In fragmented fields, stakeholders have little formal interaction and presumably no shared system of signification or common purpose that links them to each other, but each has sufficient power to question or block the actions of others. Over time, stakeholders may gradually or serendipitously come to recognize their interdependence and realize that they share a common fate (or plight) leading them to form a partnership. Alternately, institutional entrepreneurs (Maguire, et al., 2004) may engage in more deliberate efforts to convene field members (Carlson, 1999; Dorado, 2005; Gray, 1989) in order to initiate a partnership.

The Mesá case offers insight into the problems that arise when attempts at collaboration start from a volatile field—one in which some parties are substantially more powerful than others and the degree of shared purpose is low. While the case can be criticized on several bases, we focus here only on the issue of unbalanced power. In the Mesá case we argue that collaboration was ultimately not successful because powerful actors such as the Yamococha and the Ministry of Mines never shared decision-making power with lower power stakeholders, and those stakeholders did not mobilize enough to acquire standing to challenge the mine's entrenched power. Doing so would have required mobilization among the less powerful stakeholders so that the mine and the government had little choice but to fully come to the negotiating table. Nor does the CAO appear to have had sufficient convening power (Gray, 1989) to entice all the relevant actors to the table. While some indigenous people's groups did protest the Mesá's formation and refuse to participate, others elected to join it. Consequently, after five years of deliberations, these groups had made little progress in extracting concessions from the mine. Had they united and collectively mobilized to insist on an even table (as indigenous people did in the CONAIE case), efforts at collaboration would have started from a fragmented rather than volatile field, and perhaps the outcome would have been different.

The fourth pathway of institutionalization follows arrow #4 and involves moving from uncontested to quiescent fields through *compliance.* Moving from uncontested to quiescent fields requires compliance (Hardy & Phillips, 1998; Raaijmakers et al., 2015) in which rules and practices serve one group while others capitulate "with the actions they think their more powerful counterparts wish to see" (Hardy & Phillips, 1998: 227, 228). While this creates the appearance of unity of purpose, it magnifies power differences among actors in the uncontested field by creating a culture of silence and suppressed self-image among others within the field (Freire, 1971). Stakeholders who are less favored by field norms become socialized into a compliant role in deference to the signification structures imposed by the more favored actors in the field. The culture of silence prevents dominated individuals from critically responding to the culture institutionalized by the more powerful (Freire, 1971). According to Gaventa (1980), they may even become oblivious to their oppression, concluding instead that the extant power distribution is acceptable. Thus, compliance can institutionalize voicelessness and ultimately lead to quiescence in the field. Agreements reached across severe power differences without efforts to bolster the voices of the disaffected (as FERC did in its deliberations with Native American tribes) can run the risk of institutionalizing quiescence rather than empowerment and do not constitute collaboration.

Summary. In this analysis we have identified four field configurations in which multi-stakeholder partnerships unfold and four pathways of field transformation by which multistakeholder partnerships can generate field level change. Two of the pathways, consciousness raising and collaboration, occur when actors focus on examining the taken-for-granted meanings and norms in an issue field and utilize partnerships as a forum for expressing their distinct visions for the field. In the case of consciousness raising, partners need to find and construct shared frames to yield change at the field level, low-power actors must learn about their oppression and strengthen their collective voice to move the field from a quiescent to a volatile one. To move from fragmented to uncontested fields, actors need to develop shared meanings. Both pathways emphasize meaning making activities in which actors must articulate and amplify frames across the issue field through legitimation and signification.

The other two pathways, contention and compliance, emphasize the dynamics of power. Our analysis shows that actors with access to resources have the ability to influence the power dependencies within a field and to shift power differences during the collaborative process. Depending on the initial power configuration of the field, different pathways of institutional change are possible. To effect change, low-power stakeholders need to mobilize others and use social movement strategies to gain a seat at the negotiating table. Depending on their assessments of the power of contenders and the reputational damage they are incurring, powerful actors may elect to act unilaterally to preserve their systemic power or may (often in response to pressure from low power groups) work to level the playing field to support broader participation in governance decisions for the field. By combining this analysis of how change in domination structures may occur in the context of multistakeholder partnerships with our earlier discussion in this chapter about the capacity of multistakeholder partnerships to change signification and legitimation structures within fields, we offer both a means of evaluating the impact of partnerships according to whether they have yielded field change, and a set of mechanisms that describe the likelihood that such changes will unfold.

The Viability of Partnerships as Vehicles for Field-Level Change and Governance

The clamor to solve wicked societal problems using multistakeholder partnerships has increased dramatically over the last twenty-five years. Sound arguments for the utility of multistakeholder partnerships over command and control forms of governance have frequently been made. Many scholars and policy designers have extolled their promise for promoting new social innovations and advancing partners' shared aspirations for dealing with the knotty problems that we face from the local to the global levels of society. Multistakeholder partnerships have "been welcomed as a new form of democratic governance" (Glasbergen, 2007), as a critical source of needed innovation (Ansell & Torfing, 2014), as an essential avenue to preserving the planet and achieving sustainability in the broadest sense of the word. Yet, as we have articulated elsewhere (Gray, 1989; Gray & Purdy, 2014), partnerships are not panaceas. They are often fraught with difficulties, and many well-intended partnerships fail to achieve their sought-after outcomes or realize the visions of their founders. They have been criticized for their lack of representativeness and legitimacy in delivering governance instruments, their encroachment on the role of elected governments, their capture by corporations and other powerful partners, and their use as "eco-radical shakedowns" designed to cripple industries. And we still struggle to delineate, let alone measure, their short- and long-term outcomes, outputs, and impacts. Meanwhile, problems such as inequality, climate change, peace, and countless others only worsen while solutions elude us as a society. This leads us to ask, "What are our alternatives?" Can we tap the wisdom gained from our failed attempts at collaborating to rekindle our visions, sharpen our resolve, and design adaptations to our processes that bring us closer to realizing the potential of collaborative partnerships?

Without question, partnerships are often messy, confusing, and disheartening, and the problems they are designed to tackle do not stand still while we deliberate about them. The problems we face are dynamic and nonlinear. Some have called them panarchies (Gunderson & Holling, 2002), and the structures we design to address them need continued monitoring and flexibility to remain resilient (Gunderson et al., 2009; Westley et al., 2002). We believe that the institutional lens on partnerships that we have advanced here helps us to understand both the problems associated with the embeddedness of partnerships in institutional fields and their potential to transform those fields in constructive ways.

As Vurro and Dacin (2014) have observed, partnerships exhibit reciprocal relations with the fields in which they are embedded. Fields create opportunity structures (McAdam, 1996) that are more or less conducive to partnership formation and "dictate the conditions that have to be satisfied in order for [partnerships] to be considered appropriate" (Vurro and Dacin, 2014: 314). Building on our analysis above, we suggest that fragmented fields, in particular, are the most conducive for partnership success when interdependence among potential partners is high, uncertainty about key problems is high, and power differences among partners are not prohibitive to creating a level playing field for deliberations. In those conditions, partnerships have the best chance of flourishing although, of course, success also depends on the actions of the partners themselves including their attention to process design and to the quality of their interactions with each other. Extant institutional arrangements can also facilitate partnership success, as when the new frames agreed to by the partners coincide with broader discursive trends and values in the societal discourse (Pattberg, 2007) such as sustainability, or workers' rights, anti-corruption campaigns, or campaigns for a living wage. Alternately, institutional arrangements such as lack of sufficient resources, deeply embedded cultural practices, and historical mistrust can impose limitations on the likelihood that partnerships will achieve the goals to which they aspire.

Inspired by an earlier list offered by Dienhart and Ludescher (2010), we suggest that to be successful multistakeholder partnerships should cultivate the capacity to:

1. ensure that all stakeholders affected by the issue or problem have the opportunity to participate in deliberations or to select others to represent their interests in deliberations among partners;

2. take steps to level the negotiating table with respect to power and cultural differences and ensure that lower power participants have adequate voice during the proceedings;

3. thoroughly investigate the nature and source of the interdependencies that link stakeholders to each other;

4. agree upon fair procedures for the deliberations that anticipate and provide for constructive resolution of conflicts;

5. provide for periodic consultation with back-home constituencies;

6. ensure that agreements are as integrative as possible, reflecting everyone's interests while ensuring that no stakeholders carry a disproportionate burden of the costs;

7. build in sufficient redundancy of representation so that institutional memory is not lost if representatives leave the process;

8. devise governance norms that emphasize equity and fairness and allow sufficient flexibility to adapt to changing circumstances in the future;

9. err on the side of capacity building rather than efficiency; and

10. evaluate and alter governance of the partnership to ensure voice, fairness, and well-being of all partners, especially when cross-level dynamics are involved.

Waxing more philosophical, we ask: "What institutional norms do we want to govern our lives on this planet? What values do we want to champion for ourselves and future generations? What is our definition of community? And to what vision of the future do we want to commit?" We hope that the examples, models, and insights in this volume inspire thought and discussion of these important questions, and spur appropriate action. Electing to collaborate is not the easiest course to take, but it may be the best means we have of realizing a world that is more sustainable and just.

Note

1. Destabilizing change processes can be also be generated by "proximate state or non-state fields" (Fligstein & McAdam, 2012: 3) or in the interstices when two or more fields intersect (Morrill & Owen-Smith, 2002; Furnari, 2014).

References

Agranoff, R. (2007) *Managing within Networks: Adding Value to Public Organizations.* Washington, DC: Georgetown University Press.

Ählström, J. & Sjöström, E. (2005) CSOs and business partnerships: Strategies for interaction. *Business Strategy and the Environment,* 14: 230–40.

Alderfer, C. P. (1977) Group and intergroup relations. In J. R. Hackman & J. L. Suttle (eds.), *Improving Life at Work: Behavioral Science Approaches to Organizational Change,* 227–96. Santa Monica, CA: Goodyear.

Amir, Y. (1994) The contact hypothesis in intergroup relations. In W. J. Levine & R. S. Malpass (eds.), *Psychology and Culture,* 231–7. Boston: Allyn & Bacon.

Amsler, L. (2016) Collaborative governance: integrating politics and law. *Public Administration Review,* 76 (5): 700–11.

Anand, N. & Watson, M. R. (2004) Tournament rituals in the evolution of fields: The case of the Grammy Awards. *Academy of Management Journal,* 47 (1): 59–80.

Anand, S. & Segal, P. (2015) The global distribution of income. In A. B. Atkinson and F. Boualrguignon (eds.), *Handbook of Income Distribution,* Volume 2A, 937–79. Amsterdam: Elsevier.

Andersen, E. K. (2000) *Hydroelectric Power and Salmon: A Comparative Case Study of Eight Hydroelectric Power Projects and the FERC Relicensing Process.* Master's thesis, University of Washington.

Andrews, R. & Entwistle, T. (2010) Does cross-sectoral partnership deliver? An empirical exploration of public service effectiveness, efficiency, and equity. *Journal of Public Administration Research and Theory,* 20: 679–701.

Ansari, S. M., Munir, K., & Gregg, T. (2012) Impact at the "bottom of the pyramid": The role of social capital in capability development and community empowerment. *Journal of Management Studies,* 49 (4): 813–42.

Ansari, S. M., Wijen, F., & Gray, B. (2013) Averting the "tragedy of the commons": An institutional perspective on the construction and governance of transnational commons. *Organization Science,* 24: 1014–40.

Ansell, C. & Gash, A. (2008) Collaborative governance in theory and practice. *Journal of Public Administration Research and Theory,* 18 (4): 543–71.

Ansell, C. & Torfing, J. (2014) *Public Innovation through Collaboration and Design.* Oxford, UK: Routledge.

Appadurai, A. (2006) Foreword to S. Batliwana & L. D. Brown (eds.), *Transnational Civil Society: An Introduction,* xi–xvi. Bloomfield, CT: Kumarian Press.

Arbruster-Sandoval, R. (2004) *Globalization and Cross-border Labor Solidarity in the Americas: The Anti-sweatshop Movement and the Struggle for Social Justice.* New York: Routledge.

Argenti, P. A. (2004) Collaborating with activists: How Starbucks works with NGOs. *California Management Review*, 47(1): 91–116.

Argyris, C. (1970) *Intervention Theory and Method: A Behavioral Science View.* Reading, MA: Addison-Wesley.

Argyris, C. & Schon, D. (1978) *Organizational Learning.* Reading, MA: Addison-Wesley.

Argyris, C., Putnam, R., & Smith, M. C. (1985) *Action Science: Concepts, Methods and Skills for Research and Intervention.* San Francisco: Jossey-Bass.

Armstrong, E. A. (2005) From struggle to settlement: The crystallization of a field of lesbian/gay organizations in San Francisco, 1969–1973. In G. F. Davis, D. McAdam, W. R. Scott, & M. N. Zald (eds.), *Social Movements and Organization Theory*, 161–87. Cambridge: Cambridge University Press.

Asante, A. A. & Zwi, A. B. (2007) Public private partnerships and global health equity: Prospects and challenges. *Indian Journal of Medical Ethics*, 4 (4): 176–80.

Austin, J. E. (2000) Strategic collaboration between nonprofits and businesses. *Nonprofit and Voluntary Sector Quarterly*, 29 (1): 69–97.

Austin, J. E. & Elias, J. (1996) *Timberland and Community Involvement.* Harvard Business School Publishing, Case 9-796-156.

Austin, J. E. & Seitanidi, M. M. (2012) Collaborative value creation: A review of partnering between nonprofits and businesses: Part I. Value creation spectrum and collaboration stages. *Nonprofit and Voluntary Sector Quarterly*, 41 (5): 726–58.

Bäckstrand, K. (2006) Multi-stakeholder partnerships for sustainable development: Rethinking legitimacy, accountability and effectiveness. *European Environment*, 16: 290–306.

Bäckstrand, K. (2008) Accountability of networked climate governance: The rise of transnational climate partnerships. *Global Environmental Politics*, 8 (3): 74–102.

Baird, B. N. R. (1986) Tolerance for environmental health risks: the influence of knowledge, benefits, voluntariness, and environmental attitudes. *Risk Analysis*, 6 (4): 425–35.

Baker, A. (2011) How to resolve the abortion conflict. May 25. http://www.huffingtonpost.com/aspen-baker/how-to-resolve-the-aborti_b_227238.html (accessed November 13, 2016).

Balderston, K. M. (2012) Creating value through uncommon alliances: The US State Department is redefining diplomacy and development. *Stanford Social Innovation Review*, Fall, 23–4.

Baldwin, C. & Ross, H. (2012) Bridging troubled waters: Applying consensus-building techniques to water planning. *Society and Natural Resources*, 25 (3): 217–34.

Barley, S. R. (2008) Coalface institutionalism. In R. Greenwood, C. Oliver, K. Sahlin, & R. Suddaby (eds.), *The Sage Handbook of Organizational Institutionalism*, 490–515. Los Angeles, CA: Sage.

Barley, S. R. (2010) Building an institutional field to corral a government: A case to set an agenda for organization studies. *Organization Studies*, 31: 777–805.

Barley, S. R. & Tolbert, P. S. (1997) Institutionalization and structuration: Studying the links between action and institution. *Organization Studies*, 18: 93–117.

Barrett, F. (1995) Creating appreciative learning cultures. *Organizational Dynamics*, 4: 36–44.

Barsade, S. (2002) The ripple effect: Emotional contagion and its influence on group behavior. *Administrative Science Quarterly*, 47: 644–75.

Barthel, D. (1996) *Historic Preservation: Collective Memory and Historical Identity*. New Brunswick, NJ: Rutgers University Press.

Bartley, T. (2003) Certifying forests and factories. States, social movements, and the rise of private regulation in the apparel and forest products fields. *Politics and Society*, 26: 433–64.

Bartley, T. (2007) Institutional emergence in an era of globalization: The rise of transnational private regulation of labor and environmental conditions. *American Journal of Sociology*, 113 (2): 297–351.

Bartley, T. & Child, C. (2011) Movements, markets and fields: The effects of anti-sweatshop campaigns on U.S. Firms, 1993–2000. *Social Forces*, 90 (2): 425–51.

Bartley, T. & Child, C. (2014) Shaming the corporation: The social production of targets and the anti-sweatshop movement. *American Sociological Review*, 79 (4): 653–79.

Bass, S., Font, X., & Danielson, L. (2001) Standards and certification. A leap forward or a step back for sustainable development? In International Institute for Environment and Development (ed.), *The Future is Now, Vol. 2*, 21–31. London, IIED.

Batliwala, S. & Brown, L. D. (2006) Why transnational civil society matters. In S. Batliwala & L. D. Brown (eds.), *Transnational Civil Society: An Introduction*, 1–15. Bloomfield, CT: Kumarian Press.

Battelle Technology Partnership Practice (2013) The impact of genomics on the US economy. http://web.ornl.gov/sci/techresources/Human_Genome/publicat/2013 BattelleReportImpact-of-Genomics-on-the-US-Economy.pdf (accessed July 26, 2017).

Battilana, J. & Dorado, S. (2010) Building sustainable hybrid organizations: The case of commercial microfinance organizations. *Academy of Management Journal*, 53 (6): 1419–40.

Baur, D. & Schmitz, H. P. (2012) Corporations and NGOs: When accountability leads to co-optation. *Journal of Business Ethics*, 106: 9–21.

BBC News (2016) Oxfam says wealth of richest 1% equal to other 99%. Jan. 18. http://www.bbc.com/news/business-35339475 (accessed July 26, 2017).

Beech, N. & Huxham, C. (2003) Cycles of identity formation in collaboration. *International Studies of Management and Organization*, 33 (3): 28–52.

Bendell, J. (2000) A no win-win situation? GMOs, NGOs, and sustainable development. In J. Bendell (ed.), *Terms for Endearment: Business, NGOs and Sustainable Development*, 96–110. Sheffield, UK: Greenleaf.

Benford, R. & Snow, D. (2000) Framing processes and social movements: An overview and assessment. *Annual Review of Sociology*, 26: 611–39.

Berger, I. E., Cunningham, P. H., & Drumwright, M. E. (2004) Social alliances: Company/non-profit collaboration. *California Management Review*, 47(1): 58–90.

Berger, P. & Luckmann, T. (1966) *The Social Construction of Reality: A Treatise in the Sociology of Knowledge*. Garden City, NY: Anchor.

Berman, T. (2011) *This Crazy Time: Living Our Environmental Challenge*. Canada: Alfred A. Knopf.

Berryessa, C. M. & Cho, M. K. (2013) Ethical, legal, social and policy implications of behavioral genetics. *Annual Review of Genomics and Human Genetics*, 14: 515–34.

Bhattacharya, C. B., Korschun, D., & Sen, S. (2009) Strengthening stakeholder–company relationships through mutually beneficial corporate social responsibility initiatives. *Journal of Business Ethics*, 85(Supplement 2): 257–72.

Bidwell, R. D. & Ryan, C. M. (2006) Collaborative partnership design: The implications of organizational affiliation for watershed partnerships. *Society and Natural Resources* 19: 827–43.

Bingham, G. (1986) *Resolving Environmental Disputes: A Decade of Experience*. Washington, DC: Conservation Foundation.

Bingham, L. B. & O'Leary, R. (2006) Conclusion: Parallel play, not collaboration: Missing questions, missing connections. *Public Administration Review*, 66(s1): 161–7.

Bingham, L. B., Nabatchi, T., & O'Leary, R. (2005) The new governance: Practices and processes for stakeholder and citizen participation in the work of government. *Public Administration Review*, 65 (5): 547–58.

Bion, W. (1961) *Experiences in Groups*. London: Tavistock Institute.

Bitzer, V. & Glasbergen, P. (2010) Partnerships for sustainable change in cotton: An institutional analysis of African cases. *Journal of Business Ethics*, 93: 223–40.

Blumer, H. (1969) *Symbolic Interactionism: Perspective and Method*. New Jersey: Prentice-Hall.

Booher, D. E. and Innes, J. E. (2010) Governance for resilience: CALFED as a complex adaptive network for resource management. *Ecology and Society* 15 (3): 35.

Borrini-Feyerabend, G., Farvar, M. T., Nguinguiri, J. C., & Ndangang, V. (2000) *Environmental Management Co-management of Natural Resources Organising. Negotiating and Learning-by-Doing*. Eschborn: IUCN, GTZ.

Bosshard, P. (2003) *Karahnjukar: A Project on Thin Ice*. Berkeley, CA: International Rivers Network.

Bosso, C. J. (1995) The color of money: Environmental groups and the pathologies of fund raising. In A. J. Cigler & B. A. Loomis (eds.), *Interest Group Politics (4th ed.)*, 101–30. Washington, DC: CQ Press.

Bouwen, R. & Steyaert, C. (1999) From a dominant voice toward multivoiced cooperation. In D. L. Cooperrider & J. E. Dutton (eds.), *Organizational Dimensions of Global Change*, 291–319. London: Sage.

Bouwen, R. & Taillieu, T. (2004) Multi-party collaboration as social learning for interdependence: Developing relational knowing for sustainable natural resource management. *Journal of Community & Applied Social Psychology*, 14: 137–53.

Bowen, F., Newenham-Kahindi, A., & Herremans, I. (2010) When suits meet roots: The antecedents and consequences of community engagement strategy. *Journal of Business Ethics*, 95: 297–318.

Bowker, G. C. & Star, S. L. (1999) *Sorting Things Out: Classification and Its Consequences*. Cambridge, MA: MIT Press.

Brandsen, T. & van Hout, E. (2006) Co-management in public service networks: The organizational effects. *Public Management Review*, 8 (4): 537–49.

Brecher, C. & Wise, O. (2008) Looking a gift horse in the mouth: Challenges in managing philanthropic support for public services. *Public Administration Review*, (Special Issue): S146–61.

Briscoe, F. & Gray, B. (2017) Innovations in Medical Genomics: How to enable advances while managing privacy and security risks. Farrell Center, Penn State University. https://www.smeal.psu.edu/fcfe/documents/medical_genomics_innovation_sep2017.pdf

Brockmyer, B. I. (2016) *Global Standards in National Contexts: The Role of Transnational Multi-stakeholder Initiatives in Public Sector Governance Reform* (Doctoral dissertation, American University Washington, DC).

Bronen, R. (2015) Collaborative governance in Alaska: Responding to climate change threats in Alaska native communities. In K. Emerson & T. Nabatchi. *Collaborative Governance Regimes*, 120–35. Washington, DC: Georgetown University Press.

Brown, A. J. (2002) Collaborative governance versus constitutional politics: Decision rules for sustainability from Australia's South East Queensland forest agreement. *Environmental Science and Policy*, 5: 19–32.

Brown, L. D. (1980) Planned change in underorganized systems. In T. F. Cummings (ed.), *Systems Theory for Organizational Development*, 81–208. New York: Wiley.

Brown, L. D. (2008) *Creating Credibility: Legitimacy and Accountability for Transnational Civil Society*. Sterling, VA: Kumarian Press.

Brown, L. D. & Ashman, D. (1999) Social capital, mutual influence and social learning in intersectoral problem solving in Africa and Asia. In D. L. Cooperider & J. Dutton (eds.), *Organizational Dimensions of Global Change*, 139–67. Thousand Oaks, Sage.

Brummel, R. G., Nelson, K. C., Grayzeck-Souter, S., Jakes, P. J., & Williams, D. R. (2010) Social learning in a policy-mandated collaboration: Community wildfire protection in the eastern United States. *Journal of Environmental Planning and Management*, 53 (6): 681–99.

Bryan, T. (2004) Tragedy averted: The promise of collaboration. *Society & Natural Resources,* 17: 881–96.

Bryson, J. & Anderson, S. (2000) Applying large-group intervention methods in planning and implementation of major change efforts. *Public Administration Review*, 60 (2): 143–62.

Bryson, J. & Crosby, B. (1992) *Leadership for the Common Good: Tackling Problems in a Shared-Power World*. San Francisco: Jossey-Bass.

Bryson, J. & Finn, C. B. (1995) Creating the future together: Developing and using shared strategy maps. In A. Halachmi & G. Bouckaert (eds.), *The Enduring Challenges in Public Management*, 247–80. San Francisco, CA: Jossey-Bass.

Bryson, J., Crosby, B., & Stone, M. M. (2006) The design and implementation of cross-sector collaborations: Propositions from the literature. *Public Administration Review* (Special Issue): 44–55.

Bryson, J., Crosby, B., & Stone, M. M. (2015) The design and implementation of cross-sector collaborations: Needed and challenging. *Public Administration Review*, 75 (5): 647–63.

Building Consensus: History and Lessons from the Mesá de Diálogo y Consenso CAO-Cajamarca, Peru: Monograph 1. The Formation and First Steps of the Mesá (2000–2003). 2007. Washington, DC: World Bank, Office of the Compliance Advisor/Ombudsman (CAO).

Building Consensus: History and Lessons from the Mesá de Diálogo y Consenso CAO-Cajamarca, Peru: Monograph 2. The Independent Water Study (2002–2004). 2007. Washington, DC: World Bank, Office of the Compliance Advisor/Ombudsman (CAO).

Building Consensus: History and Lessons from the Mesá de Diálogo y Consenso CAO-Cajamarca, Peru: Monograph 3: Independent Water Monitoring and the Transition of the Mesá (2004–2006). 2007. Washington, DC: World Bank, Office of the Compliance Advisor/Ombudsman (CAO).

Bunker, B. B. & Albans, B. T. (1997) *Large Scale Interventions: Engaging the Whole System for Rapid Change*. San Francisco: Jossey-Bass.

Bunker, B. B. & Albans, B. T. (2006) *The Handbook of Large Group Methods: Creating Systemic Change in Organizations and Communities*. San Francisco: Jossey-Bass.

Burton, L. (2002) *Worship and Wilderness: Culture, Religion and Law in Public Lands and Resource Management*. Madison, WI: University of Wisconsin Press.

Canadian Boreal Forest Agreement (2010) http://cbfa-efbc.ca/agreement (accessed May 1, 2017).

Caneva, L. (2016) Westpac and Thrive partnership to help refugees start new businesses. Probono Australia, November 30. https://probonoaustralia.com.au/news/2016/11/westpac-thrive-partnership-help-refugees-start-businesses/ (accessed July 26, 2017).

Carlson, C. (1999) Convening. In L. Susskind, S. McKearnen, & J. Thomas-Larmer (eds.), *The Consensus Building Handbook: A Comprehensive Guide to Reaching Agreement*, 169–98. Thousand Oaks, CA: Sage.

Carlson, C. (2007) *A Practical Guide to Collaborative Governance*. Policy Consensus Initiative. Portland, OR.

Carlsson, B. (2006) Internationalization of innovation systems: A survey of the literature. *Research Policy*, 35 (1): 56–67.

Carpenter, S. (1999) Choosing appropriate consensus building techniques and strategies. In L. Susskind, S. McKearnan, & J. Thomas-Larmer (eds.), *The Consensus Building Handbook*, 61–98. Thousand Oaks, CA: Sage.

Carroll, A. B. (1979) A three-dimensional conceptual model of corporate performance. *Academy of Management Review*, 4 (4): 497–505.

Castells, M. (1997) *The Power of Identity, Vol. II of The Information Age: Economy, Society and Culture*. Oxford: Blackwell.

Castro, A. P. & Nielsen, E. (2001) Indigenous people and co-management: Implications for conflict management. *Environment: Science & Policy*, 4(4–5): 229–39.

Cavalli, A., Banba, S. I., Traore, M. N., Coulibaly, Y., Polman, K., Pirard, M., & Van Dormael, M. (2010) Interactions between global health initiatives and country health systems: The case of a neglected tropical diseases control program in Mali. *PLoS Neglected Tropical Diseases*, 401 e793, https://doi.org/10.1371/journal.pntd.0000798 (accessed April 7, 2017).

Chávez, B. V. & Bernal, A. S. (2008) Planning hydroelectric power plants with the public: A case of organizational and social learning in Mexico. *Impact Assessment and Project Appraisal*, 26 (3): 163–76.

Cheng, A. S. & Sturtevant, V. E. (2012) A framework for assessing collaborative capacity in community-based public forest management. *Environmental Management*, 49: 675–89.

Chliova, M. & Ringlov, D. (2017) Scaling impact: Template development at the base of the pyramid. *Academy of Management Perspectives*, 31 (1): 44–62.

Chrislip, D. E. & Larson, C. E. (1994) *Collaborative Leadership: How Citizens and Civic Leaders Can Make a Difference*. San Francisco: Jossey-Bass.

Clarke, A. (2011) Key structural features for collaborative strategy implementation: A study of sustainable development/local agenda 21 collaborations. *Revue Management & Avenir*, 50: 153–71.

Clarke, A. (2014) Designing social partnerships for local sustainability strategy implementation. In M. M. Seitinidi & A. Crane (eds.), *Social Partnerships and Responsible Business: A Research Handbook*, 79–102. Oxford, UK: Routledge.

Clarke, A. & Fuller, M. (2010) Collaborative strategic management: Strategy formulation and implementation by multi-organizational cross-sector social partnerships. *Journal of Business Ethics*, 94: 85–101.

Clarke, N. (2005) Transorganization development for network building. *Journal of Applied Behavioral Science*, 41 (1): 30–45.

Clegg, S. R. (1989) *Frameworks of Power*. London: Sage.

Clemens, E. (1996) Organizational form as frame: Collective identity and political strategy in the American labor movement. In J. McCarthy and M. Zald (eds.), *Comparative Perspectives on Social Movements: Opportunities, Mobilizing Structures, and Cultural Framings*, 205–26. New York: Cambridge University Press.

Cohen, P. (2010) "Culture of poverty" makes a comeback. *New York Times*, October 18: A1.

Collins, R. (2004) *Interaction Ritual Chains*. Princeton, NJ: Princeton University Press.

Colosi, T. (1985) A core model of negotiation. In R. J. Lewicki & J. A. Litterer (eds.), *Negotiation: Readings, Exercises and Cases,* 3rd ed., 313–19. Homewood, IL: Irwin.

Comments of the National Hydropower Association (2000) Federal Register Docket no. 00-1206343-0343-01, December 13.

Conga No Va (2015) An assessment of the Conga mining project in light of World Bank Standards. A report of a coalition of social organizations from the Provinces of Celendín and Hualgayoc in the Region of Cajamarca, Peru. September 2015. http://www.conganova.com.

Cooperrider, D. L. & Srivastva, S. (1987) Appreciative inquiry in organizational life. In W. A. Pasmore and R. W. Woodman (eds.), *Research in Organization Development and Change*, Vol 1: 129–69. Greenwich, CT: JAI Press.

Coser, L. (1956) *The Functions of Social Conflict*. New York: Free Press.

Creed, W. E. D., DeJordy, R., & Lok, J. (2010) Being the change: Resolving institutional contradiction. *Academy of Management Journal*, 53 (6): 1336–64.

Cronin, M., Bezrukova, K., Weingart, L. R., & Tinsley, C. A. (2011) Subgroups within teams: The role of affective and cognitive integration. *Journal of Organizational Behavior*, 32 (6): 831–49.

Cropper, S. & Palmer, I. (2008) Change, dynamics, and temporality in inter-organizational relationships. In S. Cropper, M. Ebers, C. Huxham, & P. Smith Ring (eds.), *The Oxford Handbook of Interorganizational Relations*, 635–64. Oxford: Oxford University Press.

Crosby, B. C. & Bryson, J. M. (2005) *Leadership for the Common Good: Tackling Public Problems in a Shared-Power World*, 2nd ed. San Francisco: Jossey-Bass.

Cummings, T. G. (1984) Transorganizational development. In B. Staw & I. Cummings (eds.), *Research in Organizational Behavior*, Vol. 5: 367–422. Greenwich, CT: JAI Press.

Curseu, P. & Schruijer, S. (2005) The effects of framing on group negotiation. Paper presented at the 18th Annual Conference of the International Association for Conflict Management, Budapest, Hungary, 12–15 June.

Cyert, R. & March, J. (1963/1992) *A Behavioral Theory of the Firm*, 2nd ed. New York: Wiley.

Dacin, M. T. (1997) Isomorphism in context: The power and prescription of institutional norms. *Academy of Management Journal*, 40 (1): 46–81.

Dahan, N. M., Doh, J. P., Oetzel, J., & Yaziji, M. (2010) Corporate-NGO collaboration: Co-creating new business models for developing markets. *Long Range Planning*, 43 (2-3): 326–42.

Darnall, N. & Carmin, J. (2005) Greener and cleaner? The signaling accuracy of U.S. voluntary environmental programs. *Policy Sciences*, 38: 71–90.

Das, T. K. & Teng, B. (1998) Between trust and control: Developing confidence in partner cooperation in alliances. *Academy of Management Review*, 23 (2): 491–512.

Davenport, C. (2014) December 14. A climate accord based on global peer pressure. New York Times. www.nytimes.com/2014/12/15/world/americas/lima-climate-deal.html (accessed July 27, 2017).

Davis, G. F., Mc Adam, D., Scott, W. R. & Zald, M. N. (eds.) (2005) *Social Movements and Organization Theory*, 335–50. Cambridge: Cambridge University Press.

de Bakker, F. G. A., den Hond, F., King, B., & Weber, K. (2013) Social movements, civil society and corporations: Taking stock and looking ahead. *Organization Studies*, 34: 573–94.

Dees, J. G. & Elias, J. (1996) *CityYear Enterprise*. Harvard Business School Publishing, Case 9-396-196.

den Hond, F. & de Bakker, F. G. A. (2007) Ideologically motivated activism: How activist groups influence corporate social change activities. *Academy of Management Review*, 32: 901–24.

Denis, J., Lamothe, L., & Langley, A. (2001) The dynamics of collective leadership and strategic change in pluralistic organizations. *Academy of Management Journal*, 44 (4): 809–37.

Department of Energy (2015) 10 CFR Part 430. [Docket Number EERE-2015-BT-STD-0008]. RIN: 1904-AD52. Washington, DC: United States.

Deutsch, M. (2000) Cooperation and competition. In M. Deutsch & P. T. Coleman (eds.), *The Handbook of Conflict Resolution: Theory and Practice*, 21–40. San Francisco: Jossey-Bass.

DeWinter-Schmitt, R. (2017) Addressing human rights impacts through risk management processes. Paper presented at the Workshop on Multi-stakeholder Initiatives, Occidental College, Los Angeles, CA: April 3–4.

Dewulf, A. & Bouwen, R. (2012) Issue framing in conversation for change: Discursive interaction strategies for "doing differences." *Journal of Applied Behavioral Science*, 48 (2): 168–93.

Dewulf, A., Gray, B., Putnam, L., Lewicki, R., Aarts, N., Bouwen, R., & van Woerkum, C. (2009) Disentangling approaches to framing in conflict and negotiation research: A meta-paradigmatic perspective. *Human Relations*, 62: 155–93.

Diehl, D. & McFarland, D. (2010) Toward a historical sociology of social situations. *American Journal of Sociology*, 115 (6): 1713–52.

Dienhart, J. W. & Ludescher, J. C. (2010) Sustainability, collaboration and governance: A harbinger of institutional change? *Business and Society Review*, 115 (4): 393–415.

DiMaggio, P. J. & Powell, W. W. (1983) The iron cage revisited: Institutional isomorphism and collective rationality in organizational fields. *American Sociological Review*, 48: 147–60.

Dionysiou, D. D. & Tsoukas, H. (2013) Understanding the (re)creation of routines from within: A symbolic interactionist perspective. *Academy of Management Review*, 38 (2): 181–205.

Djelic, M. L. & Quack, S. (2008) Institutions and transnationalization. In R. Greenwood, C. Oliver, K. Sahlin, & R. Suddaby (eds.), *The SAGE Handbook of Organizational Institutionalism*, 299–323. Thousand Oaks, CA: SAGE.

Doelle, M. & Sinclair, A. J. (2006) Time for a new approach to public participation in EA: Promoting cooperation and consensus for sustainability. *Environmental Impact Assessment Review*, 26 (2): 185–205.

Doh, J. P. (2003) Nongovernmental organizations, corporate strategy, and public policy: NGOs as agents of change. In J. P. Doh & H. Teegen (eds.), *Globalization and NGOs*, 1–18. Westport, CT: Praeger.

Donahue, J. D. (2010) The race: Can collaboration outrun rivalry between American business and government? *Public Administration Review*, (Special Issue): S151–2.

Dorado, S. (2005) Institutional entrepreneurship, partaking and convening. *Organization Studies*, 26 (3): 385–414.

Dorado, S. & Ventresca, M. J. (2013) Crescive entrepreneurship in complex social problems: Institutional conditions for entrepreneurial engagement. *Journal of Business Venturing*, 28 (1): 69–82.

Dovidio, J. F. & Gaertner, S. L. (1998) On the nature of contemporary prejudice: The causes, consequences, and challenges of aversive racism. In J. Eberhardt & S. T. Fiske (eds.), *Confronting Racism: The Problem and the Response*: 3–32. Thousand Oaks, CA: Sage.

Drori, G. S., Höllerer, M. A., & Walgenbach, P. (2013) The glocalization of organization and management: Issues, dimensions and themes. In G. S. Drori, M. A. Höllerer, & P. Walgenbach (eds.), *Global Themes and Local Variations in Organization and Management: Perspectives on Glocalization*, 3–24. New York: Routledge.

Dryzek, J. (2010) *Foundations and Frontiers of Deliberative Governance*. Oxford: Oxford University Press.

Dukes, E. F., Piscolish, M. A., & Stephens, B. (2000) *Reaching for Higher Ground in Conflict Resolution*. San Francisco: Jossey-Bass.

Dunn, M. B. & Jones, C. (2010) Institutional logics and institutional pluralism: The contestation of care and science logics in medical education, 1967–2005. *Administrative Science Quarterly*, 55 (1): 114–49.

Durand, R., Szostak, B., Jourdan, J. & Thornton, P. H. (2010) Institutional logics as strategic resources. In M. Lounsbury & E. Boxenbaum (eds.), *Institutional Logics in Action, Part A, Research in the Sociology of Organizations, Vol. 39A*, 165–201. Bingley, UK: Emerald Group.

Durkheim, E. 1912 (1965) *The Elementary Forms of the Religious Life*, trans. J. W. Swain. New York: Free Press.

ECOSOC (United Nations Economic & Social Council) (2016) Breaking the silos: Cross-sectoral partnerships for advancing the Sustainable Development Goals (SDGs), Dialogue 1. https://www.un.org/ecosoc/sites/www.un.org.ecosoc/files/files/en/2016doc/partnership-forum-issue-note1.pdf (accessed December 2, 2016).

Eden, C. (1989) Using cognitive mapping for strategic options development and analysis (SODA). In J. Rosenhead (ed.), *Rational Analysis in a Problematic World*, 21–42. Chichester: Wiley.

Elden, M. & Chisholm, R. F. (1993) Emerging varieties of action research: Introduction to the special issue. *Human Relations*, 46 (2): 121–42.

Elden, M. & Levin, M. (1991) Cogenerative learning: Bringing participation into action research. In W. F. Whyte (ed.), *Participatory Action Research*, 127–42. London: Sage.

Elliott, M., Gray, B., & Lewicki, R. (2003) Lessons learned about framing and reframing of intractable conflict. In R. Lewicki, B. Gray, & M. Elliott, *Making Sense of Intractable Environmental Conflict: Concepts and Cases*, 423–35. Washington, DC: Island Press.

Emerson, J. (2003) The blended value proposition: Integrating social and financial returns. *California Management Review*, 45 (4): 35–51.

Emerson, K. & Gerlak, A. K. (2014) Adaptation in collaborative governance regimes. *Environmental Management*, 54 (4), 768–81.

Emerson, K. & Nabatchi, T. (2015) *Collaborative Governance Regimes*. Washington, DC: Georgetown University Press.

Emerson, K., Nabatchi, T., & Balogh, S. (2012) An integrative framework for collaborative governance. *Journal of Public Administration Research and Theory*, 22 (1): 1–29.

Emery, F. & Emery, M. D. (1977) *A Choice of Futures*. Leiden, The Netherlands: Martinus Nijhoff.

Emery, F. & Trist, E. (1965) The causal texture of organizational environments. *Human Relations*, 18: 21–32.

Emery, M. & Purser, R. (1996) *The Search Conference: A Powerful Method for Planning Organizational Change and Community Action*. San Francisco: Jossey-Bass.

Entman, R. M. (1993) Framing: Toward clarification of a fractured paradigm. *Journal of Communication*, 43 (4): 51–8.

Esteves, A. M. & Barclay, M-A. (2011) New approaches to evaluating the performance of corporate–community partnerships: A case study from the minerals sector. *Journal of Business Ethics*, 103 (2): 189–202.

Etzioni, A. (2004) *The Common Good*. Cambridge, MA: Polity Press.

Fairclough, N. (1992) *Discourse and Social Change*. Cambridge: Polity Press.

Fals-Borda, O. and Rahman, M. A. (eds.) (1991) *Action and Knowledge: Breaking the Monopoly with Participatory Action Research*. New York: Intermediate Technology/Apex.

Fan, G. H. & Zietsma, C. (in press) Constructing a shared governance logic: The role of emotions in enabling dually embedded agency. *Academy of Management Journal*, doi:10.5465/amj.2015.0402.

Faulkner, M. & de Rond, M. (eds.) (2000) *Cooperative Strategy: Economic, Business and Organizational Issues*. New York: Oxford University Press.

Federal Energy Regulatory Commission (2004) *Handbook for Hydroelectric Project Licensing and 5 MW Exemptions from Licensing*. Washington, DC: Department of Energy.

Feiock, R. C., Lee, I. W., & Park, H. J. (2012) Administrators' and elected officials' collaboration networks: Selecting partners to reduce risk in economic development. *Public Administration Review*, 72(s1), s58–s68.

Feldman, M. S. (2000) Organizational routines as a source of continuous change. *Organization Science*, 11 (6): 611–29.

Feldman, M. S. & Pentland, B. T. (2003) Reconceptualizing organizational routines as a source of flexibility and change. *Administrative Science Quarterly*, 48: 94–118.

FEMA (2015) Private public partnerships lesson 3 summary: How partnerships enhance emergency management efforts. https://emilms.fema.gov/IS660/assets/ FEMAPrivatePublicPartnership_Lesson3Summary_pilotedits.pdf (accessed April 2, 2017).

Ferlie, E., Fitzgerald, L., Wood, M., & Hawkins, C. (2005) The non-spread of innovations: The mediating role of professionals. *Academy of Management Journal*, 48: 117–34.

Feyerherm, A. E. (1995) Changing and converging mind-sets of participants during collaborative, environmental rule making: Two negotiated regulation case studies. *Research in Corporate Social Performance and Policy*, Supplement 1: 237–57.

Field, C.B., Barros, V., & Stocker, T.F. (2012) Managing the Risks of Extreme Events and Disaster to Advance Climate Change Adoption. Special Report of the IPCC. Cambridge, UK: Cambridge University Press.

Fiol, C., Pratt, M. G., & O'Connor, E. J. (2009) Managing intractable identity conflicts. *Academy of Management Review*, 34 (1): 32–55.

Fiorino, D. J. (1999) Rethinking environmental regulation: Perspectives on law and governance. *Harvard Environmental Law Review*, 23: 1–26.

Fisher, R. & Ury, W. (1981) *Getting to Yes*. New York: Penguin.

Fisher, R., Ury, W., & Patton, B. (1991) *Getting to Yes*. New York: Penguin.

Fishkin, J. (2011) *When the People Speak*. Oxford: Oxford University Press.

Fiss, P. C. & Hirsch, P. M. (2005) The discourse of globalization: Framing and sensemaking of an emerging concept. *American Sociological Review*, 70: 29–52.

Fligstein, N. (2013) Understanding stability and change in fields. *Research in Organizational Behavior*, 33: 39–51.

Fligstein, N. & McAdam, D. (2011) Toward a general theory of strategic action fields. *Sociological Theory*, 29: 1–26.

Fligstein, N. & McAdam, D. (2012) *A Theory of Fields*. New York: Oxford University Press.

Foot, K. (2016) *Collaborating against Human Trafficking: Cross-sector Challenges and Practices*. Lanhan, MA: Rowman & Littlefield.

Foster, P. (2017) The boreal forest "agreement" was an eco-radical shakedown. Thankfully, it's finally dead. *Financial Post*, January 31. http://business.financialpost. com/fp-comment/peter-foster-the-boreal-forest-agreement-was-just-an-eco-radical-shakedown-now-thankfully-its-finally-being-killed (accessed July 27, 2017).

Foucault, M. (1979) *Discipline and Punish: The Birth of the Prison*. Harmondsworth: Penguin Books.

Freeman, E. (1984) *Strategic Management: A Stakeholder Approach*. Cambridge: Cambridge University Press.

Freire, P. (1971) *Pedagogy of the Oppressed*. New York: Herder & Herder.

Friedland, R. & Alford, R. (1991) Bringing society back in: Symbols, practices and institutional contradictions. In W. W. Powell & P. J. DiMaggio (eds.), *The New*

Institutionalism in Organizational Analysis, 232–63. Chicago: University of Chicago Press.

Furnari, S. (2014) Interstitial spaces: Microinteraction settings and the genesis of new practices between institutional fields. *Academy of Management Review*, 39 (4): 439–62.

Galvin, T. (2002) Examining institutional change: Evidence from the founding dynamics of U.S. health care interest associations. *Academy of Management Journal*, 45 (4): 673–96.

Gamson, W. A. (1992) The social psychology of collective action. In A. D. Morris & A. C. Mueller (eds.), *Frontiers in Social Movement Theory*, 53–76. New Haven, CT: Yale University Press.

Gaventa, J. (1980) *Power and Powerlessness: Quiescence and Rebellion in an Appalachian Valley*. Urbana: University of Illinois Press.

Gaworecki, M. (2016) The inside story of how Great Bear Rainforest went from a "War in the Woods" to an unprecedented environmental and human rights agreement. Feb. 22. https://news.mongabay.com/2016/02/the-inside-story-of-how-great-bear-rainforest-went-from-a-war-in-the-woods-to-an-unprecedented-environmental-and-human-rights-agreement/ (accessed July 28, 2017).

Gazley, B. (2008) Beyond the contract: The scope and nature of informal government-nonprofit partnerships. *Public Administration Review*, 68 (1): 141–51.

Geddes, M. (2008) Inter-organizational relationships in local and regional development partnerships. In S. Cropper, M. Ebers, C. Huxham, & P. S. Ring (eds.), *The Oxford Handbook of Inter-organizational Relations*, 203–30. Oxford: Oxford University Press.

Genskow, K. D. (2009) Catalyzing collaboration: Wisconsin's agency-initiated basin partnerships. *Environmental Management*, 43 (3): 411–24.

Gibson, C. C., Ostrom, E., & Ahn, T. K. (2000) The concept of scale and the human dimensions of global change: A survey. *Ecological Economics*, 32: 217–39.

Giddens, A. (1984) *The Constitution of Society*. Berkeley, CA: University of California.

Giddens, A. (1998) *The Third Way: The Renewal of Social Democracy*. Cambridge, UK: Polity.

Gieryn, T. F. (2000) A space for place in sociology, *Annual Review of Sociology*, 26: 463–96.

Glasbergen, P. (2007) Setting the scene: The partnership paradigm in the making. In P. Glasbergen, F. Biermann, & A. P. J. Mol (eds.), *Partnerships, Governance and Sustainable Development*, 1–25. Cheltenham, UK: Edward Elgar.

Glasbergen, P., Biermann, F., & Mol, A. P. J. (2007) *Partnerships, Governance and Sustainable Development*. Cheltenham, UK: Edward Elgar.

Globe & Mail (2013) AFN chiefs pan Ottawa's education plan for First Nations children, *Globe & Mail*, Oct. 11. https://www.theglobeandmail.com/news/politics/afn-chiefs-pan-ottawas-education-plan-for-first-nations-children/article14849582/ (accessed July 28, 2017).

Goffman, E. (1967) *Interaction Ritual: Essays on Face-to-Face Behavior*. Garden City, NY: Doubleday Anchor.

Goffman, E. (1974) *Frame Analysis: An Essay on the Organization of Experience*. London: Harper & Row.

Göhler, G. (2009) "Power to" and "power over." In S. R. Clegg & M. Haugaard (eds.), *The Sage Handbook of Power*, 27–40. London: Sage.

Gondo, M. B. & Amis, J. M. (2013) Variations in practice adoption: The roles of conscious reflection and discourse. *Academy of Management Review*, 38: 229–47.

Goodrick, E. & Salancik, G. R. (1996) Organizational discretion in responding to institutional practices: Hospitals and cesarean births. *Administrative Science Quarterly*, 41 (1): 1–28.

Googins, B. K. & Rochlin, S. A. (2000) Creating the partnership society: Understanding the rhetoric and reality of cross-sectoral partnerships. *Business and Society Review*, 105 (1): 127–44.

Gray, B. (1989) *Collaborating: Finding Common Ground for Multiparty Problems*. San Francisco: Jossey-Bass.

Gray, B. (1995) Obstacles to success in educational collaborations. In M. Wang and L. Rigby (eds.), *School/Community Connections: Exploring Issues for Research and Practice*, 71–100. San Francisco: Jossey-Bass.

Gray, B. (1996) Cross-sectoral partners: Collaborative alliances among business, government and communities. In C. Huxham (ed.), *In Search of Collaborative Advantage*, 58–99. London: Sage.

Gray, B. (2000) Assessing interorganizational collaboration: Multiple conceptions and multiple methods. In D. Faulkner and M. De Rond (eds.), *Cooperative Strategy: Economic, Business, and Organizational Issues*, 243–60. Oxford: Oxford University Press.

Gray, B. (2003) Freeze framing: The timeless dialogue of intractability surrounding Voyageurs National Park. In R. Lewicki, B. Gray, & M. Elliott (eds.), *Making Sense of Intractable Environmental Conflict: Concepts and Cases*, 91–126. Washington, DC: Island Press.

Gray, B. (2004) Strong opposition: Frame-based resistance to collaboration. *Journal of Community and Applied Psychology*, 14 (3): 166–76.

Gray, B. (2005) Framing in mediation and mediation as framing. In M. S. Herrman (ed.), *Handbook of Mediation: Bridging Theory, Research and Practice*, 193–216. Oxford: Blackwell.

Gray, B. (2007) Frame-based interventions for promoting understanding in multiparty conflicts. In T. Gössling, L. Oerlemans, & R. Jansen (eds.), *Inside Networks*, 223–50. Cheltenham, UK: Edward Elgar.

Gray, B. (2008) Interventions for fostering collaboration. In S. Cropper, M. Ebers, C. Huxham, & P. Smith-Ring (eds.), *Handbook of Inter-organizational Relations*, 664–90. New York: Oxford University Press.

Gray, B. & Clyman, D. (2003) Difficulties in fostering cooperation in multiparty negotiations: Cognitive, procedural, structural and social. In M. West, D. Tjosvold, and K. G. Smith (eds.), *International Handbook of Organizational Teamwork and Cooperative Working*, 401–22. Chichester: Wiley.

Gray, B. & Hay, T. M. (1986) Political limits to interorganizational consensus and change, *Journal of Applied Behavioral Science*, 22 (2), 95–112.

Gray, B. & Kish-Gephart, J. (2013) Encountering social class differences at work: How "class work" perpetuates inequality. *Academy of Management Review*, 39 (4): 670–99.

Gray, B. & Purdy, J. (2014) Conflict in cross-sector partnerships. In M. Seitanidi & A. Crane (eds.), *Social Partnerships and Responsible Business*, 205–25. Oxford, UK: Taylor & Francis.

Gray, B. & Schruijer, S. (2010) Integrating multiple voices: Working with collusion in multiparty collaborations. In C. Staeyert & B. Van Loy, *Relational Practices: Participative Organizing*, 121–35. Bingley, UK: Emerald.

Gray, B. & Stites, J. (2013) Advancing sustainable business through multi-sector "collaborative" partnerships. Systematic review prepared for Network for Sustainable Business, Western Ontario University, November 1, 2013, www.nbs.net

Gray, B. & Wondolleck, J. (2013) Environmental negotiations: Past, present and future prospects. In M. Olekans & W. Adair (eds.), *Handbook of Research in Negotiations*, 445–72. Cheltenham, UK: Edward Elgar.

Gray, B. & Yan, A. (1997) Formation and evolution of international joint ventures: Examples from U.S.–Chinese partnerships. In P. Beamish & J. P. Killing (eds.), *Cooperative Strategies: Asian Pacific Perspectives*, 57–88. San Francisco: New Lexington Press.

Gray, B., Coleman, P., & Putnam, L. (2007) Intractable conflicts: New perspectives on the causes and conditions for change. *American Behavioral Scientist,* 50 (10), 1–15.

Gray, B., Purdy, J. M. & Ansari, S. (2015) From interactions to institutions: Microprocesses of framing and mechanisms for the structuring of institutional fields. *Academy of Management Review*, 40 (1): 115–43.

Green, S. E. (2004) A rhetorical theory of diffusion. *Academy of Management Review*, 29: 653–69.

Greenwood, R. & Hinings, R. (1996) Understanding radical organizational change: Bringing together the old and the new institutionalism. *Academy of Management Review*, 21 (4): 1022–54.

Greenwood, R. & Suddaby, R. (2006) Institutional entrepreneurship in mature fields: The big five accounting firms. *Academy of Management Journal*, 49 (1): 27–48.

Greenwood, R., Raynard, M., Kodeih, F., Micelotta, E. R., & Lounsbury, M. (2011) Institutional complexity and organizational responses. *The Academy of Management Annals*, 5 (1): 317–71.

Greenwood, R., Suddaby, R., & Hinings, C. R. (2002) Theorizing change: The role of professional associations in the transformations of institutionalized fields. *Academy of Management Journal*, 45 (1): 58–60.

Gricar, B. G. & Brown, L. D. (1981) Conflict, power and organization in a changing community. *Human Relations*, 34: 877–93.

Gulati, R. (1995) Does familiarity breed trust? The implications of repeated ties for contractual choice in alliances. *Academy of Management Journal*, 38 (1): 85–112.

Gulati, R. & Nickerson, J. A. (2008) Interorganizational trust, governance choice, and exchange performance. *Organization Science*, 19 (5): 688–708.

Gunderson, L. H. & Holling, C. S. (2002) *Panarchy: Understanding Transformation in Human and Natural Systems*. Washington, DC: Island Press.

Gunderson, L. H., Allen, C. R., & Holling, C. S. (2009) *Foundations of Ecological Resilience*. Washington, DC: Island Press.

Gutman, A. & Thompson, D. (2002) Deliberative democracy beyond process. *Journal of Political Philosophy*, 10 (2): 153–74.

Hajer, M. (2003) A frame in the fields: Policymaking and the reinvention of politics. In M. A. Hajer & H. Wagenaar (eds.), *Deliberative Policy Analysis: Understanding Governance in the Network Society*, 88–112. Cambridge: Cambridge University Press.

Hall, P. D. (2006) The new globalism. In S. Batliwada & L. D. Brown (eds.), *Transnational Civil Society: An Introduction*, 16–29. Bloomfield, CT: Kumarian Press.

Hall, J. & Vredenburg, H. (2003) The challenges of innovating for sustainable development. *MIT Sloan Management Review*, 45 (1): 61–8.

Hallett, T. (2003) Symbolic power and organizational culture. *Sociological Theory*, 21 (2), 128–49.

Hallett, T. & Ventresca, M. J. (2006) Inhabited institutions: Social interactions and organizational forms in Gouldner's *Patterns of Industrial Bureaucracy*. *Theory & Society*, 35: 213–36.

Hamel, G. & Prahalad, C. K. (1994) *Competing for the Future*. Boston: Harvard Business School Press.

Hanemann, M. & Dyckman, C. (2009) The San Francisco Bay-Delta: a failure in decision making capacity. *Environmental Science and Policy*, 12 (6): 710–25.

Hanke, R., Rosenberg, A., & Gray, B. (2003) The story of Drake Chemical: A burning issue. In R. Lewicki, B. Gray, & M. Elliott (eds.), *Making Sense of Intractable Environmental Conflict: Concepts and Cases*, 275–302. Washington, DC: Island Press.

Hardy, C. & Maguire, S. (2010) Discourse, field-configuring events and change in organizations and institutions: DDT and the Stockholm convention. *Academy of Management Journal*, 53 (6): 1234–40.

Hardy, C. & Phillips, N. (1998) Strategies of engagement: Lessons from the critical examination of collaboration and conflict in an interorganizational domain. *Organization Science*, 9 (2): 217–30.

Hardy, C., Lawrence, T., & Grant, D. (2005) Discourse and collaboration: The role of conversations and collective identity. *Academy of Management Review*, 30 (1): 58–77.

Harinck, F. & Van Kleef, G. A. (2012) Be hard on the interests and soft on the values: Conflict issue moderates the effects of anger in negotiations. *British Journal of Social Psychology*, 51: 741–52.

Harrison, D. & Easton, G. (2002) Collective action in the face of international environmental regulation. *Business Strategy and the Environment*, 11: 143–53.

Hart, S. (2005) *Capitalism at the Crossroads: The Unlimited Business Opportunities in Solving the World's Most Difficult Problems*. Upper Saddle River, NJ: Wharton School Publishing.

Hart, S. & Sharma, S. (2004) Engaging fringe stakeholders for competitive imagination. *Academy of Management Executive*, 8 (1): 7–18.

Hartman, C. L. & Stafford, E. R. (2006) Chilling with Greenpeace, from the inside out. *Stanford Social Innovation Review*, 4 (2): 54–9.

Hatfield, E., Cacioppo, J. L., & Rapson, R. L. (1993) Emotional contagion. *Current Directions in Psychological Sciences*, 2: 96–9.

Haugh, H. M. & Talwar, A. (2010) How do corporations embed sustainability across the organization. *Academy of Management Learning and Education*, 9 (3): 384–96.

Hay, T. & Gray, B. (1985) The National Coal Policy Project: An interactive approach to corporate social responsiveness. In L. E. Preston (ed.), *Research in Corporate Social Performance and Policy, Vol. 7*, 191–212. Greenwich, CT: JAI Press.

Heath, R. & Isbell, M. (2015) Broadening organizational communication curricula: Collaboration as key to 21st-century organizing. *Management Communication Quarterly*, 29 (2): 309–14.

Heikkila, T. & Gerlak, A. K. (2015) Case illustration: The Everglades Restoration Task Force. In K. Emerson & T. Nabatchi, (eds.), *Collaborative Governance Regimes*, 73–80. Washington, DC: Georgetown University Press.

Held, D. (2007) Reframing global governance: Apocalypse soon or reform? In D. Held & A. McGrew (eds.), *Globalization Theory: Approaches and Controversies*, 240–60. Cambridge, UK: Polity.

Helms, W. S. & Oliver, C. (2015) Radical settlements to conflict: Conflict management and its implications for institutional change. *Journal of Management & Organization*, 21 (4): 471–94.

Hendry, J. R. (2006) Taking aim at business: What factors lead environmental non-governmental organizations to target particular businesses? *Business & Society*, 45 (1): 47–86.

Herman, M. (ed.) (2005) *Mediation from Beginning to End*. New York: Blackwell Publishers.

Hibbert, P., Siedlok, F., & Beech, N. (2016) The role of interpretation in learning practices in the context of collaboration. *Academy of Management Learning and Education*, 15 (1): 26–44.

Hicklin, A., O'Toole Jr., L. J., Meier, K. J., & Robinson, S. E. (2009) Calming the storms: Collaborative public management, Hurricanes Katrina and Rita, and disaster response. In R. O'Leary and L. B. Bingham (eds.), *The Collaborative Public Manager: New Ideas for the Twenty-first Century*, 95–114. Washington, DC: Georgetown University Press.

Himmelman, A. T. (1995) On the theory and practice of transformational collaboration: From social service to social justice. In C. Huxham (ed.), *Creating Collaborative Advantage*, 19–43. London: Sage.

Hochschild, A. R. 2016. *Strangers in Their Own Land: Anger and Mourning on the American Right*. New York: The New Press.

Hodge, G. A. & Greve, C. (2007) Public–private partnerships: An international performance review. *Public Administration Review*, 67 (3): 545–58.

Hoffman, A. J. (1999) Institutional evolution and change: Environmentalism and the US chemical industry. *Academy of Management Journal*, 42: 351–71.

Holzer, B. (2008) Turning stakeseekers into stakeholders: A political coalition perspective on the politics of stakeholder influence. *Business & Society*, 47(1): 50–67.

Hopper, T. (2016) The Great Bear Rainforest, B.C.'s new, giant protected area is a truce between loggers, greens. *National Post*. February 2. http://nationalpost.com/news/canada/the-great-bear-rainforest-b-c-s-new-giant-protected-area-is-a-truce-between-loggers-greens (accessed October 24, 2017).

Human, S. E. & Provan, K. (2000) Legitimacy building in the evolution of small-firm multilateral networks: A comparative study of success and demise. *Administrative Science Quarterly*, 45 (2): 327–65.

Hunter, F. (2016) Final agreement reached to protect B.C.'s Great Bear Rainforest. *The Globe and Mail*. February 1. http://www.theglobeandmail.com/news/british-columbia/final-agreement-reached-to-protect-bcs-great-bear-rainforest/article28475362/ (accessed July 29, 2017).

Huxham, C. (1996) Collaboration and collaborative advantage. In C. Huxham (ed.), *Creating Collaborative Advantage*, 1–19. London: Sage.

Huxham, C. & Vangen, S. (2000a) Ambiguity, complexity and dynamics in the membership of collaboration. *Human Relations*, 53 (6): 771–806.

Huxham, C. & Vangen, S. (2000b) Leadership in the shaping and implementation of collaboration agendas: How things happen in a (not quite) joined up world. *Academy of Management Journal*, 43 (6): 1159–75.

Huxham, C. & Vangen, S. (2004) Doing things collaboratively: Realizing the advantage or succumbing to inertia. *Organizational Dynamics*, 33 (2): 190–201.

Huxham, C. & Vangen, S. (2005) *Managing to Collaborate: The Theory and Practice of Collaborative Advantage*. London: Routledge.

ICLEI (2012) Local sustainability 2012: Taking stock and moving forward. *Global Review, ICLEI Global Report*. Bonn: ICLEI-Local Governments for Sustainability.

Innes, J. & Booher, D. (2003) Collaborative policymaking: Governance through dialogue. In M. A. Hajer & H. Wagenaar (eds.), *Deliberative Policy Analysis: Understanding Governance in the Network Society*. Cambridge, UK: Cambridge University Press: 33–59.

Innes, J. & Booher, D. E. (2010) *Planning with Complexity: An Introduction to Collaborative Rationality for Public Policy*. Abingdon, UK: Routledge.

Isbell, M. (2012) The role of boundary spanners as the interorganizational link in nonprofit collaborating. *Management Communication Quarterly*, 26: 159–65.

Jamali, D., Yianni, M., & Abdallah, H. (2011) Strategic partnerships, social capital and innovation: Accounting for social alliance innovation. *Business Ethics*, 20 (4): 375–91.

Jameson, K. P. (2011) The indigenous movement in Ecuador: The struggle for a plurinational state. *Latin American Perspectives*, 38 (1): 63–73.

Jaumont, F. (2016) *Unequal Partners: American Foundations and Higher Education Development in Africa*. New York: Palgrave Macmillan.

Juergensmeyer, M. (2003) *Terror in the Mind of God: The Global Rise of Religious Violence*, 3rd. ed. Berkeley: University of California Press.

Kagan, S. L. (1991) *United We Stand: Collaboration for Child Care and Early Education Services*. New York: Teachers College Press.

Kaghan, W. N. & Purdy, J. M. (2012) Capitalism, creative destruction, and the common good. Paper presented at the 2012 ESSEC Business School conference on The Role of Business in Society and the Pursuit of the Common Good. Cergy, France.

Kania, J. & Kramer, M. (2011) Collective impact. *Stanford Social Innovation Review*, Winter, 9 (1): 36–41.

Kanter, R. M. (1977) *Men and Women of the Corporation*. New York: Basic Books.

Kaplan, S. (2008) Framing contests: Strategy making under uncertainty. *Organization Science*, 19: 729–52.

Kaplan, S. & Fry, R. (2006) Whole system engagement through collaborative technology. In B. B. Bunker & B. T. Albans (eds.), *The Handbook of Large Group Methods: Creating Systemic Change in Organizations and Communities*, 66–77. San Francisco: Jossey-Bass.

Katz, L. V. (1993) Compulsory alternative dispute resolution and voluntarism: Two-headed monster or two sides of the coin? *Journal of Dispute Resolution*, 1: 1–55.

Kaufman, S. & Gray, B. (2003) Using retrospective and prospective frame elicitation to evaluate environmental disputes. In R. O'Leary & L. Bingham (eds.), *The Promise and*

Performance of Environmental Conflict Resolution, 129–47. Washington, DC: Resources for the Future Press.

KenCairn, B. (1997) The partnership phenomenon. *Chronicle of Community*, 3: 37–41.

Khagram, S. (2006) Future architectures of global governance: A transnational perspective/prospective. *Global Governance*, 12 (2): 97–117.

Khagram, S. (2017) Powerpoint presentation. Workshop on Multi-stakeholder Initiatives. Occidental College, Los Angeles, April 3–4.

Khagram, S. & Alvord, S. (2008) The rise of civic transnationalism. In S. Batilawa & L. D. Brown (eds.), *Transnational Civil Society: An Introduction*, 65–81. Bloomfield, CT: Kumarian Press.

King, B. C. (2008a) A political mediation model of corporate response so social movement activism. *Administrative Science Quarterly*, 53: 395–421.

King, B. C. (2008b) A social movement perspective of stakeholder collective action and influence. *Business and Society*, 47: 21–49.

Kolk, A. (2014) Partnerships as a panacea for addressing global problems: On rationale, context, impact and limitations. In M. M. Seitanidi & A. Crane, *Social Partnerships for Responsible Business: A Research Handbook*, 15–43. London: Routledge.

Kolk, A. & Lenfant, F. (2012) NGO-business collaboration in a conflict setting: Partnership activities in the Democratic Republic of Congo. *Business & Society*, 51 (3): 478–511.

Kolk, A. & Lenfant, F. (2015) Cross-sector collaboration, institutional gaps and fragility: The role of social innovation partnerships in a conflict-affected region. *Journal of Public Policy and Marketing*, 34 (2): 287–303.

Kolk, A., van Dolen, W., & Vock, M. (2010) Trickle effects of cross-sector social partnerships. *Journal of Business Ethics*, 94: 123–37.

Koot, W., Leisink, P., & Verweel, P. (2003) *Organizational Relationships in the Networking Age: The Dynamics of Identity Formation and Bonding*. Cheltenham: Edward Elgar.

Koppenjan, J. & Klijn, E. (2004) *Managing Uncertainties in Networks*. London: Routledge.

Koschmann, M. A., Kuhn, T. R., & Pfarrer, M. D. (2012) A communicative framework of value in cross-sector partnerships. *Academy of Management Review*, 37: 332–54.

Kourula, A. & Halme, M. (2008) Types of corporate responsibility and engagement with NGOs: An exploration of business and societal outcomes. *Corporate Governance*, 8 (4): 557–70.

Kraatz, M. S. & Block, E. S. (2008) Organizational implications of institutional pluralism. In R. Greenwood, C. Oliver, K. Sahlin, & R. Suddaby (eds.), *The Sage Handbook of Organizational Institutionalism*, 243–75. London: Sage.

Kramer, M. & Kania, J. (2006) Changing the game: Leading corporations switch from defense to offense in solving global problems. *Stanford Social Innovation Review*, 4(1): 20–7.

Krater, J. & Rose, M. (2009) Development of Iceland's geothermal energy potential for aluminium production—a critical analysis. In K. Abrahamsky (ed.), *Sparking a Worldwide Energy Revolution: Social Struggles in the Transition to a Post-Petrol World*, 311–25. Edinburgh: AK Press.

Kreiner, G., Hollensbe, E. C., & Sheep, M. L. (2006) Where is the "Me" Among the "We"? Identity Work and the Search for Optimal Balance. *Academy of Management Journal*, 49(5): 1031–57.

Kriz, M. (1993) Dueling over dams. *National Journal, 25* (December 11): 2935–7.

Laasonen, S., Fougère, M., & Kourula, A. (2012) Dominant articulations in academic business and society discourse on NGO–business relations: A critical assessment. *Journal of Business Ethics*, 109: 521–45.

Labianca, G., Brass, D., & Gray, B. (1998) Social networks and perceptions of intergroup conflict: The role of negative relationships and third parties. *Academy of Management Journal*, 41 (1): 55–67.

Lacy, P., Cooper, T., Hayward, R., & Neuberger, L. (2010) *A New Era of Sustainability (UN Global Compact-Accenture CEO Study 2010, Vol. 57)*. Retrieved from http://www.un globalcompact.org/docs/news_events/8.1/UNGC_Accenture_CEO_Study_2010.pdf (accessed on February 20, 2017).

LaFrance, J. & Lehmann, M. (2005) Corporate awakening—Why (some) corporations embrace public-private partnerships. *Business Strategy and the Environment*, 14 (4): 216–29.

Lawrence, T. B. (2008) Power, institutions and organizations. In R. Greenwood, C. Oliver, K. Sahlin, & R. Suddaby (eds.), *The Sage Handbook of Organizational Institutionalism*, 170–97. London: Sage.

Lawrence, T. B. & Suddaby, R. (2006) Institutions and institutional work. In S. R. Clegg, C. Hardy, T. B. Lawrence, & W. R. Nord (eds.), *Sage Handbook of Organization Studies*, 2nd ed., 215–54. London: Sage.

Lawrence, T. B., Winn, M. I., & Jennings, P. D. (2001) The temporal dynamics of institutionalization. *Academy of Management Review*, 29: 624–44.

Lawrence, T. B., Hardy, C., & Phillips, N. (2002) Institutional effects of interorganizational collaboration: The emergence of proto-institutions. *Academy of Management Journal*, 45: 281–90.

Laws, D. (1999) Representation of stakeholding interests. In L. Susskind, S. MacKearnan, and J. Thomas-Larmer (eds.), *The Consensus Building Handbook: A Comprehensive Guide to Reaching Agreement*, 241–85. Thousand Oaks, CA: Sage.

Lax, D. & Sebenius, J. (1986) *The Manager as Negotiator: Bargaining for Cooperation and Competitive Gain*. New York: Free Press.

Layzer, J. A. (2008) *Natural Experiments: Ecosystem-based Management and the Environment*. Cambridge, MA: MIT Press.

LeBaron, M. (2003) *Bridging Cultural Conflict*. San Francisco: Jossey-Bass.

LeBaron, M. & Carstarphan, N. (1997) Negotiating intractable conflict: The common ground dialogue process and abortion. *Negotiation Journal,* 13 (4): 341–63.

Lee, L. (2011) Business-community partnerships: understanding the nature of partnership. *Corporate Governance*, 11 (1): 29–40.

Leicht, K. T. & Fitzgerald, S. T. (2007) *Postindustrial Peasants: The Illusion of Middle Class Prosperity*. New York: Worth.

Letter from Stratus Consulting to Mesá Comité (2003).

Levy, D. & Scully, M. (2007) The institutional entrepreneur as modern prince: The strategic face of power in contested fields. *Organization Studies*, 28 (7): 1667–98.

Lewicki, R., Gray, B., & Elliott, M. (eds.) (2003) *Making Sense of Intractable Environmental Conflict: Concepts and Cases*. Washington: Island Press.

Lewicki, R., McAllister, D. J., & Bies, R. J. (1998) Trust and distrust: New relationships and realities. *Academy of Management Review*, 23 (3): 438–58.

Lewin, K. (1951) *Field Theory in Social Science: Selected Theoretical Papers*. New York: Harper.

Lewis, L., Isbell, M. G., & Koschmann, M. (2010) Collaborative tensions: Practitioners' experiences in interorganizational relationships. *Communication Monographs*, 77 (4): 460–79.

Liu, S. S. & Ngo, H. (2005) An action pattern model of inter-firm cooperation. *Journal of Management Studies*, 42 (6): 1123–53.

London, T. & Hart, S. L. (2004) Reinventing strategies for emerging markets: beyond the transnational model. *Journal of International Business Studies*, 35 (5): 350–70.

London, T. & Rondinelli, D. (2003) Partnerships for learning: Managing tensions in nonprofit organizations' alliances with corporations. *Stanford Innovation Review*, 1 (3): 28–35.

Lotia, N. & Hardy, C. (2008) Critical perspectives on collaboration. In S. Cropper, M. Ebers, C. Huxham, & P. Smith Ring (eds.), *The Oxford Handbook of Interorganizational Relations*, 366–89. Oxford: Oxford University Press.

Lounsbury, M., Ventresca, M., & Hirsch, P. 2003. Social movements, field frames and industry emergence: A cultural-political perspective on US recycling. *Socio-Economic Review*, 1: 71–104.

Loza, J. (2004) Business–community partnerships: The case for community organization capacity building. *Journal of Business Ethics*, 53 (3): 297–311.

Lu, C., Michaud, C. M., Gakidou, E., Khabn, K., & Murray, C. J. (2006) Effect of the global alliance for vaccines and immunisation on diphtheria, tetanus, and pertussis vaccine coverage: An independent assessment. *The Lancet*, 368: 1088–95.

Lukensmeyer, C. J. & Brigham, S. (2005) Taking democracy to scale: Large scale interventions—for citizens. *Journal of Applied Behavioral Science*, 41 (1): 47–60.

MSI Database (2017) www.msi-database.org.

Maasen, P. & Cloete, N. (2006) Global reform trends in higher education. In N. Cloete, P. Maasen, R. Fehnel, T. Moja, T. Gibbon, & H. Perold, (eds.), *Transformation in Higher Education—Global Pressures and Local Realities. Higher Education Dynamics*, Vol. 10, 7–33. Dordrecht: Springer.

Maguire, S., Hardy, C., & Lawrence, T. (2004) Institutional entrepreneurship in emerging fields: HIV/AIDS treatment advocacy in Canada. *Academy of Management Journal*, 47 (5): 657–79.

Maitlis, S. (2005) The social processes of organizational sensemaking. *Academy of Management Journal*, 48, 21–49.

Maitlis, S. & Sonenshein, S. (2010) Sensemaking in crisis and change: Inspiration and insights from Weick (1988). *Journal of Management Studies*, 47 (3): 551–80.

Manring, S. L. (2007) Creating and managing interorganizational learning networks to achieve sustainable ecosystem management. *Organization & Environment*, 20 (3): 325–46.

Margerum, R. D. (2007) Overcoming locally based collaboration constraints. *Society & Natural Resources*, 20 (2): 135–52.

Margerum, R. D. (2016) Theoretical perspectives on the challenges of collaboration. In R. D. Margerum & C. J. Robinson, *The Challenges of Collaboration in the Environmental Governance: Barriers and Responses*, 27–53. Cheltenham, UK: Edward Elgar.

Marquis, C. & Lounsbury, M. (2007) Vive la résistance: Competing logics and the consolidation of U.S. community banking. *Academy of Management Journal*, 50 (4): 799–820.

Marti, I. & Fernández, P. (2013) The institutional work of oppression and resistance. *Organization Studies*, 34 (8): 1195–223.

McAdam, D. (1996) Conceptual problems, future directions. In D. McAdam, J. D. McCarthy, & M. N. Zald (eds.), *Comparative Perspectives on Social Movements: Political Opportunities, Mobilizing Structures, and Cultural Framings*, 27–40. Cambridge: Cambridge University Press.

McAdam, D., Tarrow, S., & Tilly, C. (2001) *Dynamics of Contention*. Cambridge: Cambridge University Press.

McAllister, I. (2016) Unfiltered: The Great Bear Rainforest Agreement. Posted February 3. http://pacificwild.org/news-and-resources/great-bear-blog/unfiltered-the-great-bear-rainforest-agreement (accessed July 29, 2017).

McCaffrey, D., Faerman, S. R., & Hart, D. W. (1995) The appeal and difficulties of participative systems. *Organization Science*, 6 (6): 603–27.

McCann, C. (2006) Dammed if you do, damned if you don't: FERC's tribal consultation requirement and the hydropower re-licensing at Post Falls Dam. *Gonzaga Law Review*, 41 (3): 411–57.

McCann, J. & Selsky, J. W. (2014) *Mastering Turbulence: The Essential Capabilities of Agile and Resilient Individuals, Teams and Organizations*. San Francisco: Jossey-Bass.

McCann, J. E. (1983) Design guidelines for social problem-solving interventions. *Journal of Applied Behavioral Science*, 19: 177–89.

McCarthy, J. & Zald, M. (1977) Resource mobilization and social movements: A partial theory. *American Journal of Sociology*, 82: 1212–40.

McDonnell, S., Bryant, C., Harris, J., Campbell, M. K., Lobb, A., Hannon, P.A., Cross, J. L., & Gray, B. (2009) The private partners of public health: Public–private alliances for public good. *Preventing Chronic Disease*, 6 (2): 1–8. http://www.cdc.gov/pcd/issues/2009/apr/08_0213.htm (accessed July 29, 2017).

McGuire, M. (2006) Collaborative public management: Assessing what we know and how we know it. *Public Administration Review*, 66(S1): 33–43.

McHugh, L. & Stewart, I. (2012) *The Self and Perspective Taking: Contributions and Applications from Modern Behavioral Science*. Oakland, CA: New Harbinger Publications.

McKinney, M. & Field, P. (2008) Evaluating community-based collaboration on federal lands and resources. *Society and Natural Resources*, 21 (5): 419–29.

McPherson, C. A. & Sauder, M. (2013) Logics in action: Managing institutional complexity in a drug court. *Administrative Science Quarterly*, 58: 165–94.

McSheffrey, E. (2016) Thunder in the air. *National Observer*. Published February 25. http://www.nationalobserver.com/2016/02/25/canadas-coastal-indigenous-people-gain-power-through-great-bear-rainforest-agreement (accessed July 29, 2017).

Mervis, J. (1999) Minority postdocs are rare, independent breed. *Science*, 285 (5433): 1529.

Meyer, J. W. & Rowan, B. (1977) Institutionalized organizations: Formal structure as myth and ceremony. *American Journal of Sociology*, 83 (2): 340–63.

Meyer, R. E. & Höllerer, M. A. (2010) Meaning structures in a contested issue field: A topographic map of shareholder value in Austria. *Academy of Management Journal*, 53 (6): 1241–62.

Michaels, S. (2009) Matching knowledge brokering strategies to environmental policy problems and settings. *Environmental Science & Policy*, 12 (7): 994–1011.

Middleton, B. R. (2013) Just another hoop to jump through? Using environmental laws and processes to protect indigenous rights. *Environmental Management*, 52 (5): 1057–70.

Millar, C. C. J. M., Choi, C. J., & Chen, S. (2004) Global strategic partnerships between MNEs and NGOs: Drivers of change and ethical issues. *Business and Society Review*, 109 (4): 395–414.

Miller, C. & Ahmad, Y. (2000) Collaboration and partnership: An effective response to complexity and fragmentation or solution built on sand? *International Journal of Sociology and Social Policy*, 20 (5/6): 1–38.

Milward, B., Provan, K. G., Fish, A., Isett, K. R., & Huang, K. (2009) Governance and collaboration: An evolutionary study of two mental health networks. *Journal of Public Administration Research and Theory*, 20: 125–40.

Montoya, L. A., Montoya, I., & González, O. S. (2015) Lessons from collaborative governance and sociobiology theories for reinforcing sustained cooperation: A government food security case study. *Public Health*, 129 (7): 916–31.

Moore, C. W. (1986) *The Mediation Process: Practical Strategies for Resolving Conflict,* 1st. ed. San Francisco: Jossey-Bass.

Moore, C. W. (2014) *The Mediation Process: Practical Strategies for Resolving Conflict,* 4th ed. San Francisco: Jossey-Bass.

Moore, C. W., Long, G., & Palmer, P. (1999) Visioning. In L. Susskind, S. MacKearnan, & J. Thomas-Larmer (eds.), *The Consensus Building Handbook*, 557–90. Thousand Oaks, CA: Sage.

Moore, E. A. and Koontz, T. M. (2003) A typology of collaborative watershed planning groups: Citizen-based, agency-based and mixed partnerships. *Society and Natural Resources*, 16 (5): 451–60.

Morrill, C. & Owen-Smith, J. (1998) Institutional change through interstitial emergence: The growth of alternative dispute resolution in American law 1965–1995. Unpublished article.

Morrill, C. & Owen-Smith, J. (2002) The emergence of environmental conflict resolution: Subversive stories and the construction of collective action frames and organizational fields. In M. Ventresca & A. Hoffman (eds.), *Organizations, Policy, and the Natural Environment: Institutional and Strategic Perspectives*, 90–118. Stanford, CA: Stanford University Press.

Morris, J. C. & Miller-Stevens, K. (2016) *Advancing Collaboration Theory: Models, Typology and Evidence*. Oxford: Routledge.

Murphy, M. & Arenas, D. (2010) Through indigenous lenses: Cross-sector collaborations with fringe stakeholders. *Journal of Business Ethics*, 94: 103–21.

Murray, F. (2010) The oncomouse that roared: Hybrid exchange strategies as a source of productive tension at the boundary of overlapping institutions. *American Journal of Sociology*, 116: 341–88.

Myles, R. (2012) Greenpeace exits Canada's Boreal Forest Agreement citing breaches. *Digital Journal*, December 7. http://www.digitaljournal.com/article/338562 (accessed July 29, 2017).

Nalinakumari, B. & MacLean, R. (2005) NGOs: A primer on the evolution of the organizations that are setting the next generation of "regulations". *Environmental Quality Management*, 14 (4): 1–21.

Narayan, D., Patel, R., Schrafft, K., Rademacher, A., & Koch-Schulte, S. (2000) *Voices of the Poor: Can Anyone Hear Us?* Oxford: Oxford University Press.

Nathan, M. L. & Mitroff, I. (1991) The use of negotiated order theory for the analysis of an interorganizational field. *Journal of Applied Behavioral Science*, 27 (2): 163–80.

National Hydropower Association (1999) *Hydro Relicensing*. Washington, DC: National Hydropower Association.

National Hydropower Association (2016) What percentage of U.S. electric generation comes from hydropower? *NHA FAQ*. http://www.hydro.org/policy/faq/#713 (accessed August 23, 2017).

Newell, P. J. (2001) Environmental NGOs, TNC, and the question of governance. In D. Stevis and V. J. Assetto (eds.), *The International Political Economy of the Environment*, 85–107. Boulder, CO: Lynne Rienner.

Newman, J., Barnes, M., Sullivan, H., & Knops, A. (2004) Public participation and collaborative governance. *Journal of Social Policy*, 33 (2): 203–23.

Nikoloyuk, J., Burns, T. R., & de Man, R. (2010) The promise and limitations of partnered governance: The case of sustainable palm oil. *Corporate Governance*, 10 (1): 59–72.

OAS Declaration on Indigenous Peoples, 2016. (http://www.narf.org/wordpress/wp-content/uploads/2015/09/2016oas-declaration-indigenous-people.pdf).

O'Leary, R., Gazley, B., McGuire, M., & Bingham, L. B. (2009) Public managers in collaboration. In R. O'Leary & L. B. Bingham (eds.), *The Collaborative Public Manager: New Ideas for the Twenty-first Century*, 1–12. Washington, DC: Georgetown University Press.

Oliver, C. (1997) Sustainable competitive advantage: Combining institutional and resource-based views. *Strategic Management Journal*, 18 (9): 697–713.

Ollenschläger, G., Marshall, C., Qureshi, S., Rosenbrand, K., Burgers, J., Mäkelä, M., & Slutsky, J. (2004) Improving the quality of health care: using international collaboration to inform guideline programmes by founding the Guidelines International Network (G-I-N), *Quality & Safety in Health Care*, 13: 455–60.

O'Mahoney, S. & Bechky, B. A. (2008) Boundary organizations: Enabling collaboration among unexpected allies. *Administrative Science Quarterly*, 53: 422–59.

Osborn, R. N. & Hagedoorn, J. (1997) The institutionalization and evolutionary dynamics of interorganizational alliances and networks. *Academy of Management Journal*, 40 (2): 261–78.

Osgood, C. E. (1962) *An Alternative to War or Surrender*. Urbana, IL: University of Illinois Press.

Ostrom, E. (2015) *Governing the Commons: The Evolution of Institutions for Collective Action*, 2nd ed. Cambridge: Cambridge University Press.

Oxfam International (2014) Large-scale partnerships with the private sector could undermine Africans' land rights, drive inequality and damage the environment. September. http://www.oxfam.org/en/pressroom/pressreleases/2014-09-01/large-scale-partnerships-private-sector-could-undermine-africans (accessed March 23, 2017).

Pache, A-C. & Santos, F. (2010) Inside the hybrid organization: Selective coupling as a response to competing institutional logics. *Academy of Management Journal*, 56: 923–1001.

Page, S. (2003) Entrepreneurial strategies for managing interagency collaboration. *Journal of Public Administration Research and Theory*, 13 (3): 311–39.

Page, S. B. (2005) Measuring accountability for results in interagency collaboratives. *Public Administration Review*, 64 (5): 591–606.

Page, S. B., Thomas, C., & Kern, M. (2016) Innovation *and* agreement? Tensions among the outputs of collaborative governance. Paper presented at the ASPA Conference, Seattle, WA, March.

Painter, M. (2001) Multi-level governance and the emergence of collaborative federal institutions in Australia. *Policy & Politics*, 29 (2): 137–50.

Paquet, G. (2007) Intelligent accountability. *Optimum Online: The Journal of Public Sector Management*, 37 (3), 1–15.

Parkinson, J. R. (2012) *Democracy and Public Space: The Physical Sites of Democratic Performance*. Oxford: Oxford University Press.

Parmigiani, A. & Howard-Grenville, J. (2011) Routines revisited: Exploring the capabilities and practice perspectives. *Academy of Management Annals*, 5: 413–53.

Pattberg, P. (2007) Partnerships for sustainability: An analysis of transnational environmental regimes. In P. Glasbergen, F. Bierman & A. P. J. Mol (eds.), *Partnerships, Governance and Sustainable Development: Reflections on Theory and Practice*, 173–93. Cheltenham, UK: Edward Elgar.

Pattberg, P., Bierman, F., Chan, S., & Mert, A. (2012) *Public–Private Partnerships for Sustainable Development. Emergence, Influence and Legitimacy*. Cheltenham: Edward Elgar.

Patton, L. K. (1981) Problems in environmental mediation: Human, procedural and substantive. *Environmental Consensus*, Nov.: 7–10.

PCP Dialogue Tools (1999). http://www.whatisessential.org/sites/default/files/toolbox.pdf (accessed November 13, 2016).

Pearce, J., Albritton, S., Grant, G., Steed, G., & Zelenika, I. (2012) A new model for enabling innovation in appropriate technology for sustainable development. *Sustainability: Science Practice & Policy*, 8 (2): 42–53.

Perez-Aleman, P. & Sandilands, M. (2008) Building value at the top and the bottom of the global supply chain: MNC–NGO partnerships. *California Management Review*, 51 (1): 24–50.

Pestoff, V. (2006) Citizens and co-production of welfare services: Childcare in eight European countries. *Public Management Review*, 8 (4): 503–19.

Phillips, N., Lawrence, T. B., & Hardy, C. (2000a) Discourse and institutions. *Academy of Management Review*, 29 (4): 635–52.

Phillips, N., Lawrence, T. B., & Hardy, C. (2000b) Inter-organizational collaboration and the dynamics of institutional fields. *Journal of Management Studies*, 37 (1): 23–43.

Pinkse, J. & Kolk, A. (2012) Addressing the climate change—sustainable development nexus: The role of multistakeholder partnerships. *Business & Society*, 51(1): 176–210.

Plantz, M. C., Greenway, M. T., & Hendricks, M. (1997) Outcome measurement: Showing results in the nonprofit sector. *New Directions for Evaluation*, 1997 (75): 15–30.

Podolny, J. M. (2001) Networks as pipes and prisms of the market. *American Journal of Sociology*, 107 (1), 33–60.

Poffenberger, M. (1996) *Communities and Forest Management*. Washington DC: International Union for Conservation of Nature.

Policy Consensus Institute (2007) *A Practical Guide to Collaborative Governance*.

Polonsky, M. J. (2001) Strategic bridging within firm-environmental group alliances: Opportunities and pitfalls. *Journal of Marketing Theory and Practice*, 9 (1): 38–47.

Poole, M. S., Seibold, D. R., & McPhee, R. D. (1985) Group decision-making as a structurational process. *Quarterly Journal of Speech*, 71, 74–102.

Porac, J. F., Thomas, H., & Baden-Fuller, C. (1989) Competitive groups as cognitive communities: The case of Scottish knitwear manufacturers. *Journal of Management Studies*, 26: 397–416.

Potapchuk, W. R. & Polk, C. R. (1993) *Building the Collaborative Community*. Washington: National Institute for Dispute Resolution, National Civic League and Program for Community Problem Solving.

Prahalad, C. K. (2004) *The Fortune at the Bottom of the Pyramid: Eradicating Poverty through Profits*. Upper Saddle River, NJ: Wharton School Publishing.

Prahalad, C. K. & Hamel, G. (1990) The Core Competence of the Corporation. *Harvard Business Review*, May–June, 71–91.

Provan, K. & Kenis, P. (2008) Modes of network governance: Structure, management and effectiveness. *Journal of Public Administration Research and Theory*, 18 (2): 229–52.

Provan, K. G., Kenis, P. N., & Human, S. E. (2008) Legitimacy building in organizational networks. In L. B. Bingham & R. O'Leary (eds.), *Big Ideas in Collaborative Public Management*, 121–37. Armonk, NY: M. E. Sharpe.

Provan, K. G., Huang, K., & Milward, H. B. (2009) The evolution of structural embeddedness and organizational social outcomes in a centrally governed health and human services network. *Journal of Public Administration Research and Theory*, 19(4): 873–93.

Pruitt, D. & Kim, S-H. (2004) *Social Conflict: Escalation, Stalemate and Settlement*, 3rd ed. New York: McGraw Hill.

Public Conversations Project (1999) An overview of PCP's work on abortion. http://www.whatisessential.org/resource/overview-public-conversations-work-abortion (accessed August 24, 2017).

Purdy, J. M. (2012) A framework for assessing power in collaborative governance processes. *Public Administration Review*, 72(3): 409–17.

Purdy, J. M. (2016) The role of power in collaborative governance. In R. Margerum & C. Robinson (eds.), *The Challenges of Collaboration in Environmental Governance*, 246–66. Cheltenham, UK: Edward Elgar Publishing.

Purdy, J. M. & Gray, B. (1994) Government agencies as mediators in public policy conflicts. *International Journal of Conflict Management*, 5 (2): 379–82.

Purdy, J. M. & Gray, B. (2009) Conflicting logics, mechanisms of diffusion and multi-level dynamics in emerging institutional fields. *Academy of Management Journal*, 52 (2): 355–80.

Purdy, J., Ansari, S., & Gray, B. (2017) Are logics enough? Framing as an alternative tool for understanding institutional meaning making. *Journal of Management Inquiry*, in press. DOI: 10.1177/1056492617724233.

Putnam, R. (1988) Diplomacy and domestic politics: The logic of two-level games. *International Organization*, 42 (3): 427–60.

Raaijmakers, A. G. M., Vermeulen, P. A. M., Meeus, M. T. H., & Zietsema, C. (2015) I need time!: Exploring pathways to compliance under institutional complexity, *Academy of Management Journal*, 58 (1): 85–110.

Rao, H. & Kenney, M. (2008) New forms as settlements. In R. Greenwood, C. Oliver, K. Sahlin, & R. Suddaby (eds.), *The Sage Handbook of Organizational Institutionalism*, 352–70. Los Angeles: Sage.

Rao, H., Morrill, C., & Zald, M. N. (2000) Power plays: How social movements and collective action create new organizational forms. *Research in Organizational Behavior*, 22: 239–82.

Rao, H., Monin, P., & Durand, R. (2003) Institutional change in Toque Ville: Nouvelle cuisine as identity movement in French gastronomy. *American Journal of Sociology*, 108: 795–843.

Rauschmayer, F. & Risse, N. (2005) A framework for the selection of participatory approach for SEA. *Environmental Impact Assessment Review*, 25: 650–66.

Reason, P. (1994) Three approaches to participatory action research. In N. K. Denzin & Y. S. Lincoln (eds.), *Handbook of Qualitative Research*, 324–39. Thousand Oaks, CA: Sage.

Reay, T. & Hinings, C. R. (2005) The recomposition of an organizational field: Health care in Alberta. *Organization Studies*, 26: 351–84.

Reay, T. & Hinings, C. R. (2009) Managing the rivalry of competing institutional logics. *Organization Studies*, 30: 629–52.

Redford, R. (1987) Search for common ground. *Harvard Business Review*, 65 (May–June): 107–12.

Reed, A. M. & Reed, D. (2009) Partnerships for development: Four models of business involvement. *Journal of Business Ethics*, 90: 3–37.

Reed, I. A. (2013) Power: Relational, discursive and performative dimensions. *Sociological Theory*, 31 (3): 193–218.

Reed, M. G. (2004) *Taking Stands: Gender and the Sustainability of Rural Communities*. Vancouver, B.C.: University of British Columbia Press.

Regéczi, D. (2005) Limited partnerships: The lack of sustainable development in relation to participation in Hungarian public-private partnerships. *Business Strategy and the Environment*, 14: 205–15.

Rein, M. & Stott, L. (2009) Working together: Critical perspectives on six cross-sector partnerships in Southern Africa. *Journal of Business Ethics*, 90 (1): 79–89.

Reineke, J. & Ansari, S. (2015) Occupy London: Co-constructed issues, frames & relationships. Academy of Management 75th Annual Meeting, Aug. 7–11, Vancouver, Canada.

Remond, M-A. (2014) What's the future of health care? It's collaboration. *Health Care News*, July 15. http://www.healthcareitnews.com/blog/whats-future-healthcare-its-collaboration (accessed July 29, 2017).

Riddell, D. (2014) Multi-paradigm perspectives on social innovation and systems change: Agency and cross-scale strategies in the Great Bear Rainforest and Canadian Boreal Forest Agreements. Ph.D. Thesis, University of Waterloo, Waterloo, CA.

Riisgaard, L., Lund-Thomsen, P., & Coe, N. M. (2017) The challenges of cooperation in multistakeholder initiatives: Competing policy concerns in the formulation of the Better Cotton Standards System. Paper presented at the Multistakeholder Initiatives Workshop, Occidental University, Los Angeles, April 3–4.

Ring, P. S. & Van de Ven, A. H. (1994) Developmental processes of cooperative inter-organizational relationships. *Academy of Management Review*, 19 (1): 90–118.

Rittel, H. W. J. & Webber, M. W. (1983) Dilemmas in a general theory of planning. Policy Sciences, 4 (2): 155–69.

Roberts, N. (2000) Wicked problems and network approaches to resolution. *International Public Management Review,* 1 (1): 1–19.

Rodriguez, C., Langley, A., Beland, F., & Denis, J-L. (2007) Governance, power and mandated collaboration in an interorganizational network. *Administration and Society*, 39 (2): 150–93.

Rojas, F. (2010) Power through institutional work: Building academic authority in the 1968 Third World strike. *Academy of Management Journal*, 53: 1263–80.

Rolle, S. (2002) Measures of progress for collaboration: Case study of the Applegate Partnership. General Technical Report PNW-GTR-565 US Department of Agriculture Forest Service, Pacific Northwest Research Station, October.

Rondinelli, D. & London, T. (2003) How corporations and environmental groups cooperate: Assessing cross-sector alliances and collaborations. *Academy of Management Journal*, 17 (1): 61–76.

Rosenau, J. (1992) Governance, order and change in world politics. In J. Rosenau & E-O. Czempiel (eds.), *Governance without Government: Order and Change in World Politics*, 1–29. Cambridge: Cambridge University Press.

Roser, M. & Ortiz-Ospina, E. (2017) Global extreme poverty. https://ourworldindata.org/extreme-poverty/ (accessed July 29, 2017).

Rothman, J. (1997) *Resolving Identity-Based Conflict: In Nations, Organizations, and Communities*. San Francisco: Jossey-Bass.

Rowley, T. J. (1997) Moving beyond dyadic boundaries: A network theory of stakeholder influences. *Academy of Management Review*, 22 (4): 887–910.

Ruffin, C. & Rivera-Santos, M. (2013) Cross-sector governance: From institutions to partnerships, and back to institutions. In M. M. Seitanidi & A. Crane (eds.), *Social Partnerships and Responsible Business*, 125–42. Oxford, UK: Routledge.

Saarikoski, H., Raitio, K., & Barry, J. (2013) Understanding "successful" conflict resolution: Policy regime changes and new interactive arenas in the Great Bear Rainforest. *Land Use Policy*, 32: 271–80.

Sagawa, S. & Segal, E. (2000) Common interest, common good: Creating value through business and social sector partnerships. *California Management Review*, 42 (2): 105–22.

Sampat, P. (2016) Conga No Va! Newmont mothballs Conga mine as Máxima wins Goldman Prize. Earthworks, April 18. https://www.earthworksaction.org/earthblog/detail/conga_no_va/#.V-Qcr3pu5Ms (accessed September 22, 2016).

Sandfort, J. & Milward, H. B. (2008) Collaborative service provision in the public sector. In S. Cropper, M. Ebers, C. Huxham, & P. Smith Ring (eds.), *The Oxford Handbook of Interorganizational Relations*, 147–75. New York: Oxford University Press.

Sawyer, S. & Gomez, E. T. (2008) Transnational governmentality and resource extraction, identities, conflict and cohesion programme. Paper Number 13 (UN-RISD, Geneva).

Saz-Carranza, A. & Ospina, S. (2011) The behavioral dimension of governing interorganizational goal-directed networks—Managing the unity-diversity tension. *Journal of Public Administration Research and Theory*, 21 (2): 327–65.

Schaeffer, H. L. & Edin, K. (2012) Extreme poverty in the United States, 1996–2011. National Poverty Center Policy Brief no. 28, February. http://www.npc.umich.edu/publications/policy_briefs/brief28/policybrief28.pdf (accessed April 10, 2017).

Schäferhoff, M., Campe, S., & Kaan, C. (2009) Transnational public–private partnerships in international relations: Making sense of concepts, research frameworks, and results. *International Studies Review*, 11 (3): 451–74.

Schein, E. (1978) *Process Consultation*. Reading, MA: Addison-Wesley.

Schneiberg, M. & Lounsbury, M. (2008) Social movements and institutional analysis. In R. Greenwood, C. Oliver, K. Sahlin, & R. Suddaby (eds.), *The Sage Handbook of Organizational Institutionalism*, 650–72. London: Sage.

Schneiberg, M. & Soule, S. A. (2005) Institutionalization as a contested, multilevel process. The case of rate regulation in American fire insurance. In G. F. Davis, D. McAdam, W. R. Scott, & M. N. Zald (eds), *Social Movements and Organization Theory*: 122–60. Cambridge UK: Cambridge University Press.

Schon, D. A. & Rein, M. (1994) *Frame Reflection: Toward the Resolution of Intractable Policy Controversies*. New York: Basic Books.

Schumaker, P. D. (1975) Policy responsiveness to protest-group demands. *The Journal of Politics*, 37 (2): 488–521.

Schuman, S. P. (1996) Intervention processes for collaboration. In C. Huxham (ed.), *Creating Collaborative Advantage*, 126–40. London: Sage.

Schuman, S. P. (2006) *Creating a Culture of Collaboration: International Association of Facilitators' Handbook*. San Francisco: Jossey-Bass.

Schwab, K. (ed.) (2015) The Global Competitiveness Report 2015–2016. World Economic Forum. Geneva. http//www.weforum.org/gcr.

Schwab, K. (ed.) (2016) The Global Competitiveness Report 2016–2017. World Economic Forum. Geneva. http//www.weforum.org/gcr.

Scott, W. R. (1995) *Institutions and Organizations*. Thousand Oaks, CA: Sage.

Scott, W. R. (2003) *Organizations: Rational, Natural, and Open Systems*, 5th ed. Upper Saddle River, NJ: Prentice Hall.

Scott, W., Martin, R., Ruef, M., Mendel, P. J., & Caronna, C.A. (2000) *Institutional Change and Healthcare Organizations: From Professional Dominance to Managed Care*. Chicago: University of Chicago Press.

Selden, S. C., Sowa, J. E., & Sandfort, J. (2006) The impact of nonprofit collaboration in early child care and education on management and program outcomes. *Public Administration Review*, 66 (3): 412–25.

Selsky, J. W. & Parker, B. (2005) Cross-sector partnerships to address social issues: Challenges to theory and practice. *Journal of Management*, 31 (6): 849–73.

Selsky, J. W., Wilkinson, A., & Mangalagiu, D. (2014) Using futures methods in cross-sector partnership research: Engaging wicked problems responsibly. In M. M. Seitanidi & A. Crane (eds.), *Social Partnerships and Responsible Business: A Research Handbook*, 267–87. London: Routledge.

Selznick, P. (1957) *Leadership and Administration*. Evanston, Ill.: Row, Peterson.

Senge, P. M., Dow, M., & Neathe, G. (2006) Learning together: New partnerships for new times. *Corporate Governance*, 6 (4): 420–30.

Senge, P. M., Lichtenstein, B. B., Kaeufer, K., Bradbury, H., & Carroll, J. S. (2007) Collaborating for systemic change. *MIT Sloan Management Review*, 48 (2): 44–53.

Seo, M. & Creed, W. E. D. (2002) Institutional contradictions, praxis, and institutional change: A dialectical perspective. *Academy of Management Review*, 27: 222–47. Cambridge: Cambridge University Press.

Serafin, T. (2013) Action plans to alleviate global poverty. September 17. https://www.forbes.com/sites/tatianaserafin/2013/09/17/action-plans-to-alleviate-global-poverty/#71c7fb84b0c6 (accessed July 29, 2017).

Sharfman, M. K., Gray, B., & Yan, A. (1991) The context of inter-organizational collaboration in the garment industry. *Journal of Applied Behavioral Science*, 27 (2): 181–208.

Sheppard, B. H. (1995) Negotiating in long-term mutually interdependent relationships among relative equals. In R. J. Bies, R. J. Lewicki, & B. H. Sheppard (eds.), *Research on Negotiation in Organizations*, Vol. 5, 3–44. Greenwich, CT: JAI Press.

Sherif, M. (1958) Superordinate goals in the reduction of intergroup conflict. *American Journal of Sociology*, 63: 349–56.

Simanis, E. & Hart, S. (2008) The base of the pyramid protocol: Toward next generation BoP strategy. https://www.johnson.cornell.edu/portals/32/sge/docs/BoP_Protocol_2nd_ed.pdf (July 29, 2017).

Simanis, E., Hart, S., & Duke, D. (2008) The base of the pyramid protocol: Beyond basic needs business strategies. *Innovations*, 3 (1): 57–84.

Slovic, P. (1992) Perceptions of risk. In S. Krimsky & D. Golding (eds.), *Social Theories of Risk*, 117–52. Santa Barbara: Praeger.

Smith, J. (2016) Reforesting the Amazon. *Nature Conservancy*, April/May, 47–57.

Smith, K. K. & Berg, D. N. (1997) *Paradoxes of Group Life: Understanding Conflict, Paralysis, and Movement in Group Dynamics*. San Francisco, CA: New Lexington Press.

Smith, L. W. & Roberts, J. W. (2003) Death for a terrorist: Media coverage of the McVeigh execution as a case study in interorganizational partnering between the public and private sectors. *Public Administration Review*, 63 (5): 515–24.

Snow, D. A., Rochford, E. B., Worden, S. K., & Benford, R. D. (1986) Frame alignment processes, micromobilization, and movement participation. *American Sociological Review*, 51 (4): 464–81.

Sobczak, A. & Martins, L. C. (2010) The impact and interplay of national and global CSR discourses: Insights from France and Brazil. *Corporate Governance*, 10 (4): 445–55.

Sørensen, E. & Torfing, J. (2011) Enhancing collaboration innovation in the public sector. *Administration & Society*, 43 (8): 842–68.

Sousa, D. J. & Klyza, C. M. (2007) New directions in environmental policy making: An emerging collaborative regime or reinventing interest group liberalism? *Natural Resources Journal* 47: 377–444.

Steensma, H. K. & Lyles, M. (2000) Explaining IJV survival in a transitional economy through social exchange and knowledge-based perspectives. *Strategic Management Journal*, 21 (8): 831–51.

Stinchcombe, A. L. (1968) *Constructing Social Theories*. Chicago: University of Chicago Press.

Strang, D. & Soule, S. (1998) Diffusion in organizations and social movements: From hybrid corn to poison pills. *Annual Review of Sociology*, 24: 265–90.

Strauss, D. A. (1999) Designing a consensus building process using a graphic road map. In L. Susskind, S. McKearnan, and J. Thomas-Larmer (eds.). *Consensus Building Handbook*: 137–68. Thousand Oaks, CA: Sage.

Suárez, D. F. (2011) Collaboration and professionalization: The contours of public sector funding for nonprofit organizations. *Journal of Public Administration Research and Theory*, 21 (2): 307–26.

Suchman, M. C. (1995) Managing legitimacy: Strategic and institutional approaches. *Academy of Management Review*, 20: 571–610.

Suddaby, R. & Greenwood, R. (2005) Rhetorical strategies of legitimacy. *Administrative Science Quarterly*, 50 (1): 35–68.

Sullivan, H. & Skelcher, C. (2002) *Working across Boundaries: Collaboration in Public Services*. New York: Palgrave Macmillan.

Sullivan, H., Barnes, M. & Matka, E. (2007) Building collaborative capacity for collaborative control: Health action zones in England. In T. Gössling, L. Oerleamns, & R. Jansen (eds.), *Inside Networks: A Process View on Multi-Organizational Partnerships, Alliances and Networks*, 67–91. Cheltenham, UK: Edward Elgar.

Susskind, L. (1999) An alternative to Robert's Rules of Order for groups, organizations and ad hoc assemblies that want to operate by consensus. In L. Susskind, S. McKearnan, & J. Thomas-Larmer (eds.), *Consensus Building Handbook*, 3–60. Thousand Oaks, CA: Sage.

Susskind, L. & Cruikshank, J. (1987) *Breaking the Impasse: Consensual Approaches to Resolving Public Disputes*. New York: Basic Books.

Susskind, L. & Madigan, D. (1984) New approaches to designing disputes in the public sector. *The Justice System Journal*, 9 (2): 179–203.

Susskind, L. & Thomas-Larmer, J. (1999) Conducting a conflict assessment. In L. Susskind, S. MacKearnan, and J. Thomas-Larmer (eds.), *The Consensus Building Handbook*, 99–136. Thousand Oaks, CA: Sage.

Swiger, M. A. & Burns, S. A. (1998) Cost-effective relicensing: Choosing the right process. *Hydro Review*, 17 (4): 52–61.

Swiger, M. A. & Grant, M. M. (2004) Creating a new FERC licensing process. *Hydro Review*, 22 (5): 20–2.

Szulecki, K., Pattberg, P., & Biermann, F. (2011) Explaining variation in the effectiveness of transnational energy partnerships. *Governance: An International Journal of Policy, Administration and Institutions*, 24 (4): 713–36.

Takahashi, I. M. & Smutny, G. (2002) Collaborative windows and organizational governance: Exploring the formation and demise of social service partnerships. *Nonprofit and Voluntary Sector Quarterly*, 31 (2): 165–85.

Tandon, R. (1989) Participatory research and social transformation. *Convergence*, 21 (2–3): 5–15.

Tarlock, D. (2012) Hydro law and the future of hydroelectric power generation in the United States. *Vanderbilt Law Review*, 65: 1723.

Taylor, B. D. & Schweitzer, L. (2005) Assessing the experience of mandated collaborative inter-jurisdictional transport planning in the United States. *Transport Policy*, 12: 500–11.

Taylor, D. E. (2000) Advances in environmental justice: Research, theory and methodology. *American Behavioral Scientist*, 43 (4): 504–80.

Teegan, H., Doh, J. P., & Vachani, S. (2004) The importance of non-governmental organizations (NGOs) in global governance and value creation: An international business research agenda. *Journal of International Business Studies*, 35 (6): 463–83.

Tenkasi, R. V. & Chesmore, M. C. (2003) Social networks and planned organizational change: The impact of strong ties on effective change implementation and use. *Journal of Applied Behavior Science*, 39 (3): 281–300.

Tenkasi, R. V. & Mohrman, S. A. (1999) Global change as contextual collaborative knowledge creation. In D. A. Cooperrider & J. E. Dutton (eds.), *Organizational Dimensions of Global Change: No Limits to Cooperation*, 114–36. Thousand Oaks, CA: Sage.

Termeer, C. J. A. M., Dewulf, A. R. P. J., & van Lieshout, M. (2010) Disentangling scale approaches in governance research: Comparing monocentric, multilevel and adaptive governance. *Ecology & Society*, 15 (4): 29–42.

Termeer, C. J. A. M., Dewulf, A., Breeman, G., & Stiller, S. J. (2015) Governance capabilities for dealing wisely with wicked problems. *Administration and Society*, 47 (6): 680–710.

Tetlock, P. E., Peterson, R., & Lerner, J. (1996) Revising the value pluralism model: Incorporating social content and context postulates. In C. Seligman, J. Olson, and M. Zanna (eds.), *Values: Eighth Annual Ontario Symposium on Personality and Social Psychology*: 25–51. Hillsdale, NJ: Erlbaum.

Thomlinson, J. (2003) Globalization and cultural identity. In D. Held & A. McGrew (eds.), *The Global Transformation Reader*, 269–78. Cambridge, UK: Polity Press.

Thompson, A. M., Perry, J., & Miller, T. (2008) Linking collaboration processes and outcomes. In R. O'Leary and L. Bingham (eds.), *Collaborative Public Management*, 97–120. Armonk, NY: M. E. Sharpe.

Thórhallsdóttir, T. E. (2002) Evaluating nature and wilderness in Iceland. *USDA Forest Service Proceedings*, RMRS-P-26: 96–104.

Thornton, P. H. (2004) *Markets from Culture: Institutional Logics and Organizational Decisions in Higher Education Publishing*. Stanford, CA: Stanford University Press.

Thornton, P. H. & Ocasio, W. (1999) Institutional logics and the historical contingency of power in organizations: Executive succession in the higher education publishing industry 1958–1990. *American Journal of Sociology*, 105, 801–43.

Thornton, P. H., Ocasio, W., & Lounsbury, M. (2012) *The Institutional Logics Perspective: A New Approach to Culture, Structure and Process*. New York: Oxford University Press.

Tjosvold, D. & Field, R. H. G. (1983) Effects of social context on consensus and majority vote decision making. *Academy of Management Journal*, 26: 500–6.

Todd, S. (2002) Building consensus on divisive issues: A case study of the Yukon wolf management team. *Environmental Impact Assessment Review*, 22 (6): 655–84.

Tolbert, P. S. & Zucker, L. G. (1996) The institutionalization of institutional theory. In S. Clegg, C. Hardy, and W. Nord (eds.), *Handbook of Organization Studies*, 175–90. London: Sage.

Torfing, J. (2016) *Collaborative Innovation in the Public Sector*. Washington, DC: Georgetown University Press.

Torfing, J. & Ansell, C. (2017) Strengthening political leadership and policy innovation through the expansion of collaborative forms of governance. *Public Management Review*, 19 (1): 37–54.

Touval, S. & Zartman, I. W. (1985) *International Mediation in Theory and Practice*. Boulder, CO: Westview Press.

Treakle, K. (1998) Ecuador: Structural adjustment and indigenous and environmentalist resistance. In J. Fox and L. D. Brown (eds.), *The Struggle for Accountability: The World Bank, NGOs and Grassroots Movements*, 219–42. Cambridge, MA: MIT Press.

Trist, E. (1977) A concept of organizational ecology. *Australian Journal of Management*, 2: 162–75.

Trist, E. (1983) Referent organizations and the development of interorganizational domains. *Human Relations*, 36 (3): 247–68.

Turner, M. G., Dale, V. H., & Gardner, R. H. (1989) Predicting across scales: theory development and testing. *Landscape Ecology*, 3 (3/4): 245–52.

Twidale, S. & Chestney, N. (2013) Green groups quit Warsaw climate talks over lack of progress. November 21. http://www.reuters.com/article/2013/11/21/us-climate-talks-ngo-idUSBRE9AK0OM20131121#Ic7HKyOl75pOkoaI.97 (accessed July 29, 2017).

Ulbert, C. (2008) The effectiveness of global health partnerships: What determines their success or failure? Paper presented at the 49th Annual ISA Convention, San Francisco, March 26–29.

UNDRIP (UN Declaration on the Rights of Indigenous Peoples, 2006. (http://www.un.org/esa/socdev/unpfii/documents/DRIPS_en.pdf).

UNFAO. National Aquaculture Legislation Overview Canada. (http://www.fao.org/fishery/legalframework/nalo_canada/en (accessed March 8, 2017).

Utting, P. & Zammit, A. (2009) United Nations-business partnerships: Good intentions and contradictory agendas. *Journal of Business Ethics*, 90 (1): 39–56.

Valente, M. (2012) Indigenous resource and institutional capital: The role of local context in embedding sustainable community development. *Business and Society*: 409–49.

Van de Kerkhof, M. (2006) Creating and managing interorganizational learning networks to achieve sustainable ecosystem management. *Organization and Environment*, 20 (3): 325–46.

Van Gestel, N. & Hillebrand, B. (2011) Explaining stability and change: The rise and fall of logics in pluralistic fields. *Organization Studies*, 32 (2): 231–52.

Van Huijstee, M. & Glasbergen, P. (2010a) Business–NGO interactions in a multi-stakeholder context. *Business and Society Review*, 115 (3): 249–84.

van Huijstee, M. & Glasbergen, P. (2010b) NGOs moving business: An analysis of contrasting strategies. *Business & Society*, 49 (4): 591–618.

van Lieshout, M., Dewulf, A., Aarts, N., & Termeer, C. (2011) Do scale frames matter? Scale frame mismatches in the decision making process of a "mega farm" in a small Dutch village. *Ecology & Society*, 16 (1): 38–52.

Van Marrewijk, M. & Werre, M. (2003) Multiple levels of corporate sustainability. *Journal of Business Ethics*, 44: 107–19.

Van Sandt, C. V. & Sud, M. (2012) Poverty alleviation through partnerships: A road less travelled for business, governments, and entrepreneurs. *Journal of Business Ethics*, 110: 321–32.

Vangen, S. & Huxham, C. (2003) Nurturing collaborative relations: Building trust in inter-organizational collaboration. *Journal of Applied Behavioral Science*, 39 (1): 5–31.

Vansina, L. (2000) The relevance and perversity of psychodynamic interventions in consulting. *Concepts and Transformation*, 5: 321–48.

Vansina, L., Taillieu, T., & Schruijer, S. (1998) "Managing" multiparty issues: Learning from experience. In W. Pasmore & R. Woodman (eds.), *Research in Organizational Change and Development, Vol. 11*, 159–83. Greenwich, CT: JAI Press.

Vickers, Sir G. (1965) *The Art of Judgment*. London: Chapman & Hall.

Viers, J. H. (2011) Hydropower relicensing and climate change. *Journal of the American Water Resources Association*, 47 (4): 655–61.

Vij, N. (2011) Collaborative governance: Analysing social audits in MGNREGA in India. *IDS Bulletin*, 42 (6), 28–34.

Vurro, C. and Dacin, T. (2014) An institutional perspective on cross-sector partnerships. In M. M. Seitinidi & A. Crane (eds.), *Social Partnerships and Responsible Business: A Research Handbook*: 306–19. London: Routledge.

Vurro, C., Russo, A., & Perrini, F. (2009) Shaping sustainable value chains: Network determinants of supply chain governance models. *Journal of Business Ethics*, 90 (4): 607–21.

Vurro, C., Dacin, M. T., & Perrini, F. (2010) Institutional antecedents of partnering for social change: How institutional logics shape cross-sector social partnerships. *Journal of Business Ethics*, 94 (1): 39–53.

Waddell, S. & Khagram, S. (2007) Multi-stakeholder global networks: Emerging systems for the global common good. In P. Glasbergen, F. Bierman, & A. P. J. Mol (eds.), *Partnerships, Governance and Sustainable Development: Reflections on Theory and Practice*, 261–87. Cheltenham, UK: Edward Elgar.

Waldorff, S. B., Kristensen, L. S., & Ebbesen, B. V. (2014) The complexity of governance: Challenges for public sector innovation. In C. Ansell & J. Torfing (eds.), *Public Innovation through Collaboration and Design*, 70–88. London: Routledge.

Walker, P. A. & Hurley, P. T. (2004) Collaboration derailed: The politics of "community-based" resource management in Nevada County. *Society and Natural Resources*, 17(8): 735–51.

Walker, G. B., & Senecah, S. L. (2011) Collaborative governance: Integrating institutions, communities, and people. In E. F. Dukes, K. E. Firehock, & J. E. Birkhoff (eds.),

Community-based Collaboration: Bridging Socio-Ecological Research and Practice, 111–45. Charlottesville, VA: University of Virginia Press.

Warren, R., Rose, S., & Bergunder, A. (1974) *A Structure of Urban Reform.* Lexington, MA: Heath.

Weber, E. P. (2009) Explaining institutional change in touch cases of collaboration: "Ideas" in the Blackfoot Watershed. *Public Administration Review,* 69 (2): 314–27.

Weber, M. (1947) *The Theory of Social and Economic Organization.* Translated by A. M. Henderson and Talcott Parsons. London: Collier Macmillan Publishers.

Weible, C. M., Pattison, A., & Sabatier, P. A. (2010) Harnessing expert-based information for learning and the sustainable management of complex socio-ecological systems. *Environmental Science and Policy,* 13 (6): 522–34.

Weick, K. & Roberts, K. (1993) Collective mind in organizations: Heedful interrelating on flight decks. *Administrative Science Quarterly,* 38: 357–81.

Weisbord, M. & Janoff, S. (2000) *Future Search: An Action Guide to Finding Common Ground in Organizations and Communities,* 2nd ed. San Francisco: Berrett-Koehler.

Weisbord, M. & Janoff, S. (2005) Faster, shorter, cheaper may be simple; it's never easy. *Journal of Applied Behavior Science,* 41 (1): 70–82.

Westley, F., Carpenter, S., Brock, W., Holling, C. S., & Gunderson, L. (2002) Why systems of people and nature are not just social and ecological systems. In L. H. Gunderson & C. S. Holling, *Panarcy: Understanding Transformations in Human and Natural Systems,* 103–19. Washington, DC: Island Press.

Westley, F. & Vredenberg, H. (1991) Strategic bridging: The alliances of business and Environmentalists. *Journal of Applied Behavioral Science,* 27 (1): 65–90.

Westley, F. & Vredenberg, H. (1997) Interorganizational collaboration and the preservation of biodiversity. *Organization Science,* 8 (4): 381–403.

Wheeler, D., McKague, K., Thomson, J., Davies, R., Medalye, J., & Prada, M. (2005) Creating sustainable local enterprise networks. *MIT Sloan Management Review,* 47 (1): 33–40.

Whiteman, G. (2009) All my relations: Understanding perceptions of justice and conflict between companies and indigenous peoples. *Organization Studies,* 30 (1): 101–20.

Whiteman, G. & Mamen, K. (2002) Examining justice and conflict between mining companies and indigenous peoples: Cerro Colorado and the Ngäbe-Buglé in Panama. *Journal of Business and Management,* 8 (3): 293–329.

Whittington, R. (2006) Completing the practice turn in strategy research. *Organization Studies,* 27 (5): 613–34.

Wijen, F. & Ansari, S. (2007) Overcoming inaction through collective institutional entrepreneurship: Insights from regime theory. *Organization Studies,* 28 (7): 1079–1100.

Wildavsky, A. (1979) *Speaking Truth to Power—The Art and Craft of Policy Analysis.* Boston: Little Brown.

Winslade, J. & Monk, G. D. (2000) *Narrative Mediation: A New Approach to Conflict Resolution.* San Francisco: Jossey-Bass.

Wondolleck, J. (1985) The importance of process in resolving environmental disputes. *Environmental Impact Assessment Review,* 5: 341–56.

Wondolleck, J. M. & Yaffee, S. L. (2000) *Making Collaboration Work: Lessons from Innovation in Natural Resource Management.* Washington: Island Press.

Wood, D. J. & Gray, B. (1991) Toward a comprehensive theory of collaboration. *Journal of Applied Behavioral Science,* 27 (2): 139–62.

Wooten, M. E. & Hoffman, A. J. (2008) Organizational fields: Past, present and future. In R. Greenwood, C. Oliver, R. Suddaby, & K. Sahlin (eds.), *The Sage Handbook of Organizational Institutionalism,* 129–47. Los Angeles: Sage.

World Bank (2014) Health expenditure. http://data.worldbank.org/indicator/SH.XPD. TOTL.ZS (accessed February 1, 2017).

World Economic Forum (2015) *Outlook on the Global Agenda.* http://reports.weforum. org/outlook-global-agenda-2015/top-10-trends-of-2015/10-growing-importance-of-health-in-the-economy/ (accessed July 29, 2017).

World Economic Forum (2016) *The Global Risks Report 2016,* 11th ed. Geneva: World Economic Forum.

World Wildlife Fund UK and Banktrack (2006) *Shaping the Future of Sustainable Finance: Moving from Paper Promises to Performance.*

Worthington, S. (2014) Disspelling the myth: An evolving relationship between NGOs and private businesses. November 13. https://www.interaction.org/blog/dispelling-myth-evolving-relationship-between-ngos-and-private-businesses (accessed July 29, 2017).

Yarnold, D. (2007) Partners for the planet: How environmental defense builds alliances to protect the environment. *Stanford Social Innovation Review,* 5 (3): 23–4.

Yashar, D. J. (1998) Contesting citizenship: Indigenous movements and democracy in Latin America. *Comparative Politics,* 31 (1): 23–42.

Yaziji, M. (2004) Turning gadflies into allies. *Harvard Business Review,* 82 (2): 110–15.

Yaziji, M. & Doh, J. (2009) *NGOs and Corporations: Conflict and Collaboration.* New York: Cambridge University Press.

Zadek, S. (2008) Global collaborative governance: There is no alternative. *Corporate Governance,* 8 (4): 374–88.

Zald, M. N. (1999) Transnational and international social movements in a globalizing world: Creating culture, creating conflict. In Cooperider, D. & Dutton, J. (eds.), *Organizational Dimensions of Global Change: No Limits to Cooperation,* 168–84. Thousand Oaks, CA: Sage.

Zammit, A. (2003) *Development at Risk: Rethinking UN–Business Partnerships.* Geneva: UNRISD.

Zartman, I. W. (2001) The timing of peace initiatives: Hurting stalemates and ripe moments. *The Global Review of Ethnopolitics,* 1 (1): 8–18.

Zietsma, C. & Lawrence, T. (2010) Institutional work in the transformation of an organizational field: The interplay of boundary work and practice work. *Administrative Science Quarterly,* 55: 189–221.

Zilber, T. (2002) Institutionalization as an interplay between actions, meanings and actors: The case of a rape crisis center in Israel. *Academy of Management Journal,* 45 (1): 234–54.

Zilber, T. (2008) The work of meanings in institutional processes and thinking. In R. Greenwood, C. Oliver, K. Sahlin, & R. Suddaby (eds.), *The Sage Handbook of Organizational Institutionalism,* 151–69. Los Angeles: Sage.

Index

Note: The page numbers in italics '*f*' and '*t*' indicate the figures and tables.

accountability 4, 18, 60, 142, 143, 146*t*, 166
  developing standards 148
  environmental governance 129
  intelligent 129
  public 109, 149
action research 71, 78
  participatory 74*t*, 90–1
Africa 2, 6, 25, 154, 180
  digital access to classrooms 150
African Americans 34, 39
agenda-setting 74*t*, 82, 161
Agenda 21 (environmental action) 22, 134
Agranoff, R. 163
agreement(s)
  acceptable 118, 191
  binding 110
  collaborative 11, 91, 154, 190, 191, 197
  collectively establishing 36
  commitment 74*t*
  compromise 189*t*
  crafting 56–7, 187
  creative 159, 163
  enforcing 110
  fair 76, 152
  fear that partners will renege on 89
  final 152, 175
  fragile 189*t*
  global frustration with slow progress on 122
  greater ease in finding 123
  implementation of 34, 71*f*, 72, 75*t*, 77, 92,
    94, 96, 102, 143, 169, 172, 175
  importance of partners finding 124
  institutional memory of 79
  integrative 159, 200
  international 23
  joint 33, 152
  just 152
  lasting 100
  local 175, 176
  need to ratify with back-home
    constituents 91
  operationalization of 93, 96
  organization to execute 75*t*
  overarching 175, 176–6
  partnership 72, 74*t*, 92, 172, 175
  preliminary 71, 74*t*
  procedural suggestions for addressing 82
  quality diminished 69
  realistic 87
  replication in other contexts 94
  routinized and monitored for consistency 93
  seeds of 10
  settlement 161
  suboptimal 85
  sustainable 118
  tactics that help to produce 168
  tentative 94
  terms of 11
  timely 81
  trade-offs between innovation and 153
  unprecedented 104
  violation of 104, 175
  widespread support for 84
  see also CBFA; Paris Agreement; Queensland
    Forestry Agreement
agricultural development areas (ADAs) 180
Ählström, J. 30, 31, 32, 141, 148
Ahmad, Y. 5
Alaska 157
Albans, B. T. 84, 85
Alcoa 12
Alderfer, C. P. 115
Alford, R. 37, 107, 108, 119
AlphaMundi 6
Alvord, S. 4
Alzheimer's 102
American Declaration on the Rights of
    Indigenous Peoples 152
Amir, Y. 89
Amis, J. M. 43
amplification 46
  scope and 41, 42–4
Amsler, L. 3, 158, 160
Anand, N. 38

Anand, S. 17
Andean lakes 67
Andersen, E. K. 152
Anderson, S. 84
Andrews, R. 149, 150
Ansari, S. M. 23, 40, 46, 93, 100, 109, 111, 120,
    129, 182, 188
Ansell, C. 3, 4, 9, 14, 15, 26, 39, 87, 133, 156,
    164, 165, 198
Appadurai, A. 23–4
Applegate Partnership 70
appreciative inquiry 74t, 90
Arbruster-Sandoval, R. 176
Arctic wilderness 12
Arenas, D. 143, 151, 152
Argenti, P. A. 30, 148
Argyris, C. 87, 90
Armstrong, E. A. 38, 108, 126, 185, 191
Ashman, D. 5, 18
ASHOKA 6
Asia-Pacific Partnership on Clean Development
    and Climate 166
Aspen Institute 35n.(4)
asylum seekers 25
Austin, J. E. 4, 5, 7, 39, 48, 137, 142, 145,
    146, 148
Australia 24, 25, 159
    New South Wales 85
    Queensland 115, 150, 159, 163
Aweenak'ola 177

back home buy-in 74t, 91–2, 167, 177–8, 200
Bäckstrand, K. 128, 166
Baird, B. N. R. 102
Baker, A. 102
Balderston, K. M. 27
Baldwin, C. 87, 115, 150
Bangladesh 20
Banktrack 67n.(1)
Baños del Inca 61
Barclay, M-A. 30
Barley, S. R. 40, 41, 123, 178, 187
Barsade, S. 45
Barthel, D. 46
Bartley, T. 176, 178, 186, 194, 194
Base of the Pyramid (BOP) strategies 18, 19, 30,
    93, 94, 110–11, 132, 137, 138f
Bass, S. 154, 177
Batliwala, S. 26, 154
Battelle Technology Partnership Practice 162
Battilana, J. 108
Baur, D. 140, 191
BCI (Better Cotton Initiative) 134, 153,
    181, 183
Bechky, B. A. 196
Beech, N. 69
Benbrook 7

Bendell, J. 30
Benford, R. 41, 99, 108, 193, 194
Berg, D. N. 183
Berger, I. E. 69
Berger, P. 44
Berman, T. 36
Bernal, A. S. 97
Berryessa, C. M. 103
Bidwell, R. D. 96, 100
Bill and Melinda Gates, see Gates Foundation
Bingham, L. B. 77, 148, 156
biodiversity 22
Birdlife International 12
Bitzer, V. 143
Block, E. S. 126
Blumer, H. 41
Bogotá Nutrition System 162
Booher, D. E. 5, 39, 46, 160, 168
Boreal Forest 36, 104, 174–6, 195
    see also Canadian Boreal Forest Agreement
Borrini-Feyerabend, G. 158
Bosshard, P. 12
Bosso, C. J. 48, 49
Bouwen, R. 10, 68, 90, 100, 110, 115, 152
Bowen, F. 138
Brandsen, T. 165, 168
Brazil 25, 142, 162, 194
    Amazon deforestation 7, 187
Brecher, C. 150
Brent Spar 30–1
Brigham, S. 85
Briscoe, F. 103
British Columbia 144, 175
Brockmyer, B. I. 161
Bronen, R. 157
Brown, A. J. 22, 86
Brown, L. D. 5, 7, 18, 26, 27, 31–2, 40, 128,
    147, 148, 154, 185, 191, 194, 195
Brummel, R. G. 101, 164
Bryan, T. 22, 98, 113, 182, 183
Bryson, J. 5, 7, 11, 15, 22, 75, 83, 84, 97, 133
Building Consensus 59–66
Bunker, B. B. 84, 85
Burkina Faso 20
Burns, S. A. 51, 52
Burton, L. 151

Cajamarca 58–62, 64, 66–7
California Public Utilities Commission 161
    see also Quincy Library Group (QLG)
Canada 110, 145
    Government-First Nations partnership
        143–4
    see also British Columbia; Canadian Boreal
        Forest Agreement; Forest Products
        Association of Canada (FPAC); Great
        Bear Rainforest (GBR), Loblaw; Montreal

Canadian Boreal Forest Agreement 2010
  (CBFA) 36, 104, 174–6, 195
cancer 102
Caneva, L. 24
CAO (IFC Office of the Compliance
  Advisor/Ombuds-man) 58–61, 63, 64–6,
  67n.(4), 71, 95n.(1)
capacity-building 5, 143, 153, 170, 182, 183, 200
  commitment to 21
  extent of 169, 171
  grants for 136
  promoting 147
  technical programs 61
Carlson, C. 15, 73, 75, 77–8, 79, 196
Carmin, J. 147
Carroll, A. B. 132
Carstarphan, N. 34
Castells, M. 23
Castro, A. P. 97, 113, 148, 149
Catholic Church 91, 195–6
Cavalli, A. 21
change(s) 28, 56, 57, 108, 124t, 151, 168
  adaptive 171
  contextual 14–15, 123
  disruptive 143
  domination structure 188–90, 195, 196
  evaluation of 170
  exogenous and endogenous sources of 192
  field 36–40, 123, 125, 126, 129, 178, 179,
    190, 198–200
  global 16
  gradual 129
  incremental 126, 129
  institutional boundaries to implement 162
  leadership 70
  licensing 52, 54
  need to internalize 75t
  outcomes 184
  pathways in field configurations 190, 192–8
  political 23
  positive 32, 143, 154
  real 148, 177
  routines in flux and subject to 44
  social-psychological resistance to 90
  structures of domination 188–90
  supply chain 32, 135f, 136, 138f, 146
  sustainable 18, 154
  technical 171
  water quality 64
  willingness to accept 87
  see also climate change; institutional change
Chattanooga 34
Chávez, B. V. 97
Cheng, A. S. 142
Chesmore, M. C. 84, 89
Chestney, N. 122
Child, C. 176, 194, 195

child mortality 6
Chisholm, R. F. 70, 90
Chliova, M. 93
Cho, M. 103
Chrislip, D. E. 11, 78, 94
Church of Jesus Christ of the Latter Day
  Saints 25
CityYear 39
civic society 4, 181f
  governments and 5, 7, 134, 185
  NGOs broker relationships between
    businesses and 2
  outcomes for 149–52
  well-being, empowerment and peace of 155
Clarke, A. 22, 84, 145, 160, 161, 169
Clegg, S. R. 118
Clemens, E. 123
climate change 16, 22–3, 121–2, 166, 188
  acceptance of 46
  action on 174
  commitment to 105
  global 182
  increasing consumer concern about 51f
  rising importance of 49
  violent weather events triggered by 25
Cloete, N. 10
Clyman, D. 68
Cohen, P. 17
collaboration 8–11
  dealing with wicked problems 14–15
  globalization context 16–27
  government-led 160–1
  mandated/mandatory 101, 163–4
  multiparty 13 n.
  power and 117–30
collaborative efforts 22, 52–4, 69, 121f
  acceptability of 128
  factors that motivate and block 70
collaborative governance 3f, 118, 135f, 137,
    149, 155, 156–71, 184
  broad participation in 121
  need to balance power and effectiveness
    in 21
  network 128
  non-statutory approaches 147
  useful way to map types of 134
collaborative partnerships 1, 22, 38, 56, 118,
    123, 129, 141, 155, 173, 182–3
  actions acceptable to other organizational
    members 167
  attempt to dominate 109
  competitive or collaborative relationships
    within 165
  conditions favorable to formation 39–40
  development of 39
  evaluating power dynamics in 120
  evaluation of 169

collaborative partnerships (*cont.*)
 field structure impacted by 189*t*
 learning in 90
 managing meaning in 119–20
 mutually valued by all participants 128
 necessary to shift levels of analysis when
  examining 179
 need for 16, 52
 outcomes of 130
 potential of 163, 199
 powerful motivator for forming 72–3
 PPPs may be constituted as 162
 problems of scaling up 23
 regional 165
 well-intended 12
Collins, R. 41, 42, 45
Colombia, *see* Bogotá
Comité Directivo 62, 63, 65, 67n.(3)
CONAIE (Confederation of Indigenous
  Nationalities of Ecuador) 193, 194, 195–6
conflict-handling 74*t*, 85–95, 111
Conga No Va 67
Congo, *see* DRC
consensus-building 8, 74*t*, 87–8, 111
convening 67, 71, 73–8, 84, 85, 94, 197
cooperative/competitive context 164–5
Coser, L. 102
Council on Environmental Quality 52
Creed, W. E. D. 38, 42, 126, 193, 194
Cronin, M. 160
Cropper, S. 80
Crosby, B. 75, 97
cross-level dynamics 170, 172–83, 200
cross-sector partnerships 68, 94
 building appreciation among 83
 intended purposes of 33–5
 intervening in different phases of 70
 motivations for joining 27–33
 outcomes of 145
 see also social partnerships
Cruikshank, J. 88
CSR (corporate social responsibility) 50, 131,
  132–3
 business-NGO partnerships linked to 136
 commitment by businesses and/or
  partnerships to 137
CSSPs (cross-sector social partnerships) 13 n.
cultural fit 139, 142–4
Cummings, T. G. 90
Curseu, P. 69
Cyert, R. 44

Dacin, M. T. 7, 13, 37, 185, 186, 199
Dahan, N. M. 19, 30, 140
Darnall, N. 147
Das, T. K. 88
Davenport, C. 122

De Bakker, F. G. A. 36, 176, 194–5
Dees, J. G. 39
Democratic Republic of Congo (DRC) 143, 154
Den Hond, F. 194–5
Denis, J. 68, 69
Denmark 20
DeWinter-Schmitt, R. 183
Dewulf, A. 10, 38, 41, 90, 100, 110, 115
Dienhart, J. W. 4, 22, 199, 200
differences 80, 85, 96, 97, 152, 168, 172
 class 62
 constructively dealing with 8, 9–10
 cultural 69, 72*t*, 73, 142, 200
 designing partnerships to capitalize on 11
 exploring 34
 gender 62
 identity 102, 112
 individual, respect of 63
 irreconcilable 113
 national 16
 options for overcoming 89
 race 62
 religious 72*t*, 73
 resolving 68
 risk perception 102–3
 scale 173, 176, 180
 sectoral 110
 techniques used by mediators to reconcile 87
 understanding, in partners' motivations 27
 value 101–2
 see also power differences
differing frames 99–100, 191
 synergistic 39
DiMaggio, P. J. 36, 186
Dionysiou, D. D. 44, 45
distrust 98, 106, 118, 168
Djelic, M. L. 110, 115, 128
Doelle, M. 87, 149, 150, 152–3
Doh, J. 4, 32, 108, 148
Donahue, J. D. 8, 157
Dorado, S. 73, 75, 93, 108, 196
DRC (Democratic Republic of Congo) 143, 154
Drori, G. S. 16
Dryzek, J. 26
Dukes, E. F. 22, 88, 89
Dunn, M. B. 37, 109
Dupont 19, 136
Durand, R. 126
Durkheim, E. 45
Dutch banks 80*f* 105, 125, 179
 see also Rabobank
Dutch Relief Alliance 25–6
Dyckman, C. 128

EADD (East African Dairy Development) 150
Easton, G. 145
eco-labeling 5, 135*f*, 136, 138*f*,

economy 12, 35n.(3)
  governments play minimal role in
      directing 135
  growing importance of health in 16, 20–1
  indigenous peoples and distinctiveness of 143
ECOSOC (UN Economic and Social Council) 15
Ecuador 91, 100, 115 *see also* CONAIE
Eden, C. 83
EDF (US Environmental Defense Fund) 31, 33,
      136, 148
Edin, K. 17
Elden, M. 70, 90
Electric Power Research Institute 52
Elias, J. 39
Elliott, M. 34, 102, 109
Emerson et al., 2012; 5, 22, 28, 30, 35n.(4),
      156–7, 159–60, 170
Emery, F. 15, 83, 186
Emery, M. 83, 84
ENGOs (environmental NGOs) 29, 36, 113,
      159, 163, 174, 175, 177
  conflicts over sustainability between business
      and 39
Entman, R. M. 41
Entwistle, T. 149, 150
environmental impacts 60, 97
  assessment 135*f*, 136, 138*f*,
  mitigation of 184
  most significant 182
  organization for studying 66
environmental issues 4, 18, 32–3, 34, 50, 63,
      115, 119, 133, 146*t*, 151, 158, 169
  advances in science 51
  adverse impacts 59
  contamination 58
  damage 59, 173, 179
  degradation 16, 22–3
  early collaborations over 98
  exigencies 68, 79
  groups/activists 5, 12, 38, 46, 51, 78, 81, 86,
      98, 104, 105, 125, 175, 177, 187
  long-term management improvements 147
  mediated negotiations 77
  new regulations 51
  issues and outcomes 152–4
  partnerships on 129, 142–3
  problems 23, 27, 30, 32, 67, 182
  pursuing profit in inherently destructive
      ways 28
  responsibility 29
  sustainability 52, 145
  see also Council on Environmental Quality;
      EDF; ENGOs; EPA; NEEF; Rainforest
      Action Network; voluntary
      environmental programs
EPA (US Environmental Protection
      Agency) 52, 64, 136, 158

episodic power 120, 123, 125, 126, 128
  forms of 118, 119
Equator Principles 49, 147
Esteves, A. M. 30
Ethiopia 20
Ethical Trading Initiative (ETI) 147
Etzioni, A. 108
Everglades Restoration Task Force 157
expertise 26, 29*t*, 31*t*, 39, 100, 120, 156
  business-oriented 140
  contextual 29
  managerial 148
  respecting and learning from each other 8,
      10–11
  technical 148
  technological 85
Extractive Industries Transparency
      Initiative (EITI) 147, 166

Fair Labor Association (FLA) 147
Fals-Borda, O. 90
Fan, G. H. 96, 108, 109, 191
Faulkner, M. 68, 73
federal government 34, 77, 105, 106, 128,
      159, 163
  mistrust of 97
Federal Mediation and Conciliation Service 110
Feiock, R. C. 164, 165
Feldman, M. S. 44
FEMA (US Federal Emergency Management
      Agency) 25
FERC (Federal Energy Regulatory
      Commission) 51–7, 72, 91, 105–6, 121,
      160, 176, 184, 197
Ferlie, E. 90
Fernández, P. 124
FEROCAFENOP (Federation of Female Rondas
      Campesinas of Northern Peru) 58, 59, 61, 63,
      64, 67n.(3)
Feyerherm, A. E. 37
Field, P. 128
Field, R. H. G. 160, 165
field configurations
  pathways of change within 192–8
  starting points for change 190–2
fields
  changes in 36–40, 123, 125, 126, 129, 178,
      179, 190, 192–200
  cross-level analysis and 178–9
  embeddedness of partnerships within 186
  evolution of goals, norms, and practices
      within 44–6
  reciprocal influence of partnerships
      and 185–200
  see also institutional fields
Finn, C. B. 83, 84
Fiol, C. 97, 101, 112

Fiorino, D. J. 15, 159
First Nations 102, 143–4, 158, 174, 177
  rights of 175
Fisher, R. 9, 10, 85, 86
Fishkin, J. 26
Fiss, P. C. 46
Fitzgerald, S. T. 17
Fligstein, N. 36, 40, 126, 178, 185, 188, 191, 200 n.
Foot, K. 129
ForestEthics 36, 174
Forest Products Association of Canada
  (FPAC) 174
Forest Stewardship Council (FSC) 2, 23, 154,
  187, 195
formal ratification 74t, 92
Fort Worth 7
Foster, P. 175
Foucault, M. 191
Fougère, M. 5
France 37, 142
Franklin, Benjamin 14
Freire, P. 192, 193, 194, 197
Friedland, R. 37, 107, 108, 119
Friends of the Earth 148
  Netherlands 50, 73, 179, 186
Fry, R. 83
Fuller, M. 145, 161, 169
Furnari, S. 200 n.

Galvin, T. 190
Gash, A. 4, 9, 14, 15, 26, 39, 87, 156
Gates Foundation
  Children's Vaccine Program 6
  East African Dairy Development 150
  Grand Challenges in Global Health 20
Gaventa, J. 191, 197
GAVI (Global Alliance for Vaccines and
  Immunization) 5–6, 21
Gaworecki, M. 152
Gazley, B. 7, 109
genomics 102–3, 162
Genskow, K. D. 101, 128, 163
Gerlak, A. K. 157, 160
Giddens, A. 41, 187, 188, 190, 194
Gieryn, T. F. 173
Glasbergen, P. 22, 34, 39, 48, 49–50, 100, 105,
  141, 143, 198
global action networks (GANs) 13 n.
Global Alliance for Vaccines and
  Immunization 5–6, 21
Global Exchange 30
Global Reporting Initiative (GRI) 1, 16, 33,
  35n.(4), 147
globalization 36, 186
  collaboration in the context of 16–27
Goffman, E. 41, 42, 43
Göhler, G. 117, 118, 188

Gomez, E. T. 143
Gondo, M. B. 43
Googins, B. K. 5
governance 2, 4, 34, 37, 61–3, 118–19,
  133, 138
  accountable 143
  corporate structures 119
  creation of new infrastructures 154
  environmental 129
  flexible 182
  good 151
  meso-level practices 111
  network 134
  soft power 11
  stable arrangements 186
  superordinate systems 67
  viability of partnerships as vehicles for field-
    level change 198–200
  well-established, high-level 58
  see also collaborative governance
government
  absence of resources 20
  autocratic 128
  brokers between communities and 138
  collaboration with 97, 147
  conflict between engineers and indigenous
    peoples 115
  design and implementation of activities 137
  ethical watchdogs for 31
  fragile 128
  funding by 32
  global 23
  inability to respond 26–7
  inadequate 59
  incentives from 72t, 73
  NGOs and lobbying of 141
  outcomes for 146t, 148–9
  partnerships among 25
  policy making 38
  relations between society and 129
  responses to refugees 24
  role in promoting and convening cross-sector
    partnerships 155
  seeking competitive advantage for national
    industries 5
  shrinking/limited resources of 133, 134
  strong intervention by 142
  weakened social mandates 133
  see also city government; federal government;
    governance; local government;
    municipal government; national
    government; provincial government;
    regional government; tribal government
government agencies 38, 70, 120, 149, 160, 184
  authority to establish and enforce rules 119
  goals, planning, management and leadership
    functions 168

human and financial resources 109
reluctance to partner with social movement activists 114
see also quasi-governmental agencies
Grameen Foundation/Bank 6, 19
Grant, M. M. 52
Gray, B. 1, 2, 5, 7–9, 11, 14, 15, 22, 33, 37–44, 46–8, 68, 69, 71, 73, 75, 76, 78, 79, 81, 83, 85, 87, 89, 91, 92, 95n.(2), 96–9, 101–4, 108–15, 122, 123, 127, 128, 131, 133, 134, 141, 142, 152, 156, 157, 163, 178, 185, 187, 188, 191, 192, 195–8
Great Bear Rainforest (GBR) 175, 176, 177
Green, S. E. 43, 192
Greenpeace 30–1, 36, 39, 104, 121–2, 174
    campaign against PVC 116
Greenwood, R. 123, 126, 127, 192, 194
Greve, C. 162
Gricar, B. G. 195
ground rules 9, 11, 62, 92, 94
    common 89
    establishing 80–2, 87, 88
Gulati, R. 88, 140
Gunderson, L. H. 199
Gutman, A. 26

Hagedoorn, J. 92
Hajer, M. 44
Hall, J. 4
Hall, P. D. 24
Hallett, T. 41, 120
Halme, M. 31
Hamel, G. 27, 98
Hanemann, M. 128
Hanke, R. 114
Hardy, C. 45, 68, 69, 103–4, 119, 163, 185, 188, 192, 195, 197
Harinck, F. 102
Harrison, D. 145
Hart, S. 10, 18, 19, 132, 151
Hartman, C. L. 31
Hatfield, E. 45
Haugh, H. M. 132
Hay, T. M. 76
health 26, 34, 137, 173, 184
    growing importance in the economy 16, 20–1
    long-term effects of mercury spill on 59
    mental 1
    national 162
    public 5, 6
    water quality changes and possible effects on 64
healthcare 1, 2, 5, 30, 37, 129
    better 78
    debate over provision of 190
    forced changes to delivery 38
    increased integration of services 20

need for innovative delivery 38
Heikkila, T. 157
Held, D. 4, 16, 23, 26
Helms, W. S. 127, 129
Herman, M. 70
Hibbert, P. 90
High Level Forum on Aid Effectiveness 21
Hillebrand, B. 178
Himmelman, A. T. 69, 90
Hinings, C. R. 20, 37, 40, 108
Hinings, R. 194
Hirsch, P. M. 46
Hochschild, A. R. 17
Hodge, G. A. 162
Hoffman, A. J. 108, 111, 178, 185, 191
Höllerer, M. A. 44, 47, 124
Holling, C. S. 199
Holzer, B. 32, 154
Honey Care Africa 6
Hopper, T. 177
Howard-Grenville, J. 44
HUD (US Department of Housing and Urban Development) Community Challenge Grant 7
Human, S. E. 168
Hurley, P. T. 127
Huxham, C. 34, 68, 69, 85, 88, 95, 120, 190
hydroelectric plant, *see* FERC; Kárahnjúkar; US Hydroelectric

IAD framework 158
IBM 7, 187
ICANN (Internet Corporation for Assigned Names and Numbers) 16, 157
Iceland 12
identity conflicts 23–5
IFC (International Finance Corporation) 58–61, 66, 181–2
IFPMA (International Federation of Pharmaceutical Manufacturers Associations) 6
immunization services 6
    see also GAVI
income inequality 16, 17–20
India 20, 163, 180
Indiana 19
individual participation 166–7
Indonesia 112–13
information exchange 34, 74t, 82–3
    partnerships convened primarily for 77
Innes, J. 5, 39, 46, 160, 168
institution building 46, 75t, 92–4
institutional analysis and development (IAD) 158
institutional change 39, 42, 124, 129, 190, 191
    interpretations can affect 40
    lasting 188

institutional change (*cont.*)
  pathways by which it may occur 192
  recursive aspects of 46
institutional contexts 104, 123, 127
  how they shape conflict among
    partners 107–11
institutional fields 70, 97, 118, 172
  beliefs about 122
  changes in 13, 36, 46
  classified according to level of coherence 37
  partnerships can transform 184–200
  promise for transforming 13
interactive process 9
Interagency Hydropower Committee (IHC)
    54, 55
interdependence 8–9, 44, 45, 69, 72*t*, 83, 176,
    186, 200
  collaborative governance characterized by
    network clusters 168
  multilayered 15
  stakeholders may gradually or
    serendipitously come to recognize 196
  unrecognized 89
  varied understandings about 122
interest-based negotiation 74*t*, 85–6
Intergovernmental Commission on Climate
    Change 25
Intergovernmental Panel on Forests 148
Intermediate Technology Development Group
    (ITDG) 61
International Council for Local
    Environmental Initiatives (ICLEI) 22
International Council on Mining and Metals
    (ICMM)
International Detention Coalition 25
International Development Bank 91
International Network on Sustainability
    Indicators 35n.(4)
International Organization for Migration
    (IOM) 24–5
International Rivers Network 12
Internet 2, 16, 157
  see also ICANN
interveners 70, 73–95
interventions 18, 69–70, 74*t*, 111
  action research 90
  advocating 73
  applying the techniques 94–5
  design of 34, 70
  effective 83
  government 131, 142
  judicial 52
  large-group 84–9, 74*t*, 94
  participatory 90
  specific 21, 70
  see also process interventions
Israeli-Palestinian conflict 46

Jamali, D. 136
Jameson, K. P. 194, 195
Janoff, S. 84
Jaumont, F. 10
Johnson (SC) Company 19
Jones, C. 37, 109
Juergensmeyer, M. 23
jurisdictional authority 166

Kagan, S. L. 7
Kaghan, W. N. 108
Kania, J. 27, 28, 114, 116
Kanter, R. M. 119
Kaplan, S. 42, 43, 83
Kárahnjúkar 12
Kaufman, S. 109
Kenis, P. 134, 167, 168
Kenney, M. 40, 42, 44, 47, 126, 185, 191
Kentucky 19
Kentucky Department of Fish and Wildlife
    (Salato Wildlife Education Center) 136
Kern, M. 169
Keystone Pipeline (Nebraska) 102
Khagram, S. 4, 5, 37, 134
Kim, S-H. 98
Kimberly Clark 36, 174
King, B. C. 176, 195
Kish-Gephart, J. 123
KIVΛ 6
Klemdulxk 177
Klijn, E. 68
Klyza, C. M. 96
Kolk, A. 30, 33, 141–2, 143, 145, 146, 147, 154,
    184
Koontz, T. M. 100
Koot, W. 69
Koppenjan, J. 68
Kourula, A. 5, 31
Kraatz, M. S. 126
Kramer, M. 27, 28, 114, 116
Krater, J. 12
Kreiner, G. 101, 102
Kriz, M. 52
Kyoto Protocol 110, 157

Laasonen, S. 5, 28, 32, 153
Labianca, G. 43
Lacy, P. 134
LaFrance, J. 14, 29, 39
Lake Worth 7
Larson, C. E. 11, 78, 94
Lawrence, T. 38, 44, 80, 92, 118, 122, 123, 185,
    186, 195
Laws, D. 104
Lax, D. 9, 10, 86
Layzer, J. A. 129
leadership 80

changes of 70
city 1
effective 95
elected 55
identity 112*t*
indigenous 193
interpersonal skills of 94–5
legitimate 76
new 66
partnership 95
poor 22
powerful 113
process 94
shared 161
skillful 11
social movement 95
suspected 77–8
top 141
tribal 55–6, 61
learning 34, 113, 139, 170, 171
  collective 168, 188
  discouraged 182
  double-loop 74*t*, 90
  environmental 147
  joint 88, 90
  mutual 19, 152
  partner-centric outcomes related to 169
  potential for 188, 189*t*
  respecting and 10–11
  social 101, 123, 164, 187
  system-wide 84
LeBaron, M. 34, 89
legitimacy threats 127–9
legitimation structure changes 187–8, 196, 198
Lehmann, M. 14, 29, 39
Leicht, K. T. 17
Lenfant, F. 143, 154
levels of analysis 177–9
Levin, M. 90
Levy, D. 178
Lewicki, R. 40, 42, 43, 69, 86, 89, 98, 99, 103, 158, 169
Lewin, K. 70
Lewis, L. 78, 95
licensing rules 50–9, 72, 91, 105–6, 109, 121, 125, 159, 160, 176, 179, 184
Lima 122
Loblaw's (Sustainable Seafood Initiative) 136, 145
local government 7, 61, 96, 109, 148, 175
Lockyer 150
London, T. 4, 18, 29, 31, 87, 144, 150
Lotia, N. 103–4
Lounsbury, M. 37, 38, 39, 47, 108, 109, 185, 187, 190, 191, 192
Loza, J. 31
Lu, C. 21
Luckmann, T. 44

Ludescher, J. C. 4, 22, 199, 200
Lukensmeyer, C. J. 85
Lundin Foundation 6
Lyles, M. 85

Maasen, P. 10
MacLean, R. 31
Madigan, D. 82
Magdalene 58, 61
Maguire, S. 92, 108, 188, 192, 196
Maitlis, S. 169
Mamen, K. 152
Manring, S. L. 87
March, J. 44
Margerum, R. D. 22, 142
Marquis, C. 37, 109
Marine Stewardship Council (MSC) 134, 147
Martí, I. 124
Martins, L. C. 142
Massachusetts 100
McAdam, D. 36, 40, 126, 178, 185, 191, 194, 200 n.
McAllister, I. 177
McCaffrey, D. 68
McCann, J. 71, 78, 184, 186
McCarthy, J. 108, 195
McDonald's 33
McDonnell, S. 20, 21
McGuire, M. 5, 133, 157, 159
McHugh, L. 89
McKinney, M. 128
McPherson, C. A. 40, 108
McSheffrey, E. 177
meaning-making 197
  bottom-up approaches to 40–6
mediation 60, 70, 74*t*, 77, 78, 86–9, 95, 97, 103, 111, 114
  neutral 113
  shuttle diplomacy and 115
  see also Federal Mediation and Conciliation Service
meeting process 54–5
Merck 39
Mesá de Diálogo y Consenso 58–67, 80, 91, 95n.(1), 104, 126, 128, 151, 179, 196–7
  conflict in 106–7
Meyer, J. W. 126
Meyer, R. E. 44, 47, 124
Michaels, S. 11
Microsoft 150
Middle East 24
Middleton, B. R. 161
migration 7
  dignified management of 26
  global 23–5
  involuntary 17
  large-scale 17

migration (*cont.*)
  mass 24
  refugee 24, 173
  unskilled labor 17
  see also asylum seekers; IOM
Millar, C. C. J. M. 148
Miller, C. 5
Miller-Stevens, K. 7
Milward, H. B. 7, 14
Minera Yanococha 58–66, 179
Mitroff, I. 191
MNCs (multinational corporations) 6, 17, 151,
    153, 181*f*
  impacts of corporate practices on people
    living in poverty 96
Mohrman, S. A. 89
Monk, G. D. 70
Montoya, L. A. 162
Montreal 161
Moore, C. W. 28, 70, 84, 86, 87, 88
Moore, E. A. 100
Morrill, C. 200 n.
Morris, J. C. 7
motivations 4, 14, 26, 51, 76, 81, 132, 133,
    139, 145
  competency-oriented 27, 29–30, 32
  legitimacy-oriented 27, 28–9, 31–2
  resource-oriented 27, 30, 32
  society-oriented 27, 28, 30, 32–3
multisector partnerships 3*f*, 133
  evidence of effectiveness 152
  frequency of 3–4
  increasingly common type of 134
multistakeholder initiatives (MSIs) 13 n., 16,
    23, 39, 166, 182
  global 161
  potential to yield new and changed
    relationships 130
  sector-wide 181, 198
  conflict in 96–116
  cross-level dynamics of 172, 187
  designing 68–95
  evolution for sustainability 131
  examples of 5–7, 48–67
  governed by power dynamics 117
  institutional lens on 36–47
multistakeholder partnerships (MSPs) 1, 13 n.,
    129–30, 141–2, 178, 182, 184–5, 186
  clamor to solve wicked societal problems
    using
municipal government 62
Murphy, M. 143, 151, 152
Murray, F. 42, 44, 126
Myles, R. 104, 175

Nabatchi, T. 156, 157, 170
Nalinakumari, B. 31

Narayan, D. 150
Nathan, M. L. 191
National Coal Policy Project 81, 113
national government 6, 18, 21
  corruption of 59
National Hydropower Association 50, 52
National Institutes of Health (NIH) 20
National Public Lands Day 136
National Review Group (NRG) 52, 54
Native Americans 54, 58, 91, 102, 121,
    160, 197
Nature Conservancy 48, 187
NEEF (US National Environmental Education
    Foundation) 136
negotiated orders 196
  partnerships as 37–40
negotiating from interests, *see* interest-based
    negotiation
Netherlands 179–80 *see also* Friends of the
    Earth; WWF; *also under*
    Dutch
new entity 161
New York 69, 79, 85
Newman, J. 160, 167
Newmont Mining Corporation (US) 58, 67
Newtok Planning Group 157
NGOs (nongovernmental organizations) 1, 4,
    18, 21, 23, 34, 54–5, 56, 60, 64, 106, 110,
    123, 146*t*, 156, 165, 181*f*, 185
  advocacy 141, 162
  business partnerships 2, 3*f*, 5–7, 19, 20, 105,
    131, 134, 135–7, 139, 141, 142, 149, 150,
    153, 154, 159
  campaigns that expose unsustainable
    practices 36
  capacity-building focus 183
  confrontational 139
  co-opted 140
  global 25–6, 180
  motivations for partnering 27–33
  operational 141
  outcomes for 148
  power of 144
  Rabobank and 48–50, 51*f*, 71, 105, 134, 195
  reformative 141
  relational 139
  reliance on corporate governance and
    institutional structures 119
  see also ENGOs; Friends of the Earth;
    Greenpeace; Nature Conservancy;
    Oxfam
Nickerson, J. A. 140
Nielsen, E. 97, 113, 148, 149
Nikoloyuk, J. 110
NIPP (National Infrastructure Protection
    Plan) 25
North Carolina 24

North Central Texas Council of
    Governments 7
North Sea 31

OAS (Organizatioon of American States) 152
Ocasio, W. 107
Occupy Wall Street movement 120
Ohio River 19
O'Leary, R. 148, 156
Oliver, C. 14, 126, 127, 129
Ollenschläger, G. 7
O'Mahoney, S. 196
Osborn, R. N. 92
Osgood, C. E. 114
Ospina, S. 11
Ostrom, E. 22, 158
Owen-Smith, J. 200 n.
Oxfam 17, 19, 96, 112, 113, 180

Pache, A-C. 44
Pacific Forest and Watershed Lands
    Stewardship Council 161
Pacific Wild 177
Page, S. 153, 154, 155, 168, 169
Painter, M. 161
Palm Oil Roundtable 16, 110
Palmer, I. 80
Panamerican Highway 195
Paquet, G. 129
Paris Agreement on Climate Change (2015) 11
Paris Declaration on Aid Effectiveness
    (2005) 21
Parker, B. 4, 144
Parkinson, J. R. 172, 173
Parmigiani, A. 44
participants
    autonomous 157
    balancing power among 114
    collaborative partnerships mutually valued
        by all 128
    common experiences shared 89
    distrust among 118
    engaging others as reflective listeners 113
    erosion of trust among 175
    face-to-face facilitated round-table
        dialogues 85
    identifying 165–6
    legitimacy threats 127
    level of distinction among 61
    likely 164
    lower power 128, 200
    managing power dynamics among 160
    non-expert 164
    nongovernmental 167
    organizational cultures of 69
    paradoxes salient to 183
    potential 67

preliminary interviews with 88
private sector 109, 110
problem-solving by 57
process conflicts among 175
public sector 109
shared frames among 172, 182, 185
support for ideas and concerns of 86
training of 62
uncertainty for 80
unwitting behavior by 79
viewpoints of a wide array of 84
widely distributed 83
widespread, multisectoral commitment
    from 152
workshops attended by 59
partner selection 139–45
partnerships
    business-NGO 135–7
    collaborative 141
    conflict among/within addressing 111–16
    conflict among/within institutional contexts
        shape 107–11
    designing to capitalize on differences 11
    exchanging information 77, 82–3
    institutional fields transformed by 184–200
    joint ownership and responsibility for
        outcomes 11
    life-cycle model of evolution of 70–2
    motivating and restraining forces on 72–3
    power and, institutional perspective
        on 117–30
    previous experience 140
    private sector 153
    reciprocal influence of fields and 185–200
    reputation of partner 140–1
    rise of 1–13
    sustainability 131–55
    viability as vehicles for field-level change and
        governance 198–200
    see also collaborative partnerships; cross-
        sector partnerships; multisector
        partnerships; multistakeholder
        partnerships; phases of partnerships;
        PPPs; social partnerships
Pattberg, P. 23, 177, 184, 187, 188, 195, 199
Pearce, J. 150
Pentland, B. T. 44
Perez-Aleman, P. 139
Perrini, F. 7, 37
perspective-taking 74t, 89
Peru, see Cajamarca; FEROCAFENOP; Lima
Peruvian Ministry of Energy and Mines (MEM)
    61, 128, 179
phases of partnerships 3f, 70, 71f, 72, 78
partnerships early 93
philanthropy 6, 28, 32, 135f, 136, 137, 138f
Philippines 25

Phillips, N. 68, 69, 104, 119, 163, 187, 190, 195, 197
Pinkse, J. 141–2
Plan International USA 150
Planning for Livable Military Communities 6–7
Plantz, M. C. 29
Podolny, J. M. 192
Poffenberger, M. 148
Poland, *see* Warsaw
policy dialogues 3*f,* 136–7, 138*f,* 160
Polk, C. R. 79
Polonsky, M. J. 141
Poole, M. S. 41
Porac, J. F. 38
Potapchuk, W. R. 79
Powell, W. W. 36, 186
power, *see* episodic power; systemic power; *also under* power differences; power dynamics
power differences 72*t,* 90, 91, 103–4, 105, 107, 114, 198, 199, 200
    extent of 190*f,* 193*f,* 195
    large 190, 194
    minimal 191, 192
    repressive 191
    severe 191, 197
    substantial 190, 191, 194
    systemic 123, 196
power dynamics 122, 127, 129, 144, 190–1, 193
    evaluating in collaborative partnerships 120
    government-led collaborations managing 160
    multistakeholder partnerships are governed by 117
PPPs (public-private partnerships) 2, 3*f,* 12, 19–20, 35n.(3), 107, 157, 162
    noncontractual 109
    nonprofit 34
Prahalad, C. K. 18, 27, 98, 132
Private University of Antonio Guillermo Urrello 61
process interventions 82, 88, 90, 94
    roots of 78
    vital 80
Project Underground 58
Provan, K. 118, 134, 149, 167, 168
provincial government 159, 175
Pruitt, D. 98
Public Conversation Project (PCP) 34, 102
Purdy, J. 15, 22, 37, 40–2, 44, 47, 69, 75, 85, 104, 108–11, 114, 117, 118, 121, 123, 127, 165, 178, 185, 188, 191, 198
Purser, R. 84
Putnam, R. 91, 142

Quack, S. 110, 115, 128
quasi-governmental agencies 54

Quincy Library Group (QLG) 98, 113
Queensland Forestry Agreement 163

Rabobank 39, 125
    NGOs and 48–50, 51*f,* 71, 105, 134, 179, 186, 195
Rahman, M. 90
Rainforest Action Network 31
Rao, H. 37, 40, 42, 44, 47, 108, 126, 185, 191
Rauschmayer, F. 97, 99
Reason, P. 90
Reay, T. 20, 37, 40, 108
Redford, R. 89
Reed, A. M. & D. 30, 144
Reed, I. A. 118
Reed, M. G. 177
reframing 47, 89, 90, 100, 114, 115, 192
    externally induced 124*t*
    fundamental 194
Refugee Community Partnership (North Carolina) 24
Refugee Highway Program (RHP) 25
refugees 30, 103–4
    coordination of processing 24–5
    migration of 24, 173
    see also RHP; UNHCR
Regéczi, D. 135
regional government 59
regional forest agreements (RFAs) 159
Regional Health Authorities 38
Regional Refugee and Migrant Response Plan 24
Rein, M. 16, 37, 100, 114
Reineke, J. 120
Remond, M-A. 20
replicating 43, 75*t,* 189*t*
    scaling up and 93–4
representational status 139, 141–2
reputation 48, 97, 137, 139, 140–1, 147, 176
    boosting 31
    building 28, 29*t,* 31*t*
    damaging 72*t,* 198
    desire to enhance 4, 133
    enhancing 39, 49, 50, 76, 146*t*
    gains in 51*f,* 105, 146, 148
    improved 5, 145, 146*t,* 148
    long-standing 75
    protecting 125
    stain on 105
    tainted 146*t*
    tarnished 76, 148
    worry about 73
resource constraints 103
Responsible Business Forum 34
Responsible Care Initiative 137
Riddell, D. 36, 174, 175, 177
Riisgaard, L. 153, 176, 181, 182

Ring, P. S. 78, 88–9
Ringlov, D. 93
Risse, N. 97
Rittel, H. W. J. 15
River Oaks 7
Rivera-Santos, M. 19, 93
Roberts, J. W. 149
Roberts, K. 47
Roberts, N. 15
Rochlin, S. 5
Rockefeller Foundation 6
Rodriguez, C. 101, 163
Rojas, F. 124
Rolle, S. 70, 71
Rond, M. de 68, 73
Rondinelli, D. 4, 29, 31, 87, 144, 150
ROOT Capital 6
Rose, M. 12
Ross, H. 87, 115, 150
Rothman, J. 69, 97, 101, 102
Rowan, B. 126
Royal Society for the Protection of Birds 12
Ruffin, C. 19, 93
Ryan, C. M. 96, 100

Saarikoski, H. 175
Sagawa, S. 32
Sampat, P. 67
San Juan 58, 61
Sandfort, J. 7, 14
Sandilands, M. 139
Santos, F. 44
Sauder, M. 40, 108
Saving Iceland 12
Sawyer, S. 143
Saz-Carranza, A. 11
scale 179–80
    differences in 173, 176, 180
    organizing 173–7
    representation and 180–1
    scope and 26, 67, 110–11, 127, 164
    spanning levels of 181–2
scaling up 23, 93–4
Schaeffer, H. L. 17
Schäferhoff, M. 128, 184
Schmitz, H. P. 140, 191
Schneiberg, M. 38, 185, 190, 195
Schon, D. 90, 100, 114
Schruijer, S. 68, 69, 85, 104, 127, 163
Schuman, S. P. 78, 80
Schwab, K. 16, 17, 18, 25, 26
Schweitzer, L. 101, 163
scope 12, 23, 80, 94, 97, 101, 107, 135f, 138f,
    167, 179, 189t
    amplification and 41, 42–4
    characterization that broadens 157, 176
    differences in 176

geographic 165
limited 188
scale and 26, 67, 110–11, 127, 164
transnational 176
Scott, W. 37, 38, 178
Scully, M. 178
search conferences 74t, 84
Sebenius, J. 9, 10, 86
Securities and Exchange Commission 67
Segal, E. 32
Segal, P. 17
Seitanidi, M. M. 4, 5, 48, 137, 142, 145
Selden, S. C. 7
Selsky, J. 4, 15, 144, 186
Selznick, P. 91, 191
Senecah, S. L. 156
Senge, P. M. 97, 113, 132
Seo, M. 38, 42, 126, 193, 194
Serafin, T. 19
shared ownership 135f, 138f, 182–3
shared strategy maps 74t, 83–4
Sharfman, M. K. 68, 186
Sharma, S. 151
Shell 30–1
shuttle diplomacy 112t, 115
signification structure 197
    impact as change in 186–90
Simanis, E. 10, 18, 19
Sinclair, A. J. 87, 149, 150, 152–3
Sioux tribe 102
Sjöström, E. 30, 31, 32, 141, 148
Skelcher, C. 7
Sustainable Local Enterprise Networks
    (SLENs) 2, 3f
Slovic, P. 102
Smith, K. K. 183
Smith, L. W. 149
Smutny, G. 85
Snow, D. 41, 46, 99, 108, 193, 194
Sobczak, A. 142
social partnerships 114, 143
    cross-sector 13 n.
social responsibility
    proliferation of corporate codes on 151
    public expectations for 39
    visions for 30
    see also CSR
Solae 19
Sonenshein, S. 169
Sørensen, E. 26, 156
Soule, S. 38, 44, 185
Sousa, D. J. 96
Sowa, J. E. 7
Soya Roundtable 2, 23, 134, 159, 187
splitting 182–3
sponsorship 81, 84, 136, 138f
    government 38, 162

Stafford, E. R. 31
stakeholder input 55–6
    see also multistakeholder initiatives;
        multistakeholder partnerships
Steensma, H. K. 85
Stewart, I. 89
Steyaert, C. 68
Stites, J. 5, 7, 14, 22, 39, 48, 103, 131, 133, 134,
    152, 156
Stott, L. 16, 37
Strang, D. 44, 185
Stratus Consultants 65
Strauss, D. A. 73, 88
structuring 75*t*, 93, 111, 124, 170
    inadequate 22
Sturtevant, V. E. 142
Suárez, D. F. 142
Suchman, M. C. 27, 44, 117
Sud, M. 140
Suddaby, R. 122, 123, 126, 127
Sullivan, H. 7, 158
supply chains 30, 134, 141, 146*t*, 154
    changes in 32, 135*f*, 136, 138*f*, 146
Susskind, L. 82, 87, 88, 104, 111
sustainability 1, 30, 34, 36, 39, 48, 50, 63,
    71, 105, 120, 161, 170, 199, 200
    achieving 18, 198
    banking 179, 186
    commitments to 125
    encouraging 7
    ensuring 168
    environmental 52, 104
    farming 176
    forest management 188
    grazing practices 187
    high-level 180
    hydroelectric projects 184
    improvements in performance of
        commodities 181–2
    launching initiatives 100
    logging practices 86, 104
    need for 16, 22–3
    partnerships for 4, 7, 99, 131–55, 173
    production of commodities 5, 34
    species 127
    substantial negative impacts on 181
    timber harvesting 159, 195
    triple-bottom-line 115
    see also Palm Oil
        Roundtable; SLENs; Soya Roundtable;
        Sustainable Forestry Initiative
Sustainable Forestry Initiative 159
Swiger, M. A. 51, 52
systemic power 122–7, 128, 191
    basis for 118
    challenging 194, 196
    preserving 198
Szulecki, K. 184

Taillieu, T. 152
Takahashi, I. M. 85
Talwar, A. 132
Tandon, R. 90
Tarrant County 7
Taylor, B. D. 101, 163
Taylor, D. E. 99
Technical Commission 65, 66
Teegan, H. 10
Teng, B. 88
Tenkasi, R. V. 84, 89
Tennessee, *see* Chattanooga
Termeer, C. J. A. M. 15, 170, 182
Tetlock, P. E. 102
Thomas, C. 169
Thomas-Larmer, J. 104, 111
Thomlinson, J. 23
Thompson, A. 9
Thompson, D. 26
Thórhallsdóttir, T. E. 12
Thornton, P. H. 37, 41, 107, 108, 192
Thrive (charity) 24
Timberland 39, 142
time horizons 139, 144–5
Tjosvold, D. 160, 165
Todd, S. 97
Tolbert, P. S. 40, 45, 187
Torfing, J. 14, 26, 133, 164, 165–6,
    167, 198
Touval, S. 72
Toyota Motor Sales USA 136
translating 41, 74*t*, 89, 92, 93
Treakle, K. 91
tribal government 54, 56, 105, 106
Trist, E. 2, 8, 15, 33, 37, 75, 83, 186
trust-building 74*t*, 88–9
Tsee-Motsa 177
Tsoukas, H. 44, 45
Turner, M. G. 173
Twidale, S. 122
two-table problem 74*t*, 91–2, 142
Txalgiu 177

Ulbert, C. 5, 7, 21
UN Global Compact 16, 23
UNFAO (UN Food & Agriculture
    Organization) 144
UNHCR (UN High Commissioner for
    Refugees) 24, 25
UNICEF (UN Children's Fund) 6
Unilever 96, 112, 113
United Nations 22, 121–2, 157, 181*f*
    Draft Declaration on the Rights of
        Indigenous Peoples 152
    Post-2015 Development Agenda 18
    see also ECOSOC; UN Global Compact;
        UNFAO; UNHCR; UNICEF
United Negro College Fund 39

University of Michigan (William Davidson Institute) 6
Ury, W. 9, 10
US Departments
  Agriculture 52, 54
  Commerce 52, 54
  Energy 52, 159
  Interior 52, 54
US Hydroelectric 50–9, 72, 91, 109, 121, 125, 159, 160, 176, 179, 184
  Hydroelectric conflict in 105–6
USAID 6
Utah (Davis County) 25
Utting, P. 3, 135

vaccines 6, 20
  see also GAVI
Valente, M. 138
Van de Kerkhof, M. 87, 88, 159
Van de Ven, A. 78, 88–9
Van Gestel, N. 178
Van Hout, E. 165, 168
Van Huijstee, M. 39, 49–50, 100, 105, 141
Van Kleef, G. A. 102
Van Lieshout, M. 179
Van Marrewijk, M. 138, 139
Van Sandt, C. V. 140
Vangen, S. 34, 68, 69, 85, 88, 95, 120, 190
Vansina, L. 68, 69
Ventresca, M. J. 41, 93
Vickers, Sir G. 37, 83
Victoria's Secret 36
Viers, J. H. 184
violent weather events 25–6
visioning processes 34, 74t, 83–4, 94
voluntary environmental programs (VEPs) 147
Voluntary Principles on Human Rights 1
Voyageurs National Park (Minnesota) 97, 110
Vredenburg, H. 4, 91, 92
Vurro, C. 7, 13, 37, 38, 107, 138, 141, 185, 186, 199

Waddell, S. 134
Waglisla 177
Waldorff, S. B. 21
Walker, G. B. 156
Walker, P. A. 127
Warren, R. 37
Warsaw 122
Washington DC 53f, 56, 58
water crises 16, 22
water study 63–6

Watershed Council in Oregon 70
Watson, M. R. 38
weather, see violent weather events
Webber, M. W. 15
Weber, E. P. 2
Weber, M. 108
Weible, C. M. 87
Weick, K. 47
Weisbord, M. 84
Werre, M. 138, 139
Westley, F. 91, 92, 199
Westworth Village 7
Wheeler, D. 3, 4, 6, 149, 151
Whiteman, G. 10, 151, 152
Whittington, R. 44
WHO (World Health Organization) 6, 64
wicked problems 18
  clamor to solve 198
  dealing with 14–15, 170
Wijen, F. 129
Wildavsky, A. 15
Winslade, J. 70
Wise, O. 150
Wondolleck, J. 9, 22, 46, 68, 69, 80, 96, 99, 101, 102, 157, 158, 163
Wood, D. J. 1, 9, 127
Wooten, M. E. 108, 111, 178, 185, 191
World Bank 6, 20, 35n.(1), 58, 151
  Voices of the Poor (2000) 150
World Commission on Dams (WCD) 147
World Conservation Union Working Group 148
World Economic Forum 6, 18, 26
Worthington, S. 148, 150
WWF (World Wildlife Fund for Nature) 12, 67n.(1), 116, 145, 181–2
  Netherlands 39, 48–50, 170
  UK 49

Yaffee, S. L. 22, 68, 96, 157, 158
Yan, A. 73
Yanococha gold mine, see Minera Yanococha
Yarnold, D. 32, 145, 152
Yashar, D. J. 193, 194
Yaziji, M. 4, 31, 32, 148

Zadek, S. 134, 147
Zald, M. 108, 110, 195
Zammit, A. 3, 134, 135
Zartman, I. W. 72, 98
Zietsma, C. 38, 44, 80, 96, 108, 109, 122, 123, 185, 191, 195
Zilber, T. 40, 108
Zucker, L. G. 45